THOMAS JEFFERSON
as Social Scientist

THOMAS JEFFERSON
as Social Scientist

C. Randolph Benson

Rutherford • Madison • Teaneck
FAIRLEIGH DICKINSON UNIVERSITY PRESS

Associated University Presses, Inc.
Cranbury, New Jersey 08512

ISBN: 0-8386-7705-3
Printed in the United States of America

Contents

Acknowledgments

In my investigation of Thomas Jefferson and his thought, I have been assisted by many.

To those earlier scholars who collected and edited Jefferson's works and writings, we are all indebted. Like them I have retained his own sentence structure, spelling, and punctuation.

I am deeply indebted to Trinity University for financial support of this study; to Professors W. J. Jokinen, Perry H. Howard, and Vernon J. Parenton for reading the manuscript and for making insightful suggestions and criticisms; and to all others whose assistance has made my task both less laborious and more rewarding.

I wish to express my special gratitude to the following scholars and publishers who have granted me permission to quote from copyrighted material:

Daniel J. Boorstin for permission to quote from his *The Lost World of Thomas Jefferson*. Boston: Beacon Press, 1948. Copyright 1948 by Daniel J. Boorstin.

Columbia University Press, for Adrienne Koch, *The Philosophy of Thomas Jefferson*. Chicago: Quadrangle Books, 1964. By permission of Columbia University Press.

Harcourt, Brace and World, Inc., for Saul K. Padover, *Jefferson*. New York: Mentor Books, 1963. By permission of Harcourt, Brace and World, Inc.

Harper and Row, Publishers, Inc., for Lawrence

Henry Gipson, *The Coming of the Revolution, 1763-1775*, 1962; for Thomas Jefferson, *Notes on the State of Virginia*, ed. Thomas Perkins Abernethy, 1964; for Russel Blaine Nye, *The Cultural Life of the New Nation*, 1962; and for Louis B. Wright, *The Cultural Life of the American Colonies*, 1962.

Harvard University Press, for Roy J. Honeywell, *The Educational Work of Thomas Jefferson*, 1931.

Hill and Wang, Inc., for Albert Jay Nock, *Jefferson*, 1963.

Houghton Mifflin Company, for Claude G. Bowers, *The Young Jefferson, 1743-1789*, 1945.

The Johns Hopkins Press, for Gilbert Chinard, *Jefferson et les Idéalogues*, 1925.

The Liberal Arts Press Division of The Bobbs-Merrill Company, Inc., for Edward Dumbauld, ed., *The Political Writings of Thomas Jefferson*, copyright, 1955, by The Liberal Arts Press, Inc., reprinted by permission of The Liberal Arts Press Division of The Bobbs-Merrill Company, Inc.

Little, Brown and Company, for *Jefferson the Virginian*, copyright 1948, by Dumas Malone. By permission of Little, Brown and Company; *Jefferson and the Ordeal of Liberty*, copyright © 1962. By Dumas Malone, by permission of Little, Brown and Company, *Jefferson and the Rights of Man*, copyright 1951 by Dumas Malone. By permission of Little, Brown and Company.

David McKay Co., Inc., for Harvey Wish, *Society and Thought in Early America*, New York: Longmans, Green and Company, 1950. Used by permission of David McKay Company, Inc.

The Meredith Press, for Nathan Schachner, *Thomas Jefferson: A Biography*. New York: Appleton-Century-Crofts, Inc., 1951. By permission of The Meredith Press.

Oxford University Press, for William Nisbet Chambers, *Political Parties in a New Nation*, 1963; and Merrill S. Peterson, *The Jefferson Image in the American Mind*, 1962.

Princeton University Press, for Thomas Jefferson, *The Papers of Thomas Jefferson*, ed. by Julian P. Boyd, vol. 6, copyright 1952 by Princeton University Press; vol. 9 copyright 1954 by Princeton University Press; vol. 10, copyright 1954 by Princeton University Press; vol. 12, copyright © 1955 by Princeton University Press; vol. 13, copyright © 1956 by Princeton University Press; vol. 14, copyright © 1958 by Princeton University Press; vol. 15, copyright © 1958 by Princeton University Press; and vol. 16, copyright © 1961 by Princeton University Press. Reprinted by permission of Princeton University Press. Also, for Jackson Turner Main, *The Social Structure of Revolutionary America*, copyright 1965 by Princeton University Press. Princeton Paperback, 1969. Reprinted by permission of Princeton University Press.

G. P. Putnam's Sons, for Thomas Jefferson, *The Works of Thomas Jefferson*, ed. by Paul Leicester Ford, copyright © 1904; and Thomas Jefferson, *The Writings of Thomas Jefferson*, edited by Paul Leicester Ford, copyright © 1892-1899. By permission of Putnam's & Coward-McCann.

Random House, Inc., for Daniel J. Boorstin, *The Americans: The Colonial Experience*, copyright 1958; and for Adrienne Koch and William Peden, eds., *The Life and Selected Writings of Thomas Jefferson*, copyright 1944.

The University of California Press, for James B. Conant, *Thomas Jefferson and the Development of American Public Education*, 1963.

The University of North Carolina Press, for Lester J. Cappon, ed., *Adams-Jefferson Letters*, 1959, University of North Carolina Press and The Institute of Early American History and Culture; Thomas Jefferson, *Notes on the State of Virginia*, William Peden, editor, 1955,

Introduction

In his own day Thomas Jefferson was a symbol of those ideas which inspired both the inarticulate and the enlightened, and he has since become the symbol of America's image of itself.[1] It is unquestionably true that the life and thought of few men have so profoundly influenced the course of their nation's history as have those of Thomas Jefferson. He, more than any other single person, conceptualized and stated in lasting form the basic postulates of American democracy. It was his statements which clarified the goals and justified the philosophy of the American Revolution. As a practical and effective politician he charted the directions of popular government. He has been claimed as the founder of both major political parties. His name and principles have been called upon in support of ideologies and causes as diverse as Communism and Southern segregation, and in justification of almost every major American social and political movement. A few scholars have seen Jefferson as relevant only to the "lost world" of the early American agrarian republic;[2] however, it is the considered view of most of his biographers that he still exerts a mighty charisma from the grave, in fulfillment of John Adams's prophetic dying words, "Thomas Jefferson still survives."

1. Merrill D. Peterson, *The Jefferson Image in the American Mind* (New York: Oxford University Press, 1962), p. vii.
2. Daniel J. Boorstin, *The Lost World of Thomas Jefferson* (Boston: Beacon Press, 1948).

During his long and astonishingly productive life, Jefferson wrote only one full-length book, which with misleading modesty he entitled *Notes on the State of Virginia* and which is today recognized as the best single statement of his principles and the best index of his wide-ranging tastes and talents. In this book Jefferson discussed, in part from a social science viewpoint, many of the elements of the society in which he lived, the America of the early 1780s. He not only described his country but also revealed the nature of his thought. *Notes on the State of Virginia* is a major source of data for any study of Thomas Jefferson.

Other sources include his brief *Autobiography,* which he wrote in his old age for the use of his family and which gives a rather formal account of his career up to March 1790, when he became Secretary of State. Jefferson compiled his *Autobiography* from notes and memoranda, some taken almost a half-century earlier, as well as from letters and his own recollections. Thus, it contains a number of inconsistencies and misstatements of fact.

Jefferson's public papers are another major source of data. Most important of these are The Declaration of Independence and his less well-known *Summary View of the Rights of British America,* a vivid and uncompromising argument in somewhat intemperate language that the American colonies were, by the natural right of emigration and conquest, free of British parliamentary jurisdiction, being tied to the mother country only by a voluntary submission to the same common sovereign—a statement far too strong for the day in which it was written, a day when most American leaders were still seeking some means of accommodation with England.

The Act for Establishing Religious Freedom in Virginia, which Jefferson regarded as one of his greatest contributions, serves as a further source of data since it is a major statement of Jefferson's belief in freedom of thought, as does the First Inaugural Address, both a vivid statement of Jeffersonian political beliefs and a brilliant definition of democratic principles.

The richest source of data is, however, Jefferson's letters. He himself, in anticipation of a somewhat similar conclusion by his fellow Virginian, sociologist W. I. Thomas, observed that "the letters of a person . . . form the only full and genuine journal of his life."[3] Jefferson was a prolific letter writer; it is, in fact, estimated that he wrote perhaps between 50 and 75 thousand letters, in which he expressed his thoughts on an almost incredible variety of subjects. No complete collection of Jefferson's letters is now available, although the monumental task of collecting and preparing all his papers for publication has been undertaken under the direction of Julian P. Boyd of Princeton University. This is expected to be the definitive edition, and it is estimated that it will run to 50-odd volumes. Those volumes of this edition already published comprise one of the most reliable sources of data.

Older editions of Jefferson's papers are available and, although they lack the completeness and reliability of the Boyd edition, continue of necessity to serve as major sources of data. These include the two Ford editions and the "Memorial" edition. Other valuable sources are the Abernethy and Peden editions of Jefferson's *Notes on the State of Virginia,* and *The Life and Selected Writings of Thomas Jefferson,* edited by Adrienne Koch and William Peden. References to these works will be cited in the remainder of this study.

Some years ago Clinton Rossiter discussed seven different Jeffersons who have been pictured by various writers: Anti-Statist, States'-Righter, Isolationist, Agrarian, Ra-

---

3. Adrienne Koch and William Peden, eds., *The Life and Selected Writings of Thomas Jefferson* (New York: Random House, Inc., 1944), p. 2.

tionalist, Civil Libertarian, Constitutional Democrat.[4] One might perhaps add an equal number of additional Jeffersons in illustration of the fact that more has probably been written about Jefferson than about any other national public figure. More than any other single American he made his mark on the nation's future. It is also to be remembered that he wrote more—as he unquestionably wrote on a greater variety of subjects—than has any other major American political leader.

While Jefferson has been the subject of books, articles, and monographs by historians, philosophers, political scientists, religious leaders, educators, politicians, journalists, and others, no extensive study of the man and his ideas has yet appeared by a sociologist or from the specific orientation of sociology as it views the history and development of social thought. This study attempts to fill the gap, largely by means of presenting those elements of Jefferson's thought which are of sociological significance. He is viewed as a serious student of society who was deeply concerned with such matters as we in contemporary terms call elites, the power structure, demography and ecology, differentiation and stratification, racial minorities, social control, social conflict, social change, and human institutions. Certainly he belonged to the spirit of the times when the emphasis on progress and the search for a science of society found expression in the works of Auguste Comte.

Furthermore, Jefferson's social thought was part social science, part social policy, and part social criticism, as sociology throughout its history has always been, addressing itself from time to time in the works of various men to theoretical and empirical analyses of the structure and functions of social systems as well as articulating and recommending social practices and programs, all within

---

4. Peterson, p. 445.

the framework of existing institutions and values. Although Jefferson never constructed a systematic general theory of society, he gave careful consideration to many of those areas of interest which since his day have engaged the attention of social scientists. As he himself pointed out, he had been too active in the affairs of his time to develop a systematic statement of the regularities of human behavior. Although he lacked the training, the leisure, and the temperament to write out a sociological system or a philosophical system, his social thought was a fairly consistent reflection of those fundamental Enlightenment postulates which underlay his attitudes and values.

In this study Jefferson is also viewed as a special definer of situations, that is, one of those influential individuals who, while reflecting their cultural and social situations, inspire social change—the person of broad perspective who often fits the dominant social patterns rather poorly, but who, particularly during crises, may find a demand for his pioneering talents in positions of leadership.

Jefferson was not only something of a scientist, intellectual, student of society, and natural philosopher; he was also an innovator, activist, politician, and humanitarian. His definition and interpretation of the situations in which he found himself during the momentous events of the age in which he lived not only had their impact on his contemporaries but have echoed powerfully through the long years since his death. He was a child of the Enlightenment—indeed, he was in many respects the personification and exemplar of the American Enlightenment—and as such he reflected in his thought and work the prevailing cultural emphases of the day. It would be a mistake, however, to view Jefferson as simply mirroring the *Zeitgeist* of eighteenth and early nineteenth century America, for many of his ideas and activities outstripped the normative patterns of his day. He came into conflict with numerous contemporaries, although there were others, of course, who shared his ideas, just as there were indeed many more who followed his leadership.

The major focus in this study is on Jefferson's social thought as expressed in his own writings, and only supplementarily on the numerous later evaluations of his thought and work. Also, the events of his life and the character of Jefferson the person are considered largely in the context of their relation to his ideas, opinions, and concepts. It would not be possible to comprehend his social thought without some understanding of the man and his experiences, for the dependence of the individual upon the social organization and culture and that of the social organization and culture upon the individual in the interplay of values and attitudes, the objective and the subjective, has been clearly established by sociology. Not only are men and the ideas they propound the products of their time and culture, but their values and beliefs undergo change and reappraisal as a result of the thought and behavior of innovative influentials within the cultural and social systems of which they are a part.

The imaginative reconstruction of the relatively coherent scheme of things to which the phenomena under investigation belong is essential to an understanding of the man, the events, and the ideas under consideration. In order to project ourselves into the situation in question in search of the explanations that are most consistent with the personality and life history of the individual and the cultural complex of the group, we attempt to reconstruct the scheme of values involved in the dynamic assessment of these individuals and cultural complexes.[5] In the present instance, this requires that understanding or empathy which Max Weber called *verstehen* and which is used to

---

5. See R. M. MacIver, *Social Causation* (New York: Harper and Row, Publishers, 1964), pp. 291–393.

gain a more adequate comprehension of the meanings involved, both to Jefferson the man and to the society of which he was a part. Thus we gain a wider and deeper understanding than the mere recital of events and ideas can provide.

Jefferson's social science was pre-Darwinian and therefore based in large part on the natural law concept of the Newtonian system, whereas contemporary social science is of course post-Darwinian. But the precursors, if not indeed the founders, of all the social sciences were likewise pre-Darwinian—including, in the case of sociology, Comte, Quetelet, and other pioneers. It would therefore be a mistake to make too much of the pre-Darwinian/post-Darwinian dichotomy.

Even so, Jefferson's contributions to social science can best be understood by placing his thoughts in categories recognized by modern social scientists. It is in this sense, as W. I. Thomas said, that we understand the past from the present rather than the present from the past. The use of modern scientific intelligence in a consideration of the past aids us in comprehending it, particularly when used with the methodology of imaginative reconstruction.

Some will no doubt disagree with this approach. If so, perhaps they will still find it worthwhile to consider this work as at least a descriptive account of Jefferson's social thought as it concerns itself with topics of interest to men today.

I have, however, found the sociological approach fruitful in my investigation of Thomas Jefferson as a student of society and a precursor of modern social science, as well as a many-sided genius whose wide-ranging interests included at least *something* of almost every area of the knowledge of his day.

As a sociologist I have of course been tempted to point out the almost innumerable comparisons and similarities in the thought of Jefferson and that of various sociological theorists. I have resisted this temptation in most cases, however, since sociologists will recognize these similarities, and to other readers such comparisons would likely appear artificial or relatively meaningless. Few, however, will deny the relevance of Jefferson's thought to the understanding of men, societies, and value systems.

THOMAS JEFFERSON
as Social Scientist

Part I

Backgrounds:
The Historical Situation

1

The Cultural and Structural Context

CULTURAL BASES OF EIGHTEENTH-CENTURY
AMERICAN LIFE AND THOUGHT

In his published works as well as in his numerous letters, Jefferson—who has been called the most brilliant figure since the Renaissance, matched in his genius only by Leonardo Da Vinci[1]—expressed his thoughts on an astonishing variety of social questions. He discussed social structures and functions more fully than any other major American political figure, and his wide-ranging interests included those which since its founding have comprised the main corpus of modern social science. He displayed exceptional insight into the elements of social control and the psychosociological determinants of human behavior. He gave careful consideration to demographic and ecological factors, often utilizing a statistical approach. He discussed racial and ethnic minorities. He analyzed the elements of differentiation and stratification, the political process, communication and opinion formation, social conflict and social change. He was deeply concerned with social institutions and social processes.

Jefferson was, as all men are, in a sense a product of the culture in which his personality and character were

---

1. Saul K. Padover, *Jefferson* (New York: Mentor Books, 1963), p. 7.

shaped. Just as it would be impossible to imagine Shakespeare, for instance, as a product of the Orient, so it would be impossible to understand Jefferson aside from the America of his day. Both were geniuses, to be sure, but both were also shaped in part by the way of life of their respective place and time. The sociological investigation of ideas, within the framework of the sociology of knowledge, is based upon the hypothesis that even truths are to be held socially accountable and related to the historical society in which they emerged. Therefore, it is only in a superficial sense that history can be considered a mere succession of events. The ideas, movements, and men that make history cannot be understood apart from the structural and cultural content of the society in question.

Tocqueville remarked that the great advantage of America lay in the fact that it did not have to endure a democratic revolution, that it did not have to destroy a feudal structure. This absence of feudalism shaped every aspect of American social thought, giving early Americans a frame of mind that is unique in the eighteenth century as well as in the wider history of modern revolutions. The absence of a feudal tradition coupled with the background of generations of self-government by means of the colonial legislatures can hardly be overestimated, for they were powerful and decisive elements in the development of a distinctively American point of view.

American civilization may be seen as based upon four important foundations: the heritage of European culture, local conditions in the New World, continued contact with Europe, and the existence of the melting pot of varied ethnic and national strains.[2] Colonial Americans of the world into which Thomas Jefferson was born considered

---

2. Thomas J. Wertenbaker, *The Golden Age of American Culture* (New York: New York University Press, 1949), p. 5.

themselves a special breed of free-born citizens of the British Empire, entitled to the same rights as those enjoyed by their fellow citizens in England. Furthermore, they were convinced that they enjoyed unique advantages in the New World, with its almost limitless space and challenging opportunities for happiness and progress. From whatever nations Americans or their ancestors might have come, they shared a sense of identity with the English institutions and legal system which existed in the colonies—even though they had by this time come to think of themselves as a somewhat different people from those in England.

Not only were the Americans bound together with the other inhabitants of the British Empire by similar and often identical systems of law and types of government, but also by religious, ethical, intellectual, and social ideals which were still largely those of the English-speaking colonials and becoming increasingly those of the non-English elements of the population. These common ideals, codes, and institutions produced a considerable degree of cultural homogeneity, yet there were divergences which were perhaps equally important in the American experience.[3]

To the west of the coastal colonies lay the frontier, with its promise of cheap land and independence, a powerful factor in shaping colonial thought and culture.[4] As time elapsed the frontier created a new type of Briton, the American, a man less and less under the influence of inherited cultural patterns and British traditions, and more and more the product of his struggle to survive in the wilderness. To such a man, the King, the Privy Council, the Parliament seemed remote indeed. His recognized leader was seldom the British or colonial official but

3. Lawrence Henry Gipson, *The Coming of the Revolution, 1763–1775*, (New York: Harper and Row, Publishers, 1962), pp. 3–4.
4. Regarding Jefferson and the frontier, see chapter 9 below.

usually the most courageous and enterprising of his fellow backwoodsmen. Slowly but surely a rude but true type of democracy developed on the frontier to separate him further from strictly British ideas and values.

Yet the America of Jefferson's day was not only a frontier: Philadelphia, New York, Boston, and Charleston were growing cities with a developing merchant class (in fact, shortly after the Revolution Philadelphia was the second largest city in the English-speaking world). Although no more than four or five percent of the population lived in urban areas, cities exerted great influence on life in the colonies.[5]

Along the coast, from South Carolina to Baltimore, lay the lands of the settled planter class; and above, the lands of yeoman farmers and the establishments of merchants and traders. Certainly the eastern sections of the colonies were not frontiers but instead, by the time of Jefferson's birth in 1743, evidenced the results of well over a century of settlement and activity.

The Enlightenment had influenced the thinking of Americans. Men of the upper levels, those who held most of the economic and political power, became students of politics and government, reading avidly the works of Locke, Montesquieu, and Rousseau, and often engaging in heated discussions of the principles of human rights.

There existed a zeal for education, although circumstances of life in the colonies and the cultural emphases of the day precluded the establishment of a real public education system, even in New England.[6] Books were regularly imported from England; a number of men possessed libraries of several hundred volumes and a few of several thousand volumes, a comparable number to those

5. Russel Blaine Nye, *The Cultural Life of the New Nation* (New York: Harper and Row, Publishers, 1963), p. 124.
6. Louis B. Wright, *The Cultural Life of the American Colonies* (New York: Harper and Row, Publishers, 1962), pp. 102-3.

owned by Harvard, William and Mary, and Yale in the late colonial period. It is true that few literary works of outstanding merit were produced in the colonies; however, American authors produced both religious and secular writings from time to time, in prose, verse, and drama.

By the mid-eighteenth century colonists of the upper socioeconomic levels had become conscious of architecture and the decorative arts; some built great brick mansions and outfitted them with the finest of furnishings, as well as with paintings and works of art. The vast majority, however, continued to occupy unimpressive wooden houses furnished with locally made pieces.

Americans had developed a lively scientific interest, as the life and work of Benjamin Franklin well exemplifies. Certainly the frontier was one aspect of American colonial life, but mid-eighteenth-century America reflected the more advanced cultural elements of European life and thought as well. At the same time it developed areas of interest of its own, for a new civilization was being born.

The momentous developments of the Revolutionary period, the outgrowth of generations of separation from the mother country and of an increasingly distinctive American way of life, catapulted Americans out of the colonial period and into nationhood. Slowly, often haltingly, Americans built a new nation with its own hopes and dreams, its own heroes and myths, its own culture and social structure. The nation was born at a time when new ideas were abroad in the Western world, when science and rationalism were challenging the validity of traditional beliefs and the established order, when men were consciously seeking a science of society in order to build a world in which human beings could forge ahead into a progressively better way of life. The American national culture was no stranger to Locke, Newton, Turgot, and Bacon, and in its early years it adapted and modified their ideas to suit the demands of the new nation with its new physical and social environment. A developing American point of view patterned the new society for the trial of fire which lay ahead and which it successfully endured.

There is danger in overemphasizing the newness and difference in American culture and values, however. The new nation did not, of course, completely discard its European heritage. Indeed, it built upon European and particularly English foundations, such as the English common law, which it retained, often without even minor changes, well into the national period and which in fact it preserves in many aspects even today. This allegiance to the rule of law was a signal element in the transition from colonial to national status. The threads of English law, Locke, and the Enlightenment the Americans wove permanently into the constitutional fabric.[7] The American may have indeed been a "new man," as Crèvecoeur characterized him, but he was in large part a child of Europe. The American Revolution was a result of one hundred and fifty years of the American experience, combined with the ideas of the Enlightenment. The Revolutionary and post-Revolutionary leaders were children of the Enlightenment, optimistic and confident men who reflected the Enlightenment's faith in reason, science, and progress.

The cultural lag in the transmission of the ideas of the Enlightenment from Europe to America meant that the Revolutionary leaders were being influenced by ideas which in Europe had lost much of their impact, yet these ideas were the product of Europe—although in America they were being applied under wholly different circumstances to meet different needs and occasionally interpreted with different meanings. The stream of cultural continuity existed, but the elements involved were changed

---

7. William Nisbet Chambers, *Political Parties in a New Nation* (New York: Oxford University Press, 1963), p. 97.

by the dynamics of circumstance and innovation. Ties of custom, language, and law could not be obliterated; instead, the modifications which occurred over a period of decades produced at last a distinctively American ethos which was new in the sense that it was different from its ancestry.

In both the Revolutionary and post-Revolutionary periods, there was a general consensus regarding the "self-evident truths" based upon "natural law" and "natural rights," a consensus partaking of the nature of faith, which exerted its influence upon the cultural developments of this era. The majority of Americans appeared to believe in the perfectibility of man and the certainty of linear progress, herein following more closely their French contemporaries—Turgot, Helvetius, Condorcet —than the tentative and limited beliefs of Locke in this regard; although Locke, with his social-contract approach, was perhaps the chief influence upon the thinking of Jefferson and the other Revolutionary leaders, just as Lockeian empiricism pervaded formal philosophical thought in America.

The belief in progress and the heady optimism about the future led Americans to see themselves as a new and different kind of people for whom Nature's God had provided a magnificently rich natural laboratory to carry out their experiment in the search for human happiness. Jefferson was the most eloquent spokesman of this view, a view which made it necessary for Americans to maintain their separation from the contamination of things European. "The European nations," Jefferson wrote Von Humboldt, "constitute a separate division of the globe . . . They have a set of interests of their own in which it is our business never to engage ourselves. America has a hemisphere to itself."[8] So crucial was the experiment

---

8. Thomas Jefferson, *The Works of Thomas Jefferson,* ed. Paul Leicester Ford, 12 vols. (New York: © G. P. Putnam's Sons, 1904) 11:431.

that it had unparalleled importance for the human race. "Our experiment," Jefferson declared, "will be that men will be trusted to govern themselves without a master. Could the contrary of this be proved, I should conclude, either that there is no God, or that He is a malevolent being."[9] It is of course possible that Alexander Hamilton and his followers might not have agreed with Jefferson's view of America's divine mission, but most Americans probably did. And the importance of the American experiment, as well as the philosophy behind it, colored the development and directions of thought and culture in the Jeffersonian era as the Americans proceeded to create a new political, social, and cultural system out of the thirteen former colonies, a system based on the principles of progress, natural rights, self-government and science, the rationality of man, and the benevolence of nature and God. These Americans felt that they owed little to precedent and tradition; they thought of themselves as free individuals capable of self-improvement and self-government, whose mission it was to found a new civilization distinctively American, a mission whose goal, in Jefferson's words, was "the associated happiness of man."

The Enlightenment enshrined reason at the heart of man's being and led many to believe that man could discover universal laws of human behavior as precise as Newton's principles of gravitation. The philosophers of the Enlightenment taught that what science had achieved in the material world it could also achieve in the social world, that a valid, rational social science was not only possible but also inevitable.[10] Jefferson in particular, and others among the American Revolutionary leaders, believed that scientific principles could be applied to the study of society; that once the laws regulating human

    9. Nye, pp. 44–45.
    10. Sir Isaiah Berlin, ed., *The Age of the Enlightenment* (New York: Mentor Books, 1963), pp. 27–28.

behavior were discovered and systematized into a science of rational sociology, the creation of a just, virtuous, happy society was a practical possibility, not just a utopian dream.

American culture in the era of Jefferson mirrored in general this Enlightenment point of view—in science, politics, education, religion, literature, and social life. In Jefferson's particular case, the cultural milieu in which he was socialized was that of Virginia, to which he habitually referred as "my country." He was a man of broad national and international outlook; yet he was a Virginian, and it was in the culture of Virginia that he was nourished, reared, and educated. It was in Virginia that he spent his childhood and youth, much of his middle age, and the last years of his life. Wherever he found himself as a mature man, his heart turned often to Virginia and to his palatial home atop the "little mountain." "All my wishes end," he said, "where I hope my days will end, at Monticello." Thus, the cultural and structural context of Jefferson's life and thought may best be observed in the Virginia of his day.

The Virginia into which Thomas Jefferson was born was a strongly homogeneous agrarian society. Behind it lay almost a century and a half of experience as the oldest of the English colonies in the New World. Originally drawing to it soldiers of fortune and adventurers who sought to gain wealth and influence, by the end of the seventeenth century Virginia had become something of a frozen society, consciously patterned after that of the English gentry.[11] A slave economy based largely upon

11. Jackson Turner Main found that fairly distinct economic classes existed in all the colonies, and a social hierarchy based upon a consciousness of class distinctions in most of them. The lower economic class comprised between one-third and two-fifths of the population; the middle class of small property holders, craftsmen, and professionals accounted for about 70 percent; the upper class of large property owners, often with several generations of wealth and position behind them, comprised not more than ten percent, although they controlled about 45 percent of

tobacco had by the mid-eighteenth century produced a fairly rigidly stratified society in which political and economic power was held almost exclusively by an aristocracy of landed planters. Intermarriage between these families preserved the power in their hands. Property qualifications meant that only freeholders owning at least one hundred unsettled acres or twenty-five acres with a house could vote.[12] There was a strong tradition of public service, and men of the upper class were expected to serve as justices of the peace, vestrymen, and burgesses. Members of this aristocracy were dedicated to the spirit of local independence. They sought and secured election to office and came to constitute a power elite, an autocratic, almost dictatorial upper class which controlled the political and economic life of colonial Virginia, powerful "gentlemen of long-tailed families," as they were sometimes characterized.

Although many of the gentry were educated, few had the scholarly qualities of Jefferson and Madison. However, the Greek and Roman philosophers and historians, and the works of Milton, Locke and Montesquieu, were fairly widely read. A few of the sons of the gentry studied abroad, mostly at the University of Edinburgh or one of the Inns of Court, though the largest number attended William and Mary. Although this institution—under the administration of the Anglican church and with a faculty composed almost exclusively of Anglican clergymen—could hardly be considered a great college, it was an almost uniquely brilliant group of graduates which it sent

---

the wealth. Except for Virginia, mobility into the upper economic class was relatively open, and even in Virginia, in the late eighteenth century entrance into the lesser planter society was relatively easy. From Jackson Turner Main, *The Social Structure of Revolutionary America* (Copyright © 1965 by Princeton University Press; Princeton University Paperback, 1969), pp. 272–77. Reprinted by permission of Princeton University Press.

12. Charles S. Sydnor, *American Revolutionaries in the Making* (New York: The Free Press, 1965), pp. 35–36.

forth to play leading roles in the Revolution or in the creating of the nation: Thomas Jefferson, John Marshall, Peyton Randolph, Edmund Randolph, John Tyler, Sr., James Monroe, and others. The foundation of higher education in Virginia was the classics, of which Jefferson said, ". . . the Greeks and Romans have left us the present models which exist of fine composition, whether we examine them as works of reason, or style, or fancy. . . . To read the Latin and Greek authors in the original is a sublime luxury."[13] Many of the Virginia gentry went on to study the law, and every planter was expected to know his Coke and his Blackstone, for he had frequent occasion to make use of them as justice of the peace.

While many of the planters were lawyers, it was in their former role that they gained the experience for public service. The management of their economic, social, and political microcosms fitted them for greater tasks in the management of the colony, although the power which they exerted tended to make many of them obstinate, haughty, opinionated, and headstrong.

The great planters of late eighteenth-century Virginia all owned more than four thousand acres each, and almost half of them had ten thousand acres as well as nearly one hundred slaves. The worth of the property of each was in excess of ten thousand pounds. Approximately 80 percent inherited their wealth—members of the old established aristocracy, the F. F. V.'s, Nelsons, Lees, Fitzhughs, Randolphs, Harrisons. No more than ten percent of them were self-made men.[14] Vertical mobility into the planter class was therefore restricted, though not impossible.

The Virginia aristocracy, in spite of its great mansions

13. Thomas Jefferson, *The Writings of Thomas Jefferson,* ed. Andrew A. Lipscomb and Albert E. Bergh, 20 vols. (Washington: Thomas Jefferson Memorial Association, 1903), 14:231.
14. Jackson Turner Main, "The One Hundred," *William and Mary Quarterly,* 3rd Series, 14 (1954):354–84.

and elegant way of life, was a hard-working one with a strong sense of social responsibility and of service to the state. Its members were favorable to trade and did not consider it beneath them, as the diary of William Byrd II of Westover makes clear. He, like many other planters such as Jefferson, personally superintended the planting of his crops; he also operated a sawmill and a gristmill; he prospected for coal, iron, and copper; he bought up tobacco and shipped it to London; he continued his father's trade with the Indians and the traffic in slaves. But he was also representative of other great planters who believed that a gentleman needed learning; and he arose at three in the morning to read Hebrew, Latin, and Greek until breakfast. In the evenings he often read sermons, though he was no saint: he played at dice and cards and appeared to have an eye for every woman who passed by, whether she was a chambermaid or a planter's wife, and he apparently missed few opportunities to solicit their affections.[15] The widely held view that the upper-class Virginian was a "playboy" who considered trade beneath him is entirely insupportable, although it was certainly true that there was a great deal of extravagance —something to which Jefferson often expressed his ardent objection.

In spite of the fact that some of the elite could trace their descent from the younger sons of the English gentry, it is clear that the planter aristocracy was created in America. The families composing the power structure of Virginia were not usually so far removed from their fortune-seeking ancestors as to forget that hard work and enterprise were needed to maintain them in the affluent circumstances to which they had attained in Virginia. They were not English aristocrats; they were self-made,

15. See William Byrd, *The Secret Diary of William Byrd of Westover, 1709–1712,* ed. Louis B. Wright and Marion Tinling (Richmond: Dietz Press, Inc., 1941).

indigenous aristocrats (most of whose ancestors had established themselves as such in the colony several generations earlier), and most considered themselves Americans. To these Jefferson wished to add a "natural aristocracy of talent and virtue," thus broadening the base of the Virginia power elite. For he, perhaps more than others, was cognizant of the fact that those whom he characterized half-humorously as "the great" had themselves descended from men of little wealth but of much ability and perseverance, who had several generations before grasped the opportunities which in his day had become increasingly restricted. By the Enlightenment theory of the social contract, men were free and equal in the original state of nature, and Jefferson believed in removing those artificial inequalities set up by the state and class interests.

The "solid and independent yeomanry," as Jefferson characterized the element of the Virginia population which he saw as the strength and hope of democracy, made up the majority of voters. Many of them were dissenters—two-thirds at the beginning of the Revolution, Jefferson estimated—men who exhibited traits of independence and who made use of the franchise they enjoyed. Considering the property qualifications involved, the estimated one-third to one-half of the white male population who voted in 1790[16] indicates that the franchise was taken seriously. Bad roads, poor communication, and other factors must also be considered, in the light of which it is evident that citizen participation at the polls in Jefferson's Virginia was not unimpressive, although few of the yeomanry became candidates for public office.

Virginia maintained an important set of unwritten rules regarding politics and campaigning. One of these was that candidates be present at elections. In the days before

16. Charles S. Sydnor, *American Revolutionaries in the Making* (New York: The Free Press, 1965), p. 38.

the election the candidate was expected to maintain a dignified aloofness from the voters; the code of behavior dictated that he not personally solicit their support. Instead, he often relied on liberally dispensed food and drink to sway the voters, a practice followed by such men as Washington, John Marshall, and Jefferson. The usual beverage was rum punch. Cookies and ginger cakes were often served, and sometimes a barbecued calf or hog. Candidates often kept open house for voters on their way to elections, and on election day itself liquor was open-handedly dispensed. For instance, in 1758 George Washington's agent supplied a total of 160 gallons of alcoholic beverages to voters and their companions.[17] Such practices continued well into the national period, although Jefferson, Madison, and others strongly objected, one reason no doubt being that the expense involved contributed to closing effectively the doors of political candidacy to most of those who were not members or protégés of the affluent upper class.

Social and political position depended largely upon birth and wealth, but the road upward was still open to men of talent though of humble origin, particularly if they could engage the support of the aristocracy. It is true that almost none of the small farmers gained entrance into the power elite, but such men as John Marshall, George Wythe, and Patrick Henry were not of families belonging to the aristocracy. However, most of these men were members of locally prominent families, members of county oligarchies whose fathers had occupied local positions of power. Such men were not of the ilk of the Carters, Nelsons, Randolphs, Harrisons, and Lees; however, they usually enjoyed local prominence and prestige and not infrequently married into the upper echelons of the aristocracy, as did Jefferson's father.

---

17. *Ibid.,* p. 55.

Connection with or support from the gentry was indispensable for political success, and when a candidate had such connections or support his election was almost certain. Following the customary rise to power from the office of parish vestryman and county lieutenant, such men made their way at last into the House of Burgesses, a body to whose diligence American democracy owes much.

Virginia had a long tradition of self-government. Representative government began in the colony in 1619 when it was the only English colony in the New World. The Virginia Company, without clear precedent, selected this means of fulfilling the charter provisions of guaranteeing the settlers their rights as Englishmen. Indeed, when Virginia became a royal colony in 1624, it legislated itself powers which exceeded those claimed by Parliament, stating that "the governor shall not lay any taxes or impositions upon the colony . . . other than by the authority of the General Assembly."[18]

The burgesses were perhaps seldom concerned with the future of democracy and the long sweep of history, but their self-interest led them to develop orderly rules for the conduct of elections and to enlarge the powers of the elected branch of colonial government at the expense of the royal governor. Increasingly during the colonial period the power of the House overshadowed that of the governor, and in Virginia the American Revolution may be understood as the logical if not inevitable climax of this trend. These burgesses of wealth and ability, of whom Jefferson was the finest example, were in many respects representative men of the Enlightenment—educated, philosophically minded, and conscious of their responsibilities, "natural aristocrats" in the sense that Jefferson used the term.

---

18. Gilman Ostrander, *The Rights of Man in America* (Columbia: University of Missouri Press, 1960), pp. 26–27.

In the Piedmont, Jefferson's area, land and slaves formed the material bases of success just as they did in the Tidewater; and those who were building fortunes beyond the Blue Ridge in the fertile Shenandoah Valley were usually of the same level of society and often of the same families as those who dominated eastern Virginia. Although the Anglican Church was the established church, it was not strongly centralized; the educational system was underdeveloped, with few colleges and no universities; there was little literature, and no really concentrated intellectual centers existed. Virginia always had been and still was a predominantly rural society, with no cities of any size. Thus, Virginians of the aristocracy of birth as well as those of talent and ability channeled their energies into politics and law, producing a group of men with the genius of leadership and experience required for the Revolutionary struggle.

It has often been asked how men who engaged in a great and inspiring struggle for liberty could fail to perceive the inconsistencies between their doctrines of the rights of man and their maintenance of the institution of slavery. How could they fail to comprehend that holding other men in bondage was far more reprehensible morally than their political subjection to the British king and Parliament, which they protested so vehemently? The question is an unfair one, for many did see this inconsistency—Washington, Patrick Henry, Richard Henry Lee, and certainly Jefferson, who declared that "there is nothing I would not sacrifice to a practical plan of abolishing every vestige of this moral and political depravity."[19] Indeed, Jefferson expressed the inconsistency in question more clearly than have many of his critics. "What . . . an incomprehensible machine is man!" he said—man "who can endure toil, famine, stripes, imprisonment, and death itself, in vindication of his own liberty,

---

19. Saul K. Padover, ed., *Thomas Jefferson on Democracy* (New York: Mentor Books, 1954), p. 86.

and, the next moment be deaf to all those motives whose power supported him through his trial, and inflict on his fellowmen a bondage, one hour of which is fraught with more misery, than ages of that which he rose in rebellion to oppose."[20]

However, since its introduction by British and Dutch slavers, slavery had become a part of the Virginia way of life, primarily because it offered an easy and profitable means of conquering the frontier and of exploiting the land in the production of valuable crops. The economic element in history, if not the determinant that Charles Beard contends it to be,[21] is unquestionably often a decisive one.

The Virginia economy was a slave-based one, at least in the Piedmont and Tidewater, and most eighteenth-century Virginians believed that the whole economic structure would collapse were the institution of slavery destroyed. Perhaps there is no more eloquent testimony to the economic implications involved than the experience of an aged and nearly impoverished Jefferson, whose hatred of slavery was as genuine as it was vocal, forced into the despised practice of selling off some of his slaves because of his need to meet his debts and his desire not to saddle his descendants with the onerous financial obligations he had incurred. The American dilemma, it would seem, is no recent development.

Although the twenty Negroes who were brought to Virginia in 1619 by Dutch traders were purchased by the planters, it appears that Negroes originally assumed the status of indentured servants similar to that of the whites;[22] however, the growth of the profitable tobacco economy meant that they would soon become bondsmen.

---

20. *Ibid.,* p. 100.
21. See Lee Benson, *Turner and Beard: American Historical Writings Reconsidered* (New York: The Free Press, 1960).
22. James W. Vander Zanden, *American Minority Relations* (New York: The Ronald Press Co., 1963), p. 32. See also Oscar Handlin, *The Americans* (Boston: Little, Brown and Company, 1963), pp. 57, 69.

As slavery grew it troubled more and more Virginians, though not to such a degree as would lead them to implement the numerous plans which appeared from time to time to abolish the institution. In the contest between idealism and economic practicality, idealism lost, even with Jefferson, who considered slavery a violation of natural rights and had long and ardently advocated emancipation. Abolition of slavery in the agrarian Virginia economy appeared an utter impossibility, and the benefits at stake in a slave-based plantation system were such that even the most enlightened of the aristocracy could not surrender.

Many, however, outside the planter aristocracy maintained strong moral scruples against slavery. The gap between Virginia gentlemen and their middle- and lower-class fellow citizens was a great one. Rough, proud, individualistic, the small farmers of the Piedmont and the artisans of the towns were Calvinist or evangelical in their religion. They had little sympathy for the gentlemanly Anglicanism of the Tidewater. Few of the back-country farmers were slaveholders and those who were owned no more than two or three slaves.

These were the men to whom Jefferson looked for the solid, self-governing citizenry of the democratic republic he envisioned, in spite of his commitment to the view that "natural aristocrats of talent and virtue" should occupy the positions of leadership. These "natural aristocrats," however, might arise in any class of society, including the yeomanry, and so he devised an educational plan which would reveal such potential leaders. He saw clearly the need for at least the basics of education for all the yeomanry. How else could they govern themselves wisely through the election of worthy representatives in his ideal democratic republic? Yet in the late eighteenth century, there were no public schools for children of this class. Virginia tarried long in providing public education for its citizens. Families of the upper class employed tutors for their children, and those of the middle class often set up "old field" schools in which the sons of several families met for instruction. "Dame schools" provided some instruction, little of it of an academic nature, to the daughters of the aristocracy. Clergymen of the Anglican church operated private schools which some of the sons of the gentry and a few of the sons of the middle class attended. But opportunities for even a rudimentary education were seldom available to the sons of the small farmers and artisans.

In colonial Virginia communication depended largely upon receipt of printed matter from abroad. This was of course a slow process, as a crossing of the Atlantic required a period of six to eight weeks, with ships often forced to lie offshore for an equal length of time for a wind that would bring them into port. Communication between the colonies was often as slow in early colonial times. Finally, in 1692 Governor Andrew Hamilton of New Jersey established a reasonably effective mail service in the northern colonies, but Virginia was not included; in fact, it made no real effort to improve postal communications with the other colonies until after the middle of the eighteenth century. With the postal service at last placed under the administration of Benjamin Franklin and William Hunter of Virginia in 1753, the system improved dramatically.

The development of printing and publishing in the colony was also slow, the *Virginia Gazette,* the first real newspaper, having been established in 1730. Other newspapers appeared within a short while, and this fact, along with the improvement of roads, meant a wider dissemination of news, communications, and books in the late colonial period, a development that continued at an accelerated pace during Jefferson's lifetime.

From its inception there had been a close relationship

between the Anglican church and the official power structure of the Virginia colony. Numerous English clergymen,
including the famous poet and dean of St. Paul's, John
Donne, extolled the virtues of English settlement in
America, which they felt God had reserved from the
beginning of the world for the English nation, both for
purposes of spreading the Gospel among the heathen
and for gaining worldly goods and profit, after the fashion of what Max Weber called "the Protestant ethic."

The Established Church remained the official religion
of Virginia until Jefferson's efforts resulted in disestablishment. Many dissenters, however, made their way to
Virginia, and even the Established Church developed in
somewhat divergent ways from the Church in England,
with regulation not by patrons but by vestries which soon
came to exercise virtually independent control. Furthermore, the informality of worship services in the Virginia
church, a product of the frontier, served further to differ-
entiate it from the high-church practices of Anglicans in
the mother country.

With the growth of deism, many of the intellectually
inclined deserted the Established Church. The Enlightenment's faith in reason and belief in science were incorporated into deism, which found Calvinism particularly
difficult to deal with; and Jefferson himself was a leader
of the movement which came to consider organized
churches with their priesthood highly dangerous to man's
freedom. The deists further refused to accept the orthodox Calvinist view of revelation by Scriptural and ecclesiastical authority. By their opposition to church authority
and to the union of church and state, they laid the ground-
work for religious toleration and pluralism. In Virginia
there had for generations existed a sufficient degree of
toleration to permit a majority of the small farmers to
follow the Baptists, Methodists, and Presbyterians, and
many of the colonial laws requiring church attendance

and support were enforced either seldom or in a desultory manner in the late colonial period.[23] With disestablishment following the Revolution, the Episcopal Church in Virginia fell upon hard times as the other Protestant churches grew rapidly.

By modern standards, the Virginia system might be considered defective at nearly every point—with control in the hands of an entrenched aristocracy, a plantation economy built upon slavery, no public education system, poor communications and a timid press, a weak but official state church; yet, judged by the quality of men this system brought to power, it was extremely effective. The two-party system did not exist; local government was largely undemocratic; voting qualifications disfranchised poor men, women, and Negroes. And yet the men this system brought to power comprise a large proportion of those the American people today consider the heroes of democracy.

This may be explained in part by the cultural and economic character of the life of the day, which diminished the opportunities for selfish, unscrupulous men to prey upon society through the use of political power. The system was therefore admirably suited to the realities of the social order—the really modest amount of property required for voting, for instance, was actually designed to restrict the political power of the very rich and to encourage political participation by those who were relatively permanently settled in, and identified with the interests of, the colony itself. Perhaps even those "bad" practices on election day came closer to producing a working democracy than the more rational and sophisticated approaches of later periods, practices which at least brought out an impressive number of voters to cast their ballots. Since few counties had more than a thousand

23. Louis B. Wright, *The Cultural Life of the American Colonies* (New York: Harper and Row, Publishers, 1962), pp. 195–215.

voters, the candidates were known personally and often well; and the semi-independent status of the counties—largely through the county courts, which were beyond the effective control of the House of Burgesses—provided for a quasi-federal system which to Virginia leaders (such as Madison) suggested a national federal system.

Under the Virginia system, men of superior talents and singular dedication were sought out and elevated to positions of leadership and power, men who were ordinarily members of those families which could provide their sons with independent means, learning, and a sense of obligation to the community and the state. And this even Jefferson, who put his faith in education for the furnishing of leaders, reflected in his belief in a "natural aristocracy" of competent, educated men committed to the welfare of their country and their fellow men. The Virginia system of self-government was based on the belief that democracy and aristocracy were not mutually exclusive. Finally, the Virginia system did not founder on the quicksands of excessive concern with the mechanics of democracy. The early leaders left for each generation the opportunity of improving and refining the political process. They did not delay performing the essential tasks until they could reshape and perfect the political instruments at hand. Whatever the system's defects, it provided Washington, Jefferson, Patrick Henry, Madison, John Marshall, George Mason, Monroe, and others the pathway to greatness.

One might question whether the Virginia system, for all its encouragement of the talented, did not restrict the life chances of those from the less-favored strata of society. Undoubtedly it did; but perhaps in the cultural milieu of colonial Virginia this was to be expected, even though it must be said that at no other time again in its history has Virginia produced such a roster of men of comparable greatness.

The world into which Thomas Jefferson was born was

of course a different one from the world in which he died, and he himself was in no small measure responsible for the momentous social changes which had occurred. It was he himself who wrote the Declaration of Independence and the Virginia Act for Establishing Religious Freedom; he who was a revisor of the Virginia laws; he who established the state university; he who called upon his countrymen to abjure slavery and to establish a public education system according to his detailed plans; he who suggested the outlawing of slavery in the Northwest. It was Jefferson too who doubled the size of his country by the Louisiana Purchase; who founded the first opposition party; who in what he liked to call "the revolution of 1800" changed the direction of American life and political practice; who placed his hope for the future of representative government in the people, particularly the small farmers such as he had known in his youth in the Virginia Piedmont. And in many other ways it was Jefferson who helped inspire the changes which made the America of 1826 a different one from that of 1743.

All sociocultural phenomena have cultural, social, and personal aspects which must be seen in their interdependence if they are to be understood. Jefferson was the product of the society and culture of his day, and his ideas cannot be understood apart from that society and culture. This man, above whom none other towers in the vast company of American leaders, was a son of Virginia, socialized in the culture of an agrarian society dominated by a landed and wealthy aristocracy, which exercised rigid control over position and privilege. Where, in such a society, did Jefferson, the hero of democracy, fit?

SOCIAL BASES OF JEFFERSON THE MAN

Thomas Jefferson was an almost incredibly subtle and elusive human being whose wide-ranging interests, brilliance and inventiveness of mind, complexity of character, and far-reaching accomplishments make him as fascinating to study as he is difficult to understand. He is unquestionably one of the most important figures in our history, and he encompassed in the span of a single lifetime achievements which would have brought fame to the reputations of a dozen men, just as he was, it would appear, many men embodied in one: scientist, politician, philosopher, diplomat, scholar, executive, farmer, architect, inventor, philologist, revolutionary, patron of education and the arts, and—in the words of one of his major biographers —the quintessence of "the civilized man."[24] The social bases of Jefferson the man may best be explored by a consideration of his social position and class, his socialization and education, and his role in the power structure of his day.

Jefferson was born in 1743 in a modest frame house in what is now Albemarle County, Virginia, near the location of the present city of Charlottesville, the son of Peter and Jane Randolph Jefferson. Peter Jefferson had named his place Shadwell after the parish in London where his wife had been christened. Shadwell, though not on the real Virginia frontier, was situated in the midst of a largely unpopulated territory, which Jefferson stated that his father was one of the first to enter, probably in 1734, although he did not move his family there until 1743, the year of Thomas Jefferson's birth.

Peter Jefferson was in many ways the personification of the strong and courageous men who cleared the wilderness. His physical strength was legendary: his son Thomas told the story of how Peter lifted simultaneously two hogsheads of tobacco, each weighing almost a thousand pounds, and of how he pulled down single-handedly an old shed after three slaves had failed in the attempt! Little is known of Peter's lineage (Jefferson himself could

---

24. Albert Jay Nock, *Jefferson* (New York: Hill and Wang, 1963), p. vii.

trace his paternal ancestry only to his grandfather, and modern research has succeeded in moving only one step farther back to an obscure Tidewater farmer also named Thomas).[25]

Peter inherited little from his father, one of the "gentlemen justices" of Henrico County, except for some lands along Fine Creek off the James River; however, he was an ambitious man, and in 1737 he, along with William Randolph and four others, petitioned the Council of Virginia for fifty thousand acres in the area of the Blue Ridge Mountains. It is doubtful that this huge tract ever came into actual possession of the petitioners. The next year he did receive on his own a grant of two thousand acres, and again, in 1741, fifteen thousand additional acres, all in the Piedmont area, though the latter grant was made to Peter and two partners. Finally, upon their petition for another forty thousand acres, the partners were refused by the Council, although Peter later received other sizable grants. Among his later acquisitions were the lands along the Rivanna River in Albemarle, including the mountaintop which his son named Monticello. When he died he probably left about 7,500 acres, having thus become a man of substantial property as a result of his land speculations. He also owned more than sixty slaves, a fairly impressive number, as well as other possessions of substance, though not enough in total worth to place him among the wealthiest of the colony.[26]

Thomas Jefferson, who showed great admiration for his father, said that his formal education had been neglected, "but being of a strong mind, sound judgment and eager after information, he read much and improved himself."[27]

He mastered the art of surveying and became deputy

---

25. Dumas Malone, *Jefferson the Virginian.* (Boston: Little, Brown and Company, 1948), pp. 5–6.

26. *Ibid.,* p. 31. See also Nathan Schachner, *Thomas Jefferson: A Biography,* 2 vols. (New York: Appleton-Century-Crofts, Inc., 1951).

27. Ford, *Works,* 1:4.

surveyor of Albemarle County. Along with Joshua Fry, a professor of mathematics at William and Mary College, Peter in 1751 compiled a "Map of Inhabited Parts of Virginia." He had by this time become a citizen of prominence and considerable possessions, and in 1754, having already served as magistrate, he was elected to the House of Burgesses. He was a member of the gentry who occupied the positions of greatest importance and prestige in his home county.

Peter Jefferson's upward social mobility was not alone the result of his foresight, energy, and ability. Like some of his contemporaries seeking to attain position and influence, he married into one of the colony's most prominent families, the Randolphs. Peter was thirty-one when he married nineteen-year-old Jane, the daughter of Isham Randolph of Dungeness Plantation on the banks of the James. Peter's own father Thomas had also married upward, having taken as his wife Mary Field, daughter of Major Peter Field and of Judith Randolph, who was the widow of Henry Randolph and herself the daughter of a former speaker of the House of Burgesses.

Jane Randolph's father Isham was one of the sons of the legendary William Randolph of Turkey Island, the name of his baronial estate on the James which he settled in 1674. William of Turkey Island set himself down in his will as "Gentleman" of Warwickshire. His rise to fortune was swift and impressive, and he soon became one of the wealthiest men in the colony. He soon sired a family of nine children who survived to maturity and most of whom produced numerous progeny of their own. He and his wife Mary Isham have been called "the Adam and Eve of Virginia," and their descendants included not only Thomas Jefferson, John Marshall, and Robert E. Lee, but almost the entire body of the Virginia gentry. The Marquis de Chastellux in 1787 declared:

One must be fatigued with hearing the name of Randolph in Virginia (for it is one of the most ancient families in the country); a Randolph being among the first settlers, and it is likewise one of the most numerous and rich. It is divided into seven or eight branches, and I am not afraid of exaggerating when I say that they possess an income of upwards of a million livres.[28]

Peter Jefferson's father-in-law Isham, the Adjutant General of Virginia, was well educated. He spent a great deal of his time in England, where Jane was born in 1720. His lands at Dungeness comprised almost 10,000 acres. They were situated only ten miles from Fine Creek and the land which Peter Jefferson inherited from his father. Peter became a close friend of William Randolph of Tuckahoe, a nephew of Isham, and was a frequent visitor at Dungeness. Although he did not enjoy so high a social status as that of the Randolphs, his suit was apparently looked upon with favor by Isham Randolph, who at Jane's wedding promised a dowry of two hundred pounds sterling.

Peter and Jane Randolph Jefferson were the parents of ten children, of whom eight survived to adulthood and of which Thomas was the third born. Peter distributed his property fairly at the time of his death at the age of 49 in 1757 when Thomas was 14. Tradition has it that Peter Jefferson's dying instruction was that Thomas should receive a thorough classical education, something for which the son said he was more grateful than the not inconsiderable material possessions his father left him. He said that if he had had to choose between his estate and a liberal education he would have chosen the latter. Of course, no choice was necessary since he received both. Thomas Jefferson's praise of his father was both generous and sincere. He probably saw in him

---

28. Marquis de Chastellux, *Travels in North America,* 2 vols. (London: 1787), 2:151.

a combination of the solid yeomanry which he so highly admired and the natural aristocracy of talent and virtue which he felt should provide the leadership of democracy.

About his mother Jefferson maintained an almost unnatural silence. Various entries in his financial records indicate his concern for her material welfare but otherwise he almost never mentioned her name. He probably did not value her counsel very highly; and, for that matter, it appears that he never turned to women for serious advice anyway. She died in 1776 at the age of 57, an event which he matter-of-factly noted in his account book.[29]

Almost nothing is known of the character and personality of Jane Randolph Jefferson. "The mother of no other great man is as singularly devoid of embodiment for posterity."[30] Of her family, Jefferson said in his autobiography: "They trace their pedigree far back in England and Scotland, to which let every one ascribe the faith and merit he chooses."[31] It appears that Jefferson was not overly impressed by his mother's lineage and that he attached no great importance to his kinship with the distinguished and powerful Randolphs. But it is clear that he was a member of the gentry and that the pathways to prominence and position were open to him by virtue of his birth and connections.

The socialization of Thomas Jefferson began at Shadwell; however, when he was about two years of age the

29. Jefferson was not a man who often gave free expression to his emotions; however, the apparent lack of feeling which he demonstrated at his mother's death is in sharp contrast to the profound sorrow he expressed in the epitaphs he wrote for his sister Jane and for the closest friend of his youth, Dabney Carr, who was married to his sister Martha. He composed a mournful elegaic inscription in Latin for Jane's tomb, and of Dabney Carr he said that of all men living, he loved him most. He also expressed the profoundest grief at the death of his wife and of his daughter Mary.
30. Schachner, 1:10.
31. Ford, *Works*, 1:4.

family moved to Tuckahoe, the splendid Tidewater estate of Peter Jefferson's friend William Randolph. Upon the latter's death, he had requested that the Jefferson family move to his estate to oversee the education of his son and his two daughters, whose mother had preceded their father in death. William Randolph, for reasons unknown, specified that under no circumstance was his son to be sent to William and Mary or to England for schooling but was instead to be educated at home by tutors. Thomas Jefferson also received instruction from the tutor or tutors involved, though nothing is known of this aspect of his education. In his autobiography he refers to it as the "English School" and indicates that he began attendance there at age five.

The Jeffersons returned to Shadwell in 1752 when Thomas was nine. However, Thomas remained behind at Dover Church near Tuckahoe for instruction in Latin, Greek, and probably French by the clergyman of St. James Parish, of which his father, Peter Jefferson, was a vestryman. He boarded with his tutor, the Reverend William Douglas, a Scotsman to whom Peter Jefferson paid 16 pounds a year for both tuition and board. Later in life Jefferson remarked that his instructor knew little Latin and less Greek.

Jefferson remained under Douglas's tutelage for four years, returning to Shadwell in 1757 when his father died. The following year he began to attend the school operated by the Reverend James Maury, whose French Huguenot parents had fled their native land at the revocation of the Edict of Nantes, making their way by way of Ireland to the New World. Maury was a graduate of William and Mary. While serving a parish near Shadwell, he set up a small school, after the fashion of clergymen of his day. Jefferson was deeply impressed by Maury, an excellent scholar, and after two years of study under him was able to read Greek and Latin fluently, something he continued throughout life.[32]

While Jefferson studied under Maury, he spent his weekends and vacations at Shadwell. In 1760 he determined to discontinue private study and enroll at William and Mary. One of his guardians, Colonel Peter Randolph, was eager for him to do so, and Jefferson wrote his other guardian, John Harvie, a somewhat ingenuous letter to secure his permission, affirming that

> as long as I stay at the Mountains the Loss of one fourth of my Time is inevitable, by Company's coming here and detaining me from School. And likewise my Absence will in great Measure put a Stop to so much Company, and by that means lessen the Expenses of the Estate in House-Keeping. And on the other Hand by going to the College I shall get a more universal Acquaintance, which may hereafter be serviceable to me; and I suppose I can pursue my Studies in the Greek and Latin as well there as here, and likewise learn something of the Mathematics.[33]

Harvie readily agreed and so the young man set out on horseback, accompanied by a body servant, for the colonial capital of Williamsburg in March 1760, shortly after his 17th birthday. The young Jefferson no doubt felt some pangs of regret at leaving his family and friends, and his beloved mountains and hills along the Rivanna where he had found hunting, roaming, and boating such great pleasures. When he arrived in Williamsburg, at that time little more than a village of two hundred houses, with the Capitol situated at one end of the main street and the college at the other, the young

---

32. Maury attained dubious fame as the principal in the "Parson's Case," in which he protested the so-called Two Penny Act, which called for the salary of clergy to be paid by money rather than in tobacco. Patrick Henry argued against Maury's lawyers in this case and although the legal grounds were clear, the clergyman was awarded damages of only one penny.

33. Ford, *Works,* 1:433–34.

man found that he had a problem. Most of the students who attended William and Mary came from the grammar school attached to it, and Jefferson had to convince the faculty that his preparation was adequate. After a two-week delay they granted him admission.

William and Mary was the oldest institution of higher learning in the South. It consisted of a main building, believed to have been modeled on plans of the great English architect Sir Christopher Wren, and a smaller building called Brafferton House, where a few Indians stayed. Later in life Jefferson said that the buildings were "rude, mis-shapen piles, which but they have roofs, would be taken for brick-kilns."[34] The college consisted of the preparatory grammar school; the Indian school ("The Brafferton"); the philosophy school, in which Jefferson enrolled; and the divinity school, which he was later instrumental in abolishing. Including the president, the faculty numbered seven men, all Anglican clergymen except for William Small. There were probably about one hundred students.

Jefferson studied at William and Mary for two years. He found his first year disappointing except for Small. President Dawson, who was also the rector of Bruton Parish, was a notorious alcoholic; and the Reverend Jacob Rowe, Jefferson's professor of moral philosophy, was evidently not a very serious scholar, having been best known for leading the boys of the college in a fight with the boys of the town. The only lay faculty member, Small, was a different matter, however. He was a Scotsman, reputed to have been a friend of James Watt, Erasmus Darwin, and Joseph Priestley after his return to England in 1764 in protest against the Board of Visitors' assuming the right to remove a faculty member at

---

34. Thomas Jefferson, *The Writings of Thomas Jefferson,* ed. Paul Leicester Ford, 10 vols. (New York: G. P. Putnam's Sons, 1892–1899), 3 :258.

will. Small taught natural history, metaphysics, and moral philosophy after Rowe's dismissal, as well as mathematics. Except for Latin and Greek, all Jefferson's studies in the latter part of his first year were under Small. This Jefferson considered fortunate, later stating:

> It was my great good fortune, and what probably fixed the destinies of my life that Dr. Wm. Small of Scotland was then professor of Mathematics, a man profound in most of the useful branches of science, with a happy talent of communication, correct and gentlemanly manners, and an enlarged and liberal mind. He, most happily for me, became soon attached to me and made me his daily companion when not engaged in the school; and from his conversation I got my first views of the expansion of science and of the system of things in which we are placed.[35]

Small, Jefferson pointed out, also gave regular lectures in "Ethics, Rhetoric and Belles lettres."

Jefferson also observed that Small pursued an "even and dignified line" of conduct and was not one to become involved in student brawls. The two men became intimate friends, and Jefferson said that this unmarried teacher was like a father to him. Later in life he did not forget Small, and in 1775 sent him a gift of three dozen bottles of Madeira which he had kept in his own cellar for eight years, promising that more would follow. His old teacher, however, was then in his last year of life. Small was "a minor torchbearer of the Enlightenment" and his influence on Jefferson was profound and lasting.[36]

Jefferson was a conscientious student. Future governor of Virginia John Page, his fellow student and closest friend next to Dabney Carr, said that Jefferson would tear himself away from his friends and fly to his studies. Family tradition held that he studied fifteen hours a day,

---

35. Ford, *Works,* 1:5–6.
36. Malone, *Jefferson the Virginian,* p. 55.

and that even during vacations he devoted three-fourths of his time to books. This is doubtless an exaggerated view of his industry, for he himself referred to occasions of youthful frivolity and gaiety, particularly during his first year of law study when he grumbled about his law books and indulged in much light discussion about girls. He was, however, no doubt a serious student, for next to tyranny he hated indolence, which he indicated he considered to be the greatest fault of his fellow Virginians, and many years later he wrote to his daughter Martha, "Determine never to be idle. No person will have occasion to complain of the want of time who never loses any. It is wonderful how much may be done if we are always doing."[37]

But all was not work, and in spite of its small size, Williamsburg offered many opportunities for diversion. There was a theatre at which English traveling companies played and which Jefferson's account books indicate he frequently attended. Brilliant receptions and balls were held at the Governor's Palace, which ladies and gentlemen attended in court costumes and which Jefferson no doubt joined. The Raleigh Tavern, an excellent though not inexpensive hostelry, was the scene of many festivities and a place where Jefferson for many years danced quadrilles and minuets. He belonged to the Flat Hat Club, a convivial group of young men, and he attended the races, all in the company of the scions of the Virginia aristocracy.

At nineteen, at the end of his two years at William and Mary, Jefferson decided to follow the usual course of many of the young Virginia elite and undertake the study of law. Dr. Small introduced him to George Wythe, who was the most learned and scholarly lawyer in Virginia if, indeed, not in the colonies as a whole. Wythe

---

37. Henry S. Randall, *The Life of Thomas Jefferson*, 3 vols. (New York: Derby and Jackson, 1858), 1:24.

accepted Jefferson for the purpose of reading law under his tutelage. His influence upon Jefferson was as great as—perhaps greater than—that of William Small, and of him Jefferson wrote in later life that he "was the Cato of his country, without the avarice of the Roman"; he was "my second father," "my ancient master, my earliest and best friend; and to him I am indebted for first impressions which have had the most salutary influence on the course of my life."[38]

Although at one time Jefferson had considered going to England to study, he later came to believe that the finest education for an American was that which he got at home, one such as he received under the guidance of George Wythe in the law, and of this matter he wrote:

> Cast your eye over America; who are the men of most learning, of most eloquence, most beloved by their countrymen, and most trusted and promoted by them? They are those who have been educated among them, and whose manners, morals, and habits are perfectly homogeneous with those of the country.[39]

Not only was Wythe an outstanding lawyer; he was also reputed to be the best Greek and Latin scholar in Virginia. Thus, he and Jefferson had more than one serious interest in common. Indeed, the two became and remained throughout Wythe's life fast and devoted friends. Wythe and Small, themselves the best of friends, found the young Jefferson an excellent companion, and soon they introduced him to Royal Governor Francis Fauquier, himself a learned man and member of the Royal Society. The four comprised what Jefferson called a *partie quarée*. They enjoyed weekly evenings together at the Palace with a musical quartet, in which Jefferson played violin. This was followed by a fine dinner. Fauquier was something of a bon vivant and in addition to

38. Schachner, 1:32.
39. Lipscomb and Bergh, 5:188.

being a lover of music he was a devotee of gambling, a pastime that Jefferson looked upon with great disapproval. However, the Governor was a learned and liberal man who favored more self-government for the colony, and he was a strong influence upon the young Jefferson, who later called him "the ablest man who ever filled" the office of royal governor. And of his evenings with Fauquier, Wythe, and Small, he said, "At these dinners I have heard more good sense, more rational and philosophic conversation, than all my life besides."[40]

There is no better testimony to the genius and charm of the young Jefferson than his inclusion in the intimate company of these learned, experienced, urbane men; and it is indeed little short of remarkable that this lad of 19, only two years away from the Piedmont back country, would have been accepted on such close terms in such important company.

Jefferson's legal training under Wythe was sound and thorough. There were of course no law schools in the colonies at this time, and young men seeking to enter the profession apprenticed themselves to practicing attorneys while they learned the techniques and subject matter of the law. Jefferson, glad as he was to be under Wythe's tutelage, did not have a high opinion of the apprentice system, for he recognized the temptation of the practicing lawyer to make an office and errand boy of the student, and he himself no doubt performed many clerical duties for Wythe, even though their relationship was well grounded in friendship.

Jefferson applied himself to the study of law with diligence, as is demonstrated by his Commonplace Book, in which he recorded abstracts of cases and notes on his readings. Later he wrote, "When a student of the law

40. Adrienne Koch and William Peden, eds., *The Life and Selected Writings of Thomas Jefferson* (New York: Random House, Inc., 1944), p. 5. Fauquier was the founder of The Society for Promoting Useful Knowledge at Williamsburg.

. . . after getting through Coke Littleton, whose matter cannot be abridged, I was in the habit of abridging and common-placing what I read meriting it."[41] The reading of law followed a well-established pattern. Sir Edward Coke's commentaries on Littleton, covering the subject of property and tenures, was the first volume studied. (This was, of course, before Blackstone, for whom Jefferson had nothing but contempt since his *Commentaries* became a pillar of Toryism and the English monarchy. His opinion of Hume and Montesquieu was similar, and for similar reasons.) Next the law student took up the legal, historical, and politico-philosophical volumes of Lord Kames, whose works reflected faithfully the principles of John Locke. Jefferson was deeply impressed by the sweep of Kames's knowledge and, among other things, copied the following in his Commonplace Book from the great Englishman: ". . . man, by his nature is fitted for society, and society by its convenience, is fitted for man."[42] Such ideas were to remain with Jefferson and after some years of germination to produce a harvest of brilliant concepts and compelling conclusions.

Long after his days of law study, Jefferson advised those who wished to be lawyers to study agriculture, chemistry, anatomy, zoology, botany, ethics, "natural religion," and political philosophy. He especially recommended the reading of Locke, Condorcet, Cicero, Seneca, Sterne, and Priestley. It is clear that Jefferson felt that lawyers should be well-educated men.

He himself read widely during his student days from the works of Locke, Cicero, Montesquieu, Sterne, Smollett, Shakespeare, Milton, Dryden, and Pope. Virgil, Horace, Ovid, and Heroditus he read in the originals, as well as Homer, Euripides, and Anacreon, Racine, Vol-

---

41. Lipscomb and Bergh, 14:85.
42. Thomas Jefferson, *The Commonplace Book of Thomas Jefferson,* ed. Gilbert Chinard (Baltimore: Johns Hopkins Press, 1926), p. 107.

taire, Helvetius, and the Encyclopedists, plus Machiavelli, Beccaria, and Cervantes. He was especially interested in Anglo-Saxon, and it became his favorite study in languages. He was first led to Anglo-Saxon by the numerous legal terms stemming from that language, and he decided that the legal concept of liberty derived from the Anglo-Saxons and that the corruption of England was attributable to the Normans and their introduction of feudalism. Finally, after his student days, he was introduced to Ossian, the famous literary forgery, of which he said, "I am not ashamed to own that I think this rude bard of the north the greatest poet that ever lived."[43] His interest in Anglo-Saxon continued into old age, along with his fascination for American Indian tongues, both of which he wished to add to his knowledge of Latin, Greek, French, Italian, and Spanish, which he read fluently.

One of his favorite authors during his student days was Viscount Bolingbroke, whose attacks on revealed religion reinforced Jefferson's growing deistic beliefs. He copied numerous passages from Bolingbroke, including those which declared it nonsense to accept as proof of the "word of God" such evidence as would not stand up in a court of law, stating that the ethical writings of the "heathen moralists"—Tully, Seneca, Epictetus, and others—were more coherent and reasonable than the ethics of Jesus, a conclusion with which the mature Jefferson came to disagree. Jefferson was also careful to copy Bolingbroke's ridicule of the belief that "God sent his only begotten son, who had not offended him, to be sacrificed by man, who had offended him, that he might expiate their sins, and satisfy his own anger."[44] These ideas, too, were to prove seminal for Jefferson's later

---

43. Schachner, 1:48, citing Ford, *Works*, 2:36–37.
44. *Ibid.*, 1:49.

thought, a surprising amount of which concerned the subject of religion.

Thus, while preparing for the bar, Jefferson read widely in diverse fields, perhaps pursuing subjects which he considered not only of interest but also of essential worth—subjects for which he had had no time while a student at William and Mary. For five years he continued his studies under Wythe, although one year was the usual period of preparation for the law, and one of his contemporaries, Patrick Henry, studied for only three months before being admitted to the bar.

It is clear, however, that Jefferson's study during this period ranged far beyond the law, making him one of the best-educated men of his day. Also during this period he observed the House of Burgesses in action and participated in the life of the capital city of the colony as his ideas shaped themselves clearly for the decisive role he was to play in the revolutionary struggle that lay ahead.

The young Jefferson could hardly be considered a provincial Virginian. Indeed, his wide-ranging interests led him to familiarity with the principal writers of the contemporary Western world and of ancient Greece and Rome. His formal education, although gained entirely within the colony, was anything but provincial. The foundations for the thoughts and deeds which were to play no inconsiderable part in the momentous events that loomed ahead had been soundly and firmly laid; and although Jefferson was to enter very shortly upon his public career, his interest in intellectual pursuits and learning was never to wane. Few men, certainly of his day, ever entered the world of politics with so wide an acquaintance with the most significant ideas of the cultural heritage of the Western world.

Early in 1767 at the age of 24 Jefferson was admitted to the bar. Famous clients sought his services and his practice grew rapidly. He found his profession fairly lucrative, but soon he was devoting most of his time to Shadwell and making plans for the erection of Monticello. Shortly thereafter, in 1768, Jefferson assumed his expected place among the elite of his day, being appointed justice of the peace and elected burgess. In Williamsburg again, he wooed and won a young widow, Martha Wayles Skelton, whom he married on New Year's Day, 1772. She was the daughter of a prominent Williamsburg lawyer and a lover of music. Relatively little is known of her, but she had captured Jefferson's heart, and when she died ten years later, having borne him six children, only two of whom lived to maturity, he was prostrate with grief.

From the office of burgess, Jefferson continued his rise in the power structure, serving successfully as Delegate to the Continental Congress, Governor of Virginia, Minister to France, Secretary of State, Vice-President, and at last occupying the most powerful of all offices in the democratic republic he had helped found, that of President. Through all his long career his intellectual, scientific, philosophical, and humanitarian interests continued; and when he died at the age of 83, on the 50th anniversary of the signing of the Declaration of Independence, he left behind a wealth of records which scholars have yet to explore completely, the fruits of a uniquely brilliant and expansive mind and of a long and amazingly creative life.

Part II

Jefferson on Social Structures and Functions

2

Jefferson on Science

Thomas Jefferson wrote Du Pont de Nemours upon retiring from the presidency, "Nature intended me for the tranquil pursuits of science, by rendering them my supreme delight."[1] Only the "enormities of the times" had forced him to give these up for "the boisterous ocean of political passions," he continued. And even while he devoted himself to public service, his dedication to science continued, for he considered science within an atmosphere of freedom the most certain means of advancing social progress and human happiness, the two cardinal objectives of his entire life and career.

Jefferson was always ready to accept new discoveries based upon scientific knowledge, even where they might contradict his own beliefs. In the spirit of the Enlightenment, with its faith in human reason and science, he maintained an open and receptive frame of mind to all human discoveries and scientific endeavors. Furthermore, he actively supported the cause of science even as he spent his time in public affairs. His lifelong pursuit of scientific experimentation, particularly in agriculture, and his numerous inventions, are evidence of his vital scientific interests.

---

1. Thomas Jefferson, *The Writings of Thomas Jefferson,* ed. Andrew A. Lipscomb and Albert E. Bergh, 20 vols. (Washington: Thomas Jefferson Memorial Association, 1903), 12:260.

Jefferson visualized science as essentially utilitarian, although he unquestionably understood the role of theory in inspiring hypotheses and experimentation. In a letter written in 1822, after remarking on his "skeptical disposition" and characterizing himself as "an empiric in natural philosophy, suffering my faith to go no further than my facts," he continued by stating that he was pleased "to see the efforts of hypothetical speculation, because by the collisions of different hypotheses, truth may be elicited and science advanced in the end."[2] Yet his sight was focused upon the benefits that science could provide mankind. His interest in chemistry, for instance, lay, as he wrote the president of William and Mary in 1788, in the fact that it was "big with future discoveries for the utility and safety of the human race"; he found it "laudable to encourage investigation, but to hold back conclusion," asserting that "it is probably an age too soon, to propose the establishment of a system," such as Lavoisier's, when "one single experiment may destroy the whole filiation of his terms."[3]

Jefferson, of course, was not always right in his ideas regarding science, and he wrote on many scientific subjects on which he clearly did not imagine himself to be an expert. Furthermore, he reflected the state of scientific knowledge in his own day. His *natural philosophy* or *natural history,* terms he and others often used to encompass all science, was based upon the tenets of the Enlightenment, deism, and the underlying belief in a natural order perfected by the Creator in which no species could ever become extinct nor the physical "harmony of nature" be permanently changed. From time to time, Jefferson appeared to doubt some elements of this basic philosophy; however, his dedication to science was lifelong, and al-

---

2. Edwin T. Martin, *Thomas Jefferson: Scientist* (New York: Henry Schuman, Inc., 1952), pp. 33–34.
3. Lipscomb and Bergh, 7:76–77.

though he cultivated the sensible and useful, he did so with a transcendental aim—to advance the freedom, progress, well-being, and happiness of man. His goals were essentially humanitarian in science, as they were in all aspects of his life.

Jefferson's services to science were as varied as they were valuable. As successor to Franklin in the office of Minister to France, in which capacity he served from 1784 to 1789, he observed European developments in science, industry, agriculture, and education, and the knowledge he gained was of tremendous value to the people of America. Not only did he labor to establish better trade conditions for such American products as tobacco, rice, flax, hemp, potash, turpentine, and tar, by means of lower French tariffs and the bypassing of English middlemen; he also sought to improve the quality and increase the variety of American products by sending home seeds and plants with which his countrymen could experiment.

During the spring of 1787 he toured southern France and northern Italy, studying the crops, types of soil, agricultural implements, wages of laborers, prices of food, climatic zones of orange and olive trees, uses of canals for transportation, and the way of life of the people.[4] So eager was he to improve the agriculture of his country that, contrary to law, he even smuggled out all the Italian Piedmont rice his pockets could hold and sent it to some friends in South Carolina for seed.[5] Noth-

---

4. In anticipation of the participant observation method in the study of social facts, as proposed principally by LePlay, Jefferson advised Lafayette that if he wished to know the circumstances under which the French peasants lived he should "ferret the people out of their hovels" as he had done, "look into their kettles, eat their bread, loll on their beds." Adrienne Koch and William Peden, eds., *The Life and Selected Writings of Thomas Jefferson* (New York: Random House, Inc., 1944), p. 422.

5. Marie Kimball, *Jefferson: The Scene of Europe, 1784–1789* (New York: Coward-McCann, Inc., 1950), pp. 185–96.

ing escaped Jefferson's view. He described the country-
side and the people in great detail, and reflected upon the
poverty he saw, reacting in shock and disapproval at the
sight of women and children laboring in the fields.[6] Indicative of the thoroughness of his attention as well as
of his scientific bent is the fact that he prepared a scale
of the plants he observed, arranging them from the ten-
derest to the hardiest.[7] Jefferson reported his observations and reactions to what he saw in letters to his
friends—Washington, Jay, Madison, and others—so numerous that the results of a single day's correspondence
sometimes fill ten printed pages.[8] He observed European
culture and society, inventions and discoveries, political
and religious activity, architecture and art, commerce and
industry, all of which he duly reported to his correspondents.

When Jefferson became Secretary of State in 1790,
further opportunities to serve the cause of science presented themselves. His duties in that office were varied
and some of them brought him in contact with David
Rittenhouse, the physicist and mechanician. Together they
worked on the matter of weights and measures, as well
as on an experiment proposed by Jefferson to obtain
fresh water from sea water by a process of distillation.
As a result of his and Rittenhouse's experiment, he presented a model scientific paper in the form of a report to
the House of Representatives.[9]

After resigning the secretaryship in 1793, he returned
to Monticello and spent a great deal of his time on his
fields and crops, adapting many new agricultural implements to his local needs. In a letter to President Washington, he reported his enthusiasm over his test of the Caro-

6. Lipscomb and Bergh, 17:153–54.
7. *Ibid.*, 6:203–4.
8. Charles A. Browne, "Thomas Jefferson and the Scientific Trends
of His Times," *Chronica Botanica* 8 (Summer, 1944):382.
9. *Ibid.*, p. 386.

lina drill in sowing four rows of wheat or peas at a time, and his remodeling of a Scottish threshing machine.[10] At this time he also invented a new plow with a mould-board of least resistance, which he tested in his fields at Monticello and a report of which he later submitted to the American Philosophical Society.

Following his election to the vice-presidency in 1796, he received an honor which he may well have more highly esteemed than political success, that of election to the presidency of the American Philosophical Society, an office previously filled by such eminent scientists as Franklin and Rittenhouse. Jefferson felt unworthy of the honor, calling it "the most flattering incident of my life," and protesting that he had no qualifications for "this distinguished post, except a sincere zeal . . . to see knowledge disseminated through the masses of mankind," from beggars to kings.[11] He had maintained membership in the Society since 1780 and had found his associations with other members to be of tremendous value to him in promoting science for the welfare of the people, just as his great prominence helped to promote the scientific interests of the Society. In addition to his report covering the mouldboard plow, Jefferson shared other observations and discoveries with the Society, including the discovery of the large fossilized bones of some unknown animal unearthed in western Virginia, a creature to which he gave the name "Great-claw or Megalonyx."[12] He also proposed to the Society the study of the wheat pest known as the Hessian fly, and himself participated in the study. Jefferson continued as president of the Society until 1815, at which time his repeated requests to be relieved of an office whose duties he felt he could not

10. Lipscomb and Bergh, 9:342–43. Jefferson was also vitally interested in Eli Whitney's cotton gin and wrote the young inventor regarding his patent.
11. Browne, p. 387.
12. Martin, p. 107.

adequately discharge were finally honored. He continued his membership, however, throughout life.

When the presidential election of 1800 resulted in a tie and thus was thrown into the House of Representatives, most of the participants in the proceedings found themselves engrossed in political considerations and maneuverings. Jefferson, however, refused to allow politics to separate him completely from his interests in science, and during this period calmly wrote letters to friends and acquaintances regarding scientific matters—one upon climatic differences, another upon fossil bones, and yet another lengthy one upon Indian dialects, a subject of lifelong interest. In this letter he said:

> I have it much at heart to make as extensive a collection as possible of the Indian tongues. I have at present about thirty tolerably full . . . . It is curious to consider how such handfuls of men, came by different languages, and how they have preserved them so distinct.[13]

Just as "curious" to many, no doubt, was Jefferson's pursuit of philological considerations in the white heat of a political struggle which would hold such profound consequences for his own life.

The most outstanding feat of Jefferson's administration was, of course, the Louisiana Purchase. For many years he had thought of an expedition to discover the wonders hidden in the vast wilderness of the West. Jefferson had always maintained a lively interest in voyages of scientific exploration and discovery, and while in France had discussed with the Connecticut explorer Ledyard the latter's abortive attempt to make his way across Siberia to Kamchatka and thence across to the western side of

---

13. Lipscomb and Bergh, 10:192–93. His voluminous records of Indian tongues were lost, having been thrown into the James while being shipped from Washington to Monticello in 1809. Jefferson considered this loss a tremendous one, as no doubt it was.

North America, of which project the Empress of Russia prevented fulfillment. Later, Jefferson proposed a scientific expedition to the West, and the American Philosophical Society supported the project under the leadership of the French botanist and explorer, André Michaux, who got no further than Kentucky before his government instructed him to abandon the undertaking.

In 1803 Jefferson was at last able to see his dream brought to fruition in the Lewis and Clark Expedition. For two years and four months the expedition explored the West, collecting Indian vocabularies, botanical and mineralogical specimens, making topographical maps, seeking fossil remains, charting waterways, indicating trade routes, observing Indian cultures, and following all the other instructions Jefferson had given them. The scientific results of the expedition were of far-reaching importance. The publication of the journal kept by the expedition's leaders was long delayed, owing in part to the War of 1812. Portions of the journals appeared in 1814, but these did not include the botanical and other scientific notes, by then widely scattered, which Jefferson considered most important. At last, after persistent effort on his part, these records were assembled in 1818 and turned over to the American Philosophical Society, although they were not published until 1904. This expedition was a significant contribution to America from Jefferson, for it was he who first conceived of the project, who with great determination overcame the obstacles that delayed its execution, and who provided the instructions which its commanders faithfully followed in their long and arduous journey of discovery. Although overshadowed by the Lewis and Clark Expedition, that undertaken in 1806 by Zebulon Pike to the Colorado country was also commissioned by Jefferson.

Agriculture was among Jefferson's greatest scientific interests, and when he returned to Monticello upon his

retirement from the presidency, he turned his attention
to his house, his farm, and his intellectual interests. To
James Maury he wrote, "I have withdrawn from all
political intermeddlings, to indulge the evening of my
life with what have been the passions of every portion
of it, books, science, my farms, my family, and friends."[14]
He might also have mentioned his house, Monticello,
upon which he had lavished so many years of care and
inventiveness, as he was to continue to do. The house
was filled with Jefferson's practical inventions and innovations: the swivel chair, the polygraph, the dumb-
waiter, the double-acting doors between the hall and
salon, the windvane on the eastern portico that enabled
Jefferson to see which way the wind was blowing without
getting his feet wet, the clock that told the time of day
and the day of the week among other things, and all
the other pieces that he had designed and had made for
his house. Nor should one forget his excellent library
of about ten thousand volumes, which he sold to Congress
for $25,000 after the British burned Washington in 1814
and which formed the nucleus of the Library of Congress
—volumes on history, zoology, anatomy, surgery, medicine, agriculture, mineralogy, botany, chemistry, physics,
geography, geology, astronomy, mathematics, geometry,
ethics, religion, law, politics, design, epics, romances,
drama, rhetoric, oratory, criticism, philosophy, bibliogra-
phy, and polygraphy.[15]

At Monticello, surrounded by the people and the things
he loved, Jefferson turned his attention to agriculture.
"The greatest service which can be rendered any country," he said, "is to add an useful plant to its culture."[16]
He imported plants and trees from abroad and tried them

14. Lipscomb and Bergh, 13:148–49.
15. Saul K. Padover, *Jefferson* (New York: Mentor Books, 1963), p.
175. See E. Millicent Sowerby, *Catalogue of the Library of Thomas
Jefferson,* 5 vols. (Washington: Library of Congress, 1952–1959).
16. Lipscomb and Bergh, 1:259.

out at Monticello—olives, oranges, almonds, French grapes. But he did not limit himself to plants. He became particularly interested in improving wool production in America and in 1802 imported the first pair of Merino sheep from Spain. Jefferson, the agrarian, advocated diversified agriculture and farm industries to benefit those he usually called "the producers," to him the most important element in the nation's economic life. In 1813 he wrote, "Household manufacture is taking deep root with us. I have a carding machine, two spinning machines, and looms." He saw this development as becoming so widespread that "by the next winter this State will not need a yard of imported coarse or middling clothing," and attributed much of this progress to the improved wool production.[17]

The growing popularity of Merino sheep caused some breeders to raise prices for ewes and lambs, a development to which Jefferson reacted angrily in a letter to President Madison. "I have been so disgusted with the scandalous extortions lately practiced by the sale of these animals," he wrote, ". . . that I am disposed to consider as right, whatever is the reverse of what they have done." Then he added, "No sentiment is more acknowledged in the family of Agriculturists than that the few who can afford it should incur the risk and expense of all new improvements, and give the benefit freely to the many of more restricted circumstances."[18]

Throughout the remainder of his life Jefferson continued his agricultural experiments and activities. Crop rotation, soil cultivation, animal breeding, control of pests, improvement of seeds, and such matters were important elements in his scientific farming at Monticello. He advocated the study of agricultural science at his ideal university, and all his life promoted agrarian in-

17. *Ibid.,* 13:205.
18. *Ibid.,* 12:389.

terests, for it seemed plain to him that America had been designed by the Creator for an agricultural country.

Jefferson promoted the cause of science and participated in endeavors of a scientific nature as actively as the circumstances of his busy life permitted. He was not a builder of either philosophic or scientific systems; his approach was instead eclectic, combining ideas from diverse and often heterogeneous sources, although his views of nature and man in general were based largely on Bacon, and on Locke, the ancestor of positivistic empiricism, as well as on the ideas of Lord Kames, the Scottish realist, and, those of the French *encyclopedistes, idéalogues,* and physiocrats. The eclectic approach was fairly common in his day, and had been followed earlier, as in Roman times by Cicero, whom Jefferson studied extensively from his student days on.

Jefferson was a strong empiricist—knowledge to him was a matter of experience, and the expressions *experience shows* or *history informs us* appear often in his writings. He took history to be the record of man's experience, and he made this subject the principal one in his plan for general public education. History covered the whole range of human experience; thus he considered that even the ancients afforded wisdom based on empiricism. Jefferson was skeptical about speculation. The powerful influence of Locke reinforced his own empirical tendencies and led him to aver that we must "cling to what we know without knowledge of the beyond," since propositions "beyond finite comprehension" are "a weight which human strength cannot lift."[19] Jefferson's approach was positivistic in the Lockeian sense of considering material and natural objects and events subject to scientific verification, of limiting knowledge to the observable phenomena of the real world of experience. In morality,

---

19. *Ibid.,* 15:241.

ethics, religion, and taste, his approach may also be considered empirical and positivistic; his frame of reference was one based on the existence of a rational and benevolent Creator who, among other things, had instilled in man a "moral faculty" similar to the five senses, a faculty which in its "healthy" state governed man's behavior as surely as did his physical senses of touch, taste, sight, smell, and hearing. Even thinking was a "mode of action," a physiological process. Thus, morals and thought were not to be excepted from the other "facts of nature," and the experimental method was to reign supreme, leaving no purpose to be served by metaphysics, transcendental theology, and abstract speculation. Jefferson's approach was therefore essentially scientific, though based on the concept of natural law, and he followed the basic postulates of science: that all behavior is naturally determined, that man is a part of the natural world, that nature is orderly and regular, that nature is uniform, that nature is permanent, that all objective phenomena are eventually knowable, that all perceptions are achieved through the senses (since morality is one of the physical senses), and that man can trust his perceptions, memory, and reasoning as reliable agencies for acquiring facts.

Jefferson's most impressive scientific achievement is his *Notes on the State of Virginia,* in which he recorded his observations on flora, fauna, mountains, rivers, population, laws, politics, economics, agriculture, manufactures, ethics, religion, customs, Indians, and Negroes, demonstrating his empirical approach and discussing matters of significance in the natural sciences as well as in the social sciences. Since this is Jefferson's only organized, extensive, book-length statement of his thoughts, it occupies a place of unique importance among his varied and wide-ranging writings, and is of particular scientific interest.

Notes on the State of Virginia grew out of a questionnaire relayed in 1780 to Jefferson from the Marquis de Barbé-Marbois, Secretary of the French Legation in America. The French, having entered the war on the side of America, sought information regarding the geography, climate, people, resources, and customs of their new ally. Jefferson had already through the years compiled a collection of miscellaneous data on such matters, and thus found that the request provided him with an opportunity of organizing and presenting the facts which he had long been collecting. His familiarity with many phases of the scientific knowledge of his time became known only through the publication of this work.

The request from Barbé-Marbois arrived near the end of Jefferson's rather unsuccessful term as governor of Virginia. The war-ravaged state was near economic exhaustion; it had no effective defensive forces with which to repel the threat of invasion, and when British troops under Benedict Arnold attacked, the legislature fled. Arnold took Richmond and burned a number of buildings, with Jefferson almost powerless to meet the threat of conquest. When Cornwallis entered Virginia in the spring of 1781 with a large invasion force, despondency seemed universal. Jefferson, having fled to Charlottesville along with the legislators, called upon General Washington to save the state. Cornwallis, seeking to capture the governor and legislators, dispatched Tarleton with a troop of cavalry to carry out his plans, an undertaking which Captain Jack Jouett learned of at Louisa, about 45 miles east of Charlottesville. Jouett, in a wild ride celebrated still in Virginia, raced over little-known mountain trails, reaching Monticello at about four-thirty in the morning, in time to permit Jefferson (who reacted with almost incredible calmness) to escape the approaching British.

Jefferson made his way to the privacy of his summer estate, Poplar Forest, taking with him the Barbé-Marbois request, on which he had already begun work. When the request originally arrived, he had seriously considered resigning the governorship to devote himself entirely to the project—no doubt a reflection of his discouragement over the impossible conditions affecting his role performance as governor as well as a testimony to his interest in things scientific. During the darkest days of the war, he wrote Barbé-Marbois apologizing for his lack of progress in supplying the desired information, and at Poplar Forest he settled down in earnest to fulfill the task. He appealed to friends for further data, broadened the scope of his answers, and finally, in late 1781, finished the voluminous manuscript, with another apology to Barbé-Marbois for the long delay, explaining that

> I retired from the public service in June only, and after that the general confusion of our state put it out of my power to procure the information necessary till lately. Even now you will find them very imperfect and not worth offering but as a proof of my respect for your wishes.[20]

Originally, it appears, Jefferson had planned the *Notes* to be essentially a statistical survey of Virginia; instead, this work turned out to be a fascinating and enlightening commentary on many aspects of American life and history. It has been called perhaps the most important scientific and political work written by an American before 1785.[21] At first Jefferson did not plan to publish these commentaries, fearing that they would excite political controversy in Virginia. He retained at least one copy of the manuscript, however, and circulated it among friends for suggestions and corrections. He spent the winter of 1781 revising and enlarging the work, a project he again pursued during the winter of 1783-1784 while

20. Nathan Schachner, *Thomas Jefferson: A Biography,* 2 vols. (New York: Appleton-Century-Crofts, Inc., 1951). 1:224-25.

21. Thomas Jefferson, *Notes on the State of Virginia,* ed. William Peden (Chapel Hill: University of North Carolina Press, 1955), p. xi.

he was a delegate to the Continental Congress. More and more people expressed a desire to see a copy of the work, so Jefferson decided upon publication which, because of prohibitive costs, he delayed until his arrival in France. The work appeared in 1785 and he distributed the two hundred copies among his friends, since he intended it solely for private distribution, enjoining them all—as was his custom when writing about matters of a controversial nature—to prevent their copies from getting into the hands of those who might be offended at his outspoken expressions regarding the emancipation of slaves and the reformation of the Virginia constitution in particular.

Interest in the volume became increasingly widespread, however, in Europe as well as in America. Faced with the prospect of an unauthorized French edition, Jefferson accepted the offer of the Abbé Morellet, a member of the French Academy and translator of Beccaria, to prepare and supervise an authorized French translation. This appeared in 1787 but was badly done and a source of embarrassment to Jefferson. Finally, to correct this unfortunate turn of events, he authorized an edition printed in the summer of 1787 by John Stockdale in England, which Jefferson considered the "definitive text." From time to time he continued to enlarge the subject-matter, and even after his retirement from the presidency expressed his intention of revising the book, a project he was unable to accomplish.

The *Notes* had originally been conceived as a factual description of the resources and cultural life of one state, but it developed into much more. It begins with an "exact description" of the boundaries of the state, but at that time Virginia claimed almost a third of what became the continental United States and therefore Jefferson's commentaries included matters relevant to the vast western areas. Likewise, he advanced from the consideration of natural resources to the discussion of the nature and purpose of governments, of the relation between the individual and society, and even of the riddle of man's being.[22] The facts he set out to present suggested to him social, moral, and political implications, and in the process of considering the vastness of Virginia, he came to identify its characteristics and aspirations with those of America as an "empire of liberty," a concept undergirded by his faith in the destiny of America and his shrewd foresight regarding the economic potentiality of the West. The *Notes on Virginia* are a memorable expression of the ideas of the American Enlightenment, of which Jefferson was the best example, and of his own original and innovative thought. This important work is a veritable testament of freedom, one in which Jefferson expressed his conviction that through knowledge men could improve their lot in the brave new world of America and that the American experiment would lead to betterment for all mankind.

It is no surprise that this volume became the subject of long and sometimes violent controversy, for herein Jefferson criticized most of the vested interests of his time. He attacked religious superstition, the assumption and usurpation of power by the rich and wellborn, the tyranny of the church, slavery, ignorance, and bigotry.

The early parts of the book concern matters in the realm of natural science. Even here he maintains a cosmic outlook and seems always to be seeking an understanding of how his observations about Virginia stand with reference to what is known about the world at large. Always he sought explanations, and his wide-ranging curiosity led him to touch on many sciences in which he would have been the first to admit that he was no expert. Often he considered known scientific hypotheses, many of which failed to satisfy his empirical approach. Thus he con-

---

22. *Ibid.,* p. **xxii**.

cludes: "Ignorance is preferable to error; and he is less remote from the truth who believes nothing than he who believes what is wrong."[23]

First he discusses the limits and boundaries of the state, its physical geography, latitude, and longitude. Then he gives a description of the rivers and streams, indicating their width and depth and whether they are navigable, noting the fish which live in them, and the fertility of the lands bordering them. Moving to a broad approach concerning America as a whole, he indicates distances from city to city by way of roads following the rivers, observing, as a case in point, that "from New Orleans to the city of Mexico is about one thousand nine hundred and fifty miles; the roads after setting out from the Red river, near Natchitoches, keeping generally parallel with the coast, and about two hundred miles from it, till it enters the city of Mexico."[24]

He discusses the mountains of his home state, referring—with pride, no doubt—to "Fry and Jefferson's map of Virginia." Occasionally he describes his observations vividly and speculates on the forces producing the scenes which thrill him, such as that now known as Jefferson's Rock at the junction of the Shenandoah and Potomac Rivers:

> The passage of the Potomac through the Blue Ridge is, perhaps, one of the most stupendous scenes in nature. You stand on a very high point of land. On your right comes up the Shenandoah, having ranged along the foot of the mountain a hundred miles to seek a vent. On your left approaches the Potomac, in quest of a passage also. In the moment of their junction, they rush together against the mountain, rend it asunder, and pass off to the sea. The first glance of this scene hurries our senses into the opinion, that this earth has been created in time, that the mountains were formed first, that the rivers began to flow afterwards, that in this place, particularly,

23. *Ibid.*, p. 33.
24. *Ibid.*, p. 9.

they have been dammed up by the Blue Ridge of mountains, and have formed an ocean which filled the whole valley; that continuing to rise they have at length broken over at this spot, and have torn the mountain down from its summit to its base. The piles of rock on each hand, but particularly on the Shenandoah, the evident marks of their disrupture and avulsion from their beds by the most powerful agents of nature, corroborate the impression. But the distant finishing which nature has given to the picture is of a very different character. It is a true contrast to the fore-ground. It is as placid and delightful, as that is wild and tremendous. For the mountain being cloven asunder, she presents to your eye, through the cleft, a small catch of smooth blue horizon, at an infinite distance in the plain country, inviting you, as it were, from the riot and tumult roaring around, to pass through the breach and participate of the calm below.[25]

This passage describing what is now Harpers Ferry, West Virginia, is typical of portions of Jefferson's writing in the *Notes,* passing as it does from simple description to scientific explanation and then to a vivid and eloquent literary portrayal of the subject at hand, especially in his descriptions of nature, for Jefferson was always a nature lover who never ceased to respond to the beauties of fields, rivers, and mountains.

He also discusses the state's cascades and caverns, including a careful description of Natural Bridge, to which Jefferson secured title in 1774 and over which he exults: "So beautiful an arch, so elevated, so light, so springing as it were up to heaven! the rapture of the spectator is really indescribable!"[26]

Then follows an account of the mineral resources— lead, copper, and iron—and of coal, marble, limestone and, at the foot of some of the mountains, schist containing impressions of shells. Here Jefferson considers the possibility of a universal deluge having occurred but

25. *Ibid.,* p. 19.
26. *Ibid.,* p. 25.

rejects this explanation. Accounts of salt deposits, hot springs, and other matters follow.

From these considerations, he turns to the subject of plants, fruits, and vegetables, cataloguing over eighty plant species by both their popular and scientific names, separating those native to the state from those which had been introduced from abroad.

Then he turns to the subject of animal life, soon introducing the contentions of Count de Buffon that animals common to both the old world and the new are smaller in the new, that animals peculiar to the new world are smaller than those indigenous to the old, that those which have been domesticated in both have degenerated in America, and that America has fewer species of animals than has Europe. Jefferson sets out to refute Buffon's conclusions, stating that "our only appeal on such questions is experience."[27] As evidence, he presents a lengthy statistical table comparing the weights of European and American animals, successfully demonstrating Buffon's error, although Jefferson himself concludes that "there is no uniform difference in favor of either" Europe or America, "which is all I pretend."[28] He calls to his support accounts of American animals, wild and domestic, which have attained great weight, and indicates that Buffon's conclusions are based upon speculation rather than upon empirical observation, pointing out that the French scientist has not "measured, weighed, or seen" the animals of America.

Jefferson pursued for many years his project of disproving Buffon's contentions, since they had had such influence in Europe. He asked his explorer friend Thomas Walker to send him the heaviest weights of American animals that he knew, "from the mouse to the mammoth," the latter a creature Jefferson was convinced must

27. *Ibid.*, p. 47.
28. *Ibid.*, p. 49.

still exist in the American wilderness.[29] He sought the most precise and detailed information in his efforts to refute Buffon, at last having John Sullivan of New Hampshire forward to him in France the largest moose he could secure, a project which, undertaken as it was in winter, proved to be one of tremendous difficulties. However, when the moose reached Jefferson he presented incontrovertible evidence to Buffon, who stood corrected and chagrined.[30]

Buffon's denigration of American animals was serious enough, but his assertions regarding the American Indians were even more shocking to Jefferson, whose interest in Indians, from his boyhood on, made him both a student and a friend of the Red Man and resulted in his being called the first American anthropologist.[31] The American "savage," Buffon said, "is feeble . . . less strong in body . . . less sensitive . . . more timid and cowardly; he has no vivacity of mind. . . . Their heart is icy, their society cold, and their rule harsh."[32] Buffon's statements were elaborated upon in the work of numerous followers and popularizers, such as Corneille De Pauw and the Abbé Raynal. De Pauw reported that frogs had been discovered in Louisiana weighing 37 pounds which bellowed like calves, and that America was so cold that the ground in Illinois was often frozen to a depth of 30 feet.[33] Jefferson's refutations of such assertions comprise an important part of the early sections of the *Notes on the State of Virginia*. The views he expressed on the American Indian will be considered later.

Jefferson took particular umbrage at the Abbé Raynal's

29. Jefferson's interests in natural history, archaeology, and animal life led his critics to refer to him as "Mr. Mammoth."

30. Martin, pp. 183–86.

31. *Ibid.*, p. x. See also Alexander F. Chamberlain, "Thomas Jefferson's Ethnological Opinions and Activities," *American Anthropologist*, 9, New Series (July, 1907):499–509.

32. Peden, pp. 58–59.

33. Martin, p. 160.

statement that America had not yet produced "one good poet, one able mathematician, one man of genius in a single art or a single science."[34] These allegations Jefferson considered insufferable. He claimed no great poet for America, nor did he claim a great mathematician. But as far as other arts and sciences were concerned, in warfare America had produced a Washington, in physics a Franklin, and in astronomy a Rittenhouse, who by means of his orrery had approached nearer his "Maker than any other man who has lived from the creation to this day."[35]

Then, having disposed of these accusations, Jefferson proceeded to discuss the birdlife of America, cataloguing 94 species by their popular and scientific names, including the designations assigned to them by Linnaeus and by Catesby, as well as giving the appropriate references to them, by volume and page number, in Buffon's *Histoire Naturelle*.[36] A brief discussion of albino Negroes follows, then a short reference to fish and insects.

Jefferson also discusses climate, using in part as a basis of his treatment the five-years' observations he had made in Williamsburg and its neighborhood, from which he constructed a table showing the averages of rainfall, minimum and maximum temperatures, and the direction of winds, carefully explaining the method by which he arrived at his averages. He compares the winds at Williamsburg and Monticello, gives thermometer readings at various places in the state, recounts barometric pressures, and discusses the phenomenon of warm air-pockets. His observations and discussions give him a rank in meteorology well above that of the amateur.[37] His remarks concerning the effects of cold upon plants may be taken as indicative of his scientific approach, showing his reluc-

---

34. Peden, p. 64.
35. *Ibid.*
36. *Ibid.*, pp. 66–69, 277.
37. Browne, pp. 376–77. Jefferson began his weather observations at the suggestion of Royal Governor Fauquier.

tance to draw unwarranted generalizations from insufficient facts. "I do not know," he says, that the lack of "long moss, reed, myrtle, swamp laurel, holly and cypress in the upper country, proceeds from a greater degree of cold, nor that they were ever killed with any degree of cold in the lower country."[38]

In his *Notes on the State of Virginia*, Jefferson made significant scientific contributions in the areas of geology, meteorology, geography, botany, and plant physiology. He also applied his scientific approach to social and cultural matters.

As Sir Isaiah Berlin has pointed out, men of the Enlightenment believed that human behavior was subject to natural laws similar to those obtaining in the material world, and thus that they could develop a science of sociology.[39] Jefferson shared in this belief that science—or "philosophy," as he often called it—held the key to knowledge of society, and this outlook, coupled with his reformist, humanitarian, and utilitarian proclivities, motivated much of his life and thought; it also permeated the major part of his *Notes on the State of Virginia*, the book which was principally responsible for establishing his scientific reputation at home and abroad.

Jefferson was more concerned with the limitations of human nature than he was with the imperfection of institutions.[40] He saw human beings as naturally predatory, given to exploiting one another. From Paris he wrote in 1787 of the American people: "If once they became inattentive to the public affairs, you and I, and Congress and Assemblies, Judges and Governors, shall all become wolves. It seems to be the law of our general na-

38. Lipscomb and Bergh, 2:114.
39. Sir Isaiah Berlin, ed., *The Age of the Enlightenment* (New York: Mentor Books, 1963), p. 27.
40. Daniel J. Boorstin, *The Lost World of Thomas Jefferson* (Boston: Beacon Press, 1948), p. 177.

ture. . . ."[41] He sought general laws of human behavior, and concluded that the people themselves must be educated to understand the laws of social life that they might attain the good society. To Jefferson this human propensity to exploit and dominate his fellows was an instinct, a fatal flaw in the species. Man in society was therefore the focus of his concern, and only secondarily did he give his attention to the problem of institutions. However, he considered institutions of great importance, for it was by means of institutions that man secured his natural rights and protected himself from tyranny. Humanity he divided into wolves and sheep—a view reinforced by his European observations. He held that the best form of government was one which was "too weak to aid the wolves, yet strong enough to protect the sheep." That each man might be free from exploitation by his fellows was the essence of political liberty, and to insure such liberty was the true purpose of government. Jefferson's search for a science of society was based upon reason and experience, and therefore conducted in the spirit of the scientific method.

Many of the social and cultural matters which Jefferson discussed in the *Notes on Virginia* involved criticisms of the prevailing institutions and the power structure of his day. This, of course, meant that his book would inevitably excite controversy. During the period when Jefferson was laying the foundations of the Republican party, his Federalist opponents seized upon such passages in the *Notes* which they felt would injure him and discredit his followers.[42] The attacks on Jefferson reached a flood tide during the presidential campaigns of 1800 and 1804, and his opponents found much of their political ammunition in the *Notes on Virginia*. Details and incidents were wrenched from context and distorted to serve

41. Lipscomb and Bergh, 6:58.
42. Peden, pp. xxiii–xxiv.

as partisan propaganda.[43] He was accused of being a "howling atheist" and a "confirmed infidel," and of seeking to undermine the Bible. Others called him a traitor to his class, and some even whispered that his expressed disapproval of slavery might have arisen from his sympathy for his alleged Negro mistress and mulatto offspring.[44] This campaign of vilification was to continue into the late nineteenth century. Such were some of the results of Jefferson's *Notes on the State of Virginia*. They led him to lament in one of his letters: "O! that mine enemy would write a book! has been a well known prayer against an enemy. I had written a book, and it has furnished matter of abuse for want of something better."[45]

The *Notes on the State of Virginia* was primarily a work of scientific orientation. It was also an expression of Jefferson's considered thoughts and opinions and revealed his strong reformist tendencies. Some of his suggestions for change at last bore fruit, and the impact of his thoughts and proposals was felt throughout the land. All his life he continued to advocate social and political changes and at last his fellow citizens gave heed to his words, particularly regarding the reformations he advocated in his home state, where he left his mark on the society, the government, the church, the academy.[46] Indeed, he left his mark on the length and breadth of America and on the minds of her people. His *Notes on the State of Virginia* was not only a major expression of his thought; it was also a powerful influence on the thoughts, hopes, and actions of his fellow countrymen.

Other subjects of scientific interest which engaged Jefferson's attentions are frequently encountered in his letters. Furthermore, he kept careful records of his activ-

---

43. *Ibid.*, p. xiv.
44. See chapter 10 below.
45. Peden, p. xxiv.
46. Merrill D. Peterson, *The Jefferson Image in the American Mind* (New York: Oxford University Press, 1962), p. 130.

ities and investigations, many of these in statistical form. He took notes and made memoranda on much that he observed and experienced, and felt it "truly unfortunate" that so few did so, for without such notes "history becomes fable instead of fact."[47] From his notes grew his authoritative *Manual of Parliamentary Procedure.* His *Garden Book,* begun in 1776 and continued the rest of his life, records his interest in seeds, plants, gardening, and farming. His *Account Books* he kept from 1767 until his death, and his *Weather Memorandum Book* from 1776 to 1820. His range of interests was little short of astounding and his diversity of activities almost incredible.

In his own day he enjoyed high repute both as a statesman and as a scientist who labored for the good of his native country and for the general human welfare.

Jefferson never failed to acknowledge that in science he was "an amateur." Certainly he was a man who loved science and, had he not spent so much of his time and energy in public service, one who might have attained greater accomplishments in science. Even so, had he not gained fame as a statesman, he would still be remembered today as a scientist, if for no other reason than the scientific elements of the *Notes on Virginia.* Both his insistence upon freedom for scientists and scientific endeavors, and his emphasis upon objectivity and the accumulation of sufficient data as a basis for generalizations rather than *a priori* approaches were great contributions to science. "A patient pursuit of facts and cautious combination and comparison of them is the drudgery to which man is subjected by his Maker, if he wishes to attain sure knowledge,"[48] he said. Underlying all his concern for science was his humanitarian desire that scientific progress

47. Martin, p. 19.
48. Albert Jay Nock, *Jefferson* (New York: Hill and Wang, 1963), p. 88.

should be utilized to promote human happiness, freedom, and fulfillment.

It is furthermore true that, since Jefferson has so long been overlooked as a social scientist, we must reappraise his contributions to the development of science in America. The foregoing comments regarding his interests in science have of course referred largely to the natural sciences and are given to show his general scientific approach. Much of the remainder of this study will be concerned with Jefferson and his contributions to social science—contributions of such a nature as to justify our speaking of him as a social scientist, or at least as a proto-social scientist, that should place him properly in the vanguard of those who were convinced that the study of human behavior was as much a subject for scientific investigation as the subject matter of the natural sciences. It may well be that Jefferson's most significant and enduring accomplishments of a scientific nature were realized in the area of the social sciences.

Indeed, it may be true that his political activities were primarily efforts to apply the principles of his social science to the "American experiment" to which he so often referred and which he repeatedly stated that he considered crucially significant if freedom and equality were to be made attainable by humanity in America and elsewhere.

3

On Demography and Ecology

Demographic and ecological factors are basic to a science of society, and Jefferson gave careful attention to them. In the *Notes on Virginia* he presented a statistical analysis of the population of Virginia from its settlement in 1607 to 1782, the year in which he was compiling the information for this book. He was careful to distinguish between figures indicating the entire population, and those indicating tythes only, that is, free white males and both male and female slaves over age sixteen. Jefferson pointed out that the two figures as reported were not comparable, but that these figures, along with other considerations, "will enable us to calculate, with a considerable degree of precision, the rate at which we have increased,"[1] particularly since 1654, the year in which the Virginia Company was dissolved. The tythes in that year were 7,209, and by 1772 they had increased to 153,000. Thus, the population doubled approximately every 27 years,[2] and on the basis of this calculation, Jefferson predicted a population of "between six and

---

1. Thomas Jefferson, *Notes on the State of Virginia,* ed. Thomas Perkins Abernethy (New York: Harper and Row, Publishers, 1964), p. 81.
2. This is reminiscent of Benjamin Franklin's remark that the American population doubled about every 25 years, a statement which helped inspire the Malthusian theory.

seven millions of inhabitants within ninety-five years," which would be one hundred inhabitants per square mile, a population density similar to that of the British Isles in Jefferson's day.

He estimated the total population of the state in 1782 at 567,614. The census upon which he based his calculations was not complete, giving no figures for eight of the counties; however, this census enabled him to project the total population from that reported, which included 53,289 free males over 21, 211,698 slaves of all ages and both sexes, and 23,766 not distinguished in the returns "but said to be tytheable slaves."[3] To calculate the number of slaves which should have been reported instead of the 23,766 "tytheables," he consulted "a former census," which indicated that "the numbers of slaves above and below sixteen years of age were equal. The double of this number, therefore, to wit, 47,532 must be added to 211,698," giving a total of 259,230 slaves of all ages and sexes.

To find the number of free inhabitants we must repeat the observation that those above and below sixteen are nearly equal. But as the number 53,289 omits the males below sixteen and twenty-one, we must supply them from conjecture. On a former experiment it had appeared that about one-third of our militia, that is, of the males between sixteen and fifty, were unmarried. Knowing how early marriage takes place here, we shall not be far wrong in supposing that the unmarried part of our militia are those between sixteen and twenty-one. . . . But as men above fifty were not included in the militia, we will suppose the unmarried, or those between sixteen and twenty-one to be one-fourth of the whole number above sixteen, then we have the following calculation:
52,289 free males above twenty-one years of age.
17,762 free males between sixteen and twenty-one.

3. Jefferson showed the 1782 census as also enumerating 195,439 horses, 609,734 cattle, 5,126 "wheels of riding-carriages," and 191 taverns (from which he might have calculated, but did not, that there was one tavern for approximately every 274 free males over 21!)

17,052 free males under sixteen.
142,104 free females of all ages.
284,208 free inhabitants of all ages.
259,230 slaves of all ages.
543,438 inhabitants, exclusive of the eight counties from which were no returns. In these eight counties in the years 1779 and 1780, were 3,161 militia. Say then,
3,161 free males above the age of sixteen.
3,161 free males under sixteen.
6,322 free females.
12,644 free inhabitants in these eight counties. To find the number of slaves, say as 284,208 to 259,230, so is 12,644 to 11,352. Adding the third of these numbers to the first, and the fourth to the second, we have
296,852 free inhabitants.
270,762 slaves.
567,614 inhabitants of every age, sex and condition. But 296,852, the number of free inhabitants, are to 270,762, the number of slaves, nearly as 11 to 10.[4]

Thus did Jefferson depict the demographic composition of Virginia in 1782, in a clear and succinct presentation. His statistical computations reveal a degree of sophistication which many will no doubt find surprising, and his projections are made with care and due designation of the variables to be considered. Here, as elsewhere, he demonstrated his scientific approach in dealing with social facts.

Jefferson was concerned with both demographic and ecological matters and their implications. In America as elsewhere it was man's nature to exploit and dominate his fellows for, in Jefferson's view, "mankind soon learn to make interested uses of every right and power which they possess or may assume. . . . Human nature is the same on every side of the Atlantic, and will alike be influenced by the same causes."[5] Jefferson saw environment

4. Abernethy, pp. 84–85.
5. Daniel J. Boorstin, *The Lost World of Thomas Jefferson* (Boston: Beacon Press, 1948), pp. 178–79.

as a crucial element in attaining social harmony and the happiness of mankind. The fitness of the environment for the health and welfare of the human species was a decisive factor, for he believed that the inevitable social struggle was primarily a result of the contest between man and the environment. The health of the body and the health of society were positively correlated, and when environmental conditions enabled men to grow vigorous, society was prosperous and the social order was presumed to be natural and moral. The multiplication and lengthening of human life were signs of health, and whatever social and environmental conditions produced these results had the approval of the Creator. He did not hesitate to affirm that a republican form of government produced healthful effects; thus, demography and ecology became important elements of his political philosophy.[6]

Even though the predatory nature of man was apparently designed by the Creator to secure a demographic equilibrium, this did not signify Jefferson's approval of the predator. He believed that the few who were to provide leadership for the many should be "an aristocracy of virtue and talents," as he wrote John Adams, "the most precious gift of nature, for the instruction, the trusts, and the government of society."[7] The people, he insisted, were competent for self-government through their choice of these "natural aristocrats" to lead them.

While in Paris Jefferson observed from Buffon's mortality tables analyzing 23,994 deaths that of all persons living at any moment, half would be dead within 24 years and eight months; and he calculated that by leaving out all minors and considering only adults (those who had the power to act for society), one-half of the voting popu-

---

6. *Ibid.,* pp. 180-85.
7. Adrienne Koch and William Peden, eds., *The Life and Selected Writings of Thomas Jefferson* (New York: Random House, Inc., 1944), pp. 632-33.

lation alive at any given moment would be dead within eighteen years and eight months. This demographic conclusion had tremendous political implications in Jefferson's view. To Madison he wrote, "the earth belongs in usufruct to the living,"[8] and since each generation had a span of only about 19 years, none had a right "to contract a public debt which could not be retired within that period."[9] Indeed, all public contracts, all laws, even all constitutions should be void within 19 years after their enactment;[10] otherwise, revolutions would be necessary to rid the living of the shackles by which the dead had sought to bind them. Jefferson declared that

> no society can make a perpetual constitution, or even a perpetual law. The earth belongs always to the living. . . . The constitution and the laws of their predecessors are extinguished . . . with those whose will gave them being. . . . If it be enforced longer, it is an act of force, and not of right.[11]

Such were the implications of demographic factors—particularly the average life span—to Jefferson.

The ecological relationship of men to their environment in America gave Jefferson cause for optimism. The land which belonged to the living of his generation was vast and fertile, a land where each man could prosper from his own labors, so long as the social and political environment were as favorable as that which nature and nature's God had provided.

Jefferson's enthusiasm for America as a land offering freedom and happiness to its people led him to visualize an "empire for liberty" which would extend perhaps over both the American continents. His view was that every

8. *Ibid.*, p. 488.
9. Thomas Jefferson, *The Writings of Thomas Jefferson*, ed. Andrew A. Lipscomb and Albert E. Bergh, 20 vols. (Washington: Thomas Jefferson Memorial Association, 1903), 13:272.
10. *Ibid.*, 7:463.
11. *Ibid.*, 7:459.

man had the right to acquire and accumulate property. Thus, he looked to the Louisiana Purchase to provide a vast new territory of potential farm lands for the establishment of agrarian communities, the strength and hope of American democracy. He spoke of the Western territories as "that vast and fertile country" which the sons of its settlers were "destined to fill with arts, with science, with freedom and happiness."[12] In 1813 he wrote to John Jacob Astor, whom he compared to Columbus and Raleigh, that in the West there would arise a "great, free and independent empire on that side of our continent, and that liberty and self-government spreading from that side as well as this side, will insure their complete establishment over the whole."[13] So eager was he to see the spread of this empire of liberty that during the War of 1812 he expressed his hope for the conquest of Canada,[14] and even suggested that South America might be added.[15] To Jefferson, land and liberty went hand in hand, and wherever there was plentiful available land, the future of liberty was bright. The virtue and strength of America lay in the agrarian producers.

To John Adams he wrote that the old world was crowded and "steeped in the vices which that situation generates"; but here in America, each man "may have land to labor for himself" and "every one, by his property . . . is interested in the support of law and order," reserving "to themselves a wholesome control over public affairs, and a degree of freedom" which would be impossible in Europe.[16] America was an uncontaminated laboratory, and the American experiment held implications for the whole of the human species. The Creator's approval of this society built on the rights of man would

12. *Ibid.,* 18 :160.
13. *Ibid.,* 13 :432.
14. *Ibid.,* 13 :173.
15. *Ibid.,* 14 :21.
16. *Ibid.,* 13 :401.

be read in the nation's success and prosperity, and sooner
or later the whole world would discover the route to
human happiness.[17]

Nevertheless, Jefferson's early belief was that the
American experiment could succeed only if the immigration of Europeans with their penchant for monarchy and
their city-bred vices was severely restricted.[18] The mes-
sianic task of Americans would reach fruition only by
the exploitation of peculiarly American advantages.

Jefferson tackled the question of immigration in the
Notes on the State of Virginia, pointing out that the desire of America in his time was "to produce rapid population by as great importations of foreigners as possible."
But he questioned whether this was good policy. By
doubling its population in one year through immigration,
Virginia would have a population of four and one-half
millions in 54½ years; by natural increase it would take
81¾ years to reach that number, and this he demonstrated by use of a statistical table. Would the state be
able to support such a number at the level of living then
current? Jefferson thought not.

There were other considerations, too.

> It is for the happiness of those united in society to harmonize
> as much as possible in matters which they must of necessity
> transact together. Civil government being the sole object of
> forming societies, its administration must be conducted by com-
> mon consent. Every species of government has its specific prin-
> ciples. Ours perhaps are more peculiar than those of any other
> in the universe. It is a composition of the freest principles of
> the English constitution, with others derived from natural right
> and natural reason. To these nothing can be more opposed than
> the maxims of absolute monarchies. Yet from such are we to
> expect the greatest number of emigrants. They will bring with
> them the principles of the governments they leave, imbibed in
> their early youth; or, if able to throw them off, it will be in

17. *Ibid.,* 10:217.
18. Boorstin, *The Lost World of Thomas Jefferson,* p. 229.

exchange for unbounded licentiousness, passing, as is usual, from one extreme to another. It would be a miracle were they to stop precisely at the point of temperate liberty. These principles, with their language, they will transmit to their children. In proportion to their numbers, they will share with us the legislation. They will infuse into it their spirit, warp and bias its directions, and render it a heterogenious, incoherent, distracted mass. . . . If they come of themselves, they are entitled to all the rights of citizenship; but I doubt the expediency, of inviting them by extraordinary encouragements.[19]

Jefferson felt that consensus and cohesion could be maintained in American society only by a homogeneous population of native-born patriots. He gloried in the American separation from Europe, for America had land enough "to the hundredth and thousandth generation," he said in the First Inaugural Address, if only it did not open its doors to a flood of men socialized in the norms of despotism and monarchy. This was Jefferson's view when he wrote the *Notes on Virginia.*

But later events caused him to alter his opinions. One of them was the Federalist Naturalization Act of 1798, a part of the so-called Alien and Sedition Acts. This act was obviously political; it extended the requirement for attaining citizenship by immigrants from five to fourteen years. The Federalists complained that every new boat-load of immigrants brought more votes for Jefferson and the Republicans; the objective of the act was clear. Political considerations aside, the man who wrote the *Summary View,* in which he based the rights of the colonists to self-government partly on emigration, perhaps remembered his early principles, including his own Virginia Naturalization Bill of 1776, which provided for admission to citizenship after two years' residence. His opposition to the Federalist Naturalization Act was vigorous and lasting.

---

19. Abernethy, pp. 83–84.

He never quite lost his fears that unrestricted immigration might corrupt the principles of American society, yet he also wished America to be a haven for the world's oppressed. In his First Annual Message to Congress, he asked: "Shall we refuse the unhappy fugitives from distress that hospitality which the savages of the wilderness extended to our fathers arriving in this land? Shall oppressed humanity find no asylum on this globe?" Then, remembering the Federalist act, he asked: "Might not the general character and capabilities of a citizen be safely communicated to every one manifesting a *bona fide* purpose of embarking his life and fortunes permanently with us?"[20] In 1817 he wrote of his desire "to consecrate a sanctuary for those whom the misrule of Europe may compel to seek happiness in other climes"[21]; and to a French correspondent he declared, "I think it fortunate for the United States to have become the asylum for so many virtuous patriots of different denominations."[22] He seemed to prefer Italian immigrants, since they were among the world's best artisans, and even in the *Notes on Virginia* he had made an exception of "useful artificers," saying, "Spare no expense in obtaining them. They will after a while go to the plough and the hoe; but in the mean time, they will teach us something we do not know."[23] He also applied this later view to the Louisiana Territory, which he was convinced would be opened to immigration, with new settlers moving into the virgin lands, bringing prosperity to the United States and happiness to themselves.

In the *Notes on Virginia,* Jefferson also discussed the communities of the state. "We have no towns of any consequence," he pointed out. "Williamsburg never con-

20. Lipscomb and Bergh, 3:338.
21. *Ibid.,* 15:141.
22. Koch and Peden, p. 533.
23. Abernethy, p. 84.

tained above 1,800 inhabitants; and Norfolk, the most populous town we ever had, contained but 6,000. . . . The *laws* have said there shall be towns; but *nature* has said there shall not."[24] Jefferson no doubt found this a source of comfort, for he considered that indolence and dissipation were the universal characteristics of city dwellers and this provided a strong moral argument against an urban civilization. "The general desire of men to live by their heads rather than their hands," he remarked, "and the strong allurement of great cities to those who have any turn for dissipation, threaten to make them here, as in Europe, the sinks of voluntary misery." Artificers were the panders of vice, and thus instruments by which a country's liberties might be lost; and greed for wealth, the principal vice of commerce, could eventually destroy the virtue and morals of a whole citizenry.[25] He was convinced that most vices could not thrive in rural areas, and thus he maintained a strong preference for agriculturalists over those who earned their livings in urban occupations. "Those who labor in the earth are the chosen people of God, if ever He had a chosen people," he declared in the *Notes on Virginia*. "Corruption of morals in the mass of cultivators is a phenomenon of which no age nor nation has furnished an example."[26]

Demographic and ecological considerations were important elements in Jefferson's social science and in his design for a society in which men might find freedom, happiness, and equality.

---

24. *Ibid.*, p. 103.
25. Lipscomb and Bergh, 5:93.
26. Koch and Peden, p. 280.

4

On Economic Institutions

In the *Notes on Virginia*, Jefferson said ". . . generally speaking, the proportion which the aggregate of the other classes of citizens bears in any state to that of its husbandmen, is the proportion of its unsound to its healthy parts, and is a good enough barometer whereby to measure its degree of corruption."[1] His preference for an economic system based on agriculture was an important aspect of his ideas regarding economic institutions. "The political economists of Europe have established it as a principle, that every State should endeavor to manufacture for itself," he pointed out; but the shortage of land in Europe meant that manufacturing was necessary in order to support the population. However, in America the circumstances were different. "We have an immensity of land courting the industry of the husbandman." Since God had made "those who labor in the earth . . . His peculiar deposit for substantial and genuine virtue," it was plain to Jefferson that the agrarian life was to be desired and encouraged above all others.[2]

Corruption of morals he saw as a natural result of

---

1. Thomas Jefferson, *Notes on the State of Virginia,* ed. Thomas Perkins Abernethy (New York: Harper and Row, Publishers, 1964), p. 157.
2. *Ibid.*

urban life, in which the interdependence that Emile Durkheim characterized as the basis of organic solidarity "begets subservience and venality, suffocates the germ of virtue, and prepares fit tools for the design of ambition." Dependence upon "the casualties and caprice of customers" in a commercial society with its specialized division of labor was to Jefferson an unnatural and undesirable phenomenon, as was employment in manufacturing with its enforced separation from nature. "While we have land to labor then," he advocated, "let us never wish to see our citizens occupied at a work-bench or twirling a distaff. . . . Let our workshops remain in Europe." Manufacturing led to the growth of cities, with their heterogeneous populations and invitations to vice and corruption. And these were lethal to the freedom and happiness of man. "The mobs of great cities add just so much to the support of pure government, as sores do to the strength of the human body," he declared. Cities would therefore be disastrous to the American experiment, for "it is the manners and spirit of a people which preserve a republic in vigor. A degeneracy in these is a canker which soon eats to the heart of its laws and constitution."[3]

Jefferson at this stage in his life thus advocated economic institutions built upon agriculture. In the *Notes* he presented a table of the state's annual exports before the Revolution. These, according to his figures, represented a total value of $2,833,333, and included, in order of importance, tobacco, wheat, corn, shipping, masts, planks, scantling, shingles, staves, tar, pitch, turpentine, pelts (deer, beaver, otter, muskrat, raccoon, fox), pork, flax-seed, hemp, cotton, coal, pig iron, peas, beef, fish (sturgeon, white shad, herring), brandy (from peaches and apples), whiskey, and horses. The tobacco exports

3. *Ibid.*, pp. 157–58.

represented by far the greatest item in value ($1,650,-000), followed by wheat ($666,666), with the items of lowest value being brandy and whiskey ($1,666) and horses (also $1,666).[4]

However, Jefferson opposed the tobacco culture, pointing out that it required "an extraordinary degree of heat" as well as "an uncommon fertility of soil," making it a more satisfactory crop for the abundant fresh and fertile soils in "the western country on the Mississippi, and the midlands of Georgia," which he saw as replacing Virginia and Maryland as the chief producers of tobacco. Besides, he considered the tobacco culture to be one "productive of infinite wretchedness. Those employed in it are in a continual state of exertion beyond the power of nature to support." Such people raised few other crops, so that both men and animals were badly fed. Furthermore, tobacco exhausted the soil, robbing it of its fertility.[5] He himself abandoned the cultivation of this crop at Monticello. To Samuel Biddle, whom he wished to employ as an overseer, he wrote in 1792:

> The farm is of about five or six hundred acres of cleared land, very hilly, originally as rich as any highlands in the world but much worried by Indian corn and tobacco. . . . You will have from 12 to 15 laborers under you. They will be well clothed, and as well fed as your management of the farm will enable us, for it is chiefly with a view to place them on the comfortable footing of the laborers of other countries [states] that I come into another country to seek an overlooker for them, as also to have my lands a little more taken care. For these purposes I have long banished tobacco and wish to do the same by Indian corn in a great degree.[6]

Jefferson, however, was never a rigid doctrinaire in

4. *Ibid.,* p. 158.
5. *Ibid.,* p. 159.
6. Thomas Jefferson, *The Writings of Thomas Jefferson,* ed. Andrew A. Lipscomb and Albert E. Bergh, 20 vols. (Washington: Thomas Jefferson Memorial Association, 1903), 18:189. Jefferson often used the term "country" instead of "state."

farming, and economic conditions which brought about a great increase in the price of tobacco in 1798 caused him temporarily to return to growing this crop. To John Taylor of Caroline he wrote:

> . . . the high price of tobacco, which is likely to continue for some short time, has tempted me to go entirely into that culture, and in the meantime, my farming schemes are in abeyance, and my farming fields at nurse against the time of my resuming them.[7]

But Jefferson very much preferred wheat as the chief crop of "the producers" in the economic structure of his ideal republic, as he makes clear in the *Notes on Virginia*. "Besides clothing the earth with herbage, and preserving its fertility, it feeds the laborers plentifully, requires from them only a moderate toil, except in the season of harvest, raises great numbers of animals for food and service, and diffuses plenty and happiness among the whole."[8] Growing wheat involved one great problem, and that was the weevil. To control this pest, Jefferson proposed "subterranean granaries" with temperatures sufficiently low to prevent the hatching of weevil eggs. Or, alternatively, he suggested that the wheat might be dried in kilns of sufficient temperature to kill the eggs, and then stored in hogsheads covered with a coating of lime. But these and other methods of controlling the weevil made the production of wheat rather troublesome, and he expressed the hope that some solution to the problem might soon appear. Not only had wheat culture the advantages previously indicated, but it, "by enlarging our pasture, will render the Arabian horse an article of considerable profit," and Jefferson considered this animal a creature of "fleetness and beauty" as well as one well adapted to the needs of his state.[9]

---

7. *Ibid.,* 10:63.
8. Abernethy, p. 159.
9. *Ibid.,* pp. 160–61.

Jefferson's preference for an agricultural economy was strong and deep-seated. This preference was reinforced by his observations in France and later became a source of disagreement between his Republican party and the Federalists. His almost passionate belief in the superiority of an agrarian society he later modified, but he never abandoned his distrust of large cities and their heterogeneous populations. In the *Notes on Virginia* Jefferson was speaking not merely of Virginia but of the whole nation, and his ideas on the subjects of commerce, manufacturing, and agriculture must be viewed in this larger framework. He was a firm believer in free trade between Europe and America and did not consider American self-sufficiency a goal, as Hamilton and Clay later did. He was willing to abandon shipping in order to avoid quarrels with Europe and to insure American independence from the Old World, a policy he believed would encourage all Americans to follow the salutary occupation of farming, although he realized that this was but the dream of a "philosopher" and that some Americans would continue to engage in commerce.

Nevertheless, he felt no real enthusiasm for commerce and manufacturing, although he came to favor domestic workshops; and eventually he undertook the making of carriages, furniture, and nails at Monticello, hoping that shops of the industrial type would remain in Europe. Only home-type industries held any appeal for him, and he became enthusiastic over these.

His "nail manufactory" is a case in point. He set up his nailery at Monticello in 1794; it operated almost continuously for about ten years and intermittently until near the end of his life. To a French correspondent, he wrote:

> There is no such thing in this country as what would be called wealth in Europe. . . . In our private pursuits it is a great

advantage that every honest employment be deemed honorable.
. . . My new trade of nailmaking is to me in this country what
an additional title of nobility or the ensigns of a new order are
in Europe.[10]

By 1796 he was producing a ton of nails each month,
using both hand methods and machine methods. During
the first two years, the operation looked like a success,
and he indicated in his *Farm Book* that he could produce
enough nails in two weeks to cover the cost of his coffee,
chocolate, tea, sugar, molasses, rice, rum or French brandy
for three months. Competition from imported British
nails soon jeopardized his operation, and—as much as
he disliked retailing—he started a consignment business
in Charlottesville, Milton, and Staunton in order to place
his nails before the buyer. Difficulties in collecting payment, plus his return to public life, put a stop to his plans
for expansion. He had supervised the entire operation
before 1800, but as President of the United States he
was no longer able to oversee this rustic business; thus,
the nailery operation failed to develop as the profitable
home industry he had hoped it would be.

Jefferson characteristically viewed economic matters in
the larger social and philosophical setting. Regarding the
Constitution, he wrote Madison that if a majority approved of it, he would concur, "in hopes they will amend
it whenever they find it works wrong. This reliance can
not deceive us," he declared, "as long as we remain virtuous; and I think we shall be so long as agriculture is
our principal object, which will be the case while there
remains vacant lands in any part of America."[11] His
view of agriculture as conducive to morality, honesty,

---

10. Thomas Jefferson, *The Writings of Thomas Jefferson*, ed. Paul
Leicester Ford, 10 vols. (New York: G. P. Putnam's Sons, 1892–1899),
7:13–14.

11. Albert Jay Nock, *Jefferson* (New York: Hill and Wang, 1963),
p. 69.

democracy, and virtue colored much if not all of his thinking about the structure and function of economic institutions.

Nevertheless, Jefferson fulfilled faithfully his obligations to seek commercial treaties with Europe when he
served as a member of the commission composed of himself, Franklin, and Adams; and he worked energetically
in this regard when he became minister to France, although his efforts were largely unsuccessful. To Monroe
he wrote, "You see that my primary object in the formation of treaties is to take the commerce of the states out
of the hands of the states, and to place it under the
superintendence of Congress."[12] He had much in common
with the physiocrats, and of course he still thought agriculture the best way of life, though he later came to de-
scribe commerce as the handmaiden of agriculture. He
wished that trade might be entirely free, preferring Adam
Smith's doctrine to that of the mercantilists, in part because he believed in the maximum of individual liberty
in all things, and in part because he felt that the United
States should be able to develop its own practices for its
greatest benefit. "In political economy," he wrote his
son-in-law, Thomas Mann Randolph, "I think Smith's
Wealth of Nations is the best book extant."[13]

For European nations, however, he realized that free
trade without complex tariffs was impossible. "The establishments are fixed upon them," he wrote; "they are
interwoven with the body of their laws and the organization of their government and they make a great part of
their revenue; they cannot then get rid of them."[14] He
also observed that only when Congress indicated its disposition to regulate commerce did the European nations

12. Ford, *Writings*, 4:55.
13. Adrienne Koch and William Peden, eds., *The Life and Selected
Writings of Thomas Jefferson* (New York: Random House, 1944), p. 496.
14. Ford, *Writings*, 4:56.

display any interest in commercial treaties with the United States.[15] Thus Jefferson, the champion of local self-government, came to recognize the inevitability of national regulation of external commerce, against which his chief grievance was that it led to wars, a circumstance which meant that along with the development of commerce must come the development of naval strength—something he found it necessary at this point to advocate.[16] Furthermore, the growth of commerce led to the rise of large cities, which he continued to distrust.

This matter of commerce was, of course, a major element in the Jefferson-Hamilton controversy. Jefferson realized that Hamilton's much-debated Assumption Bill, opposed vigorously by Southern congressmen, was necessary "to save us from the greatest of all calamities, the total extinction of our credit in Europe."[17] Although he was no financier and was reluctant to agree with Hamilton, he deplored the sectionalism displayed in Congress, fearing that the dissolution of the union might result therefrom. Thus, he arranged for several Southerners to switch their votes to favor the Assumption Bill in exchange for Hamilton's agreement to support the location of the national capital in the South, on the borders of the Potomac. This shrewd bit of political maneuvering involved economic and financial implications, however, which Jefferson at the time did not foresee.

Under Hamilton's aggressive leadership, financial interests were gaining influence in the government, and speculators, whom Jefferson called "stock-jobbers," stood to gain wealth at the expense of the people. Hamilton's financial program was beginning to take effect. Congress had passed his Excise Bill, his Bank Bill, and his Assump-

---

15. Lipscomb and Bergh, 5:108.
16. Ford, *Writings*, 4:89–90.
17. Saul K. Padover, *Jefferson* (New York: Mentor Books, 1963), p. 81.

tion Bill. Even Jefferson admitted that the result had been one of great prosperity for the country. Yet, with mills and factories springing up and financiers flourishing, Jefferson was perturbed. The republic, he feared, was falling into the hands of corrupt merchants and speculators who had no commitment to liberty or equality. The business interests, under Hamilton's leadership, were gaining disproportionate power in a nation still overwhelmingly rural. These powerful men were beginning to monopolize the privileges and wealth which Hamilton's policies had secured. "Congress may go home," Senator Maclay wrote. "Mr. Hamilton is all-powerful and fails at nothing."[18]

Jefferson was no match for Hamilton in the field of finance and economics and could offer President Washington no realistic alternative to Hamilton's program; however, he viewed with alarm the growth of powerful financial interests which he was sure would undermine the democratic foundations of the republic and, if unchecked, lead at last to the realization of Hamilton's monarchist ambitions for the nation. Hamilton considered the English constitution "perfect" and advocated an elective lifetime monarch for the United States. He did not trust the people; they were a "great beast," he had said; and Jefferson feared that the Hamiltonians' exalted power would destroy the rights of the people to self-government, turning the wealth of the nation to their private plunder and robbing the people of rights that had been dearly won.

He did not understand Hamilton's financial innovations, for to Jefferson real property was the true source of wealth. He deplored the speculation in bank scrip that was rampant. Hamilton's policies had increased the wealth and importance of a rising moneyed group, who

---

18. Dumas Malone, *Jefferson and the Rights of Man* (Boston: Little, Brown and Company, 1951), p. 340.

were gaining great profits from their speculative activities. All this Jefferson regarded as financial trickery and gambling. He believed that Americans would be happier if they returned to the "plain unsophisticated common sense" from which they should never have been led astray by the "criminality of this paper system."[19] Jefferson feared debt, and the sort of wealth deriving from Hamilton's policies seemed unreal to him, for he considered land to be the basis of wealth and was a believer in hard money. And, even more, he feared what he believed to be the purpose of the Hamiltonian system: the concentration of wealth and power in the hands of the rich and wellborn.

When Jefferson became president, he proposed a "wise and frugal government." He eliminated the system of internal taxes and reduced the national debt by almost half, despite the expenditure of fifteen million dollars for Louisiana. Although he grew more sympathetic to manufacturing, he still stood largely opposed to the Hamiltonian financial system and he still considered agriculture the most desirable basis of American economic life. It was not his attitude toward a specific economic system which gave a degree of consistency to his policies but instead his unshakable faith in the right of men to rule themselves and his eternal hostility to any form of despotism, financial, political, religious, or other. Jefferson developed no theory or science of economics going beyond the principles of physiocracy and Adam Smith, which he largely accepted. In this area he was essentially less scientific than in most others, and he seems largely inadequate in his understanding of economics. His tentative gropings toward a theory of economics produced little of significance, and his concern in this area was principally with economic practices and institutions, an outgrowth of

19. Ford, *Writings*, 5:507-8.

his view of the natural order he postulated and upon which so much of this thought was based. Thus, it may be said that Jefferson thought primarily in broader terms than the strictly economic.[20]

He thought instead in terms of an underlying belief in the purposes of nature and nature's God, which, while not part of a systematic theory, was based upon the concept of natural rights. In this view, the Creator had made men and society but had not designed specific institutions. It was nature which held the key, and the object of both politics and economics was to secure what Jefferson called "the associated happiness of man." The underlying source of Jefferson's thought was a firm conviction that economic, political, and other institutions were but instruments to be utilized by man in the larger purpose of fitting himself to the scheme of the Creator as revealed in nature. Natural rights and natural reason were the decisive factors, and the history of human progress was the history of man's success in discovering and structuring institutions to fit the scheme of nature. It was man's destiny to attain adaptation to his environment in order to secure the happiness which a benevolent Creator had designed for him and for the accomplishment of which purpose institutions were the instruments. Institutions represented

20. Nock, p. 116. One of his major biographers, Albert Jay Nock, however, finds the explanation of Jefferson's economic ideas and principles in his role as representative of an economic class interest. Jefferson stood for control of government by the economic producers, that is, by those who apply labor and capital to natural resources for the production of wealth. Nock concedes that he shares the view expressed by Charles A. Beard, who saw Jefferson's political thought as largely determined by his economic outlook. See Charles A. Beard, *An Economic Interpretation of the Constitution of the United States* (New York: The Macmillan Company, 1913); also Charles A. Beard, *Economic Origins of Jeffersonian Democracy* (New York: The Macmillan Company, 1915).

Other efforts to deal with Jefferson's economic views may be found in the following: Joseph Dorfman, *The Economic Mind in American Civilization,* vol. 1 (New York: The Viking Press, 1946); Alfred Whitney Griswold, *Farming and Democracy* (New Haven: Yale University Press, 1948); and William D. Grampp, "Re-examination of Jeffersonian Economics," *Social Economics Journal* 12 (January, 1946): 263–82.

the attempts of men to secure their natural rights, and as the only vehicles available, they were important—though their structure was neither sacred nor permanent. Nature itself, and nature's God, were alone unchanging and unchangeable, and it was to secure the rights of nature—life, liberty, and the pursuit of happiness—that institutions were to be utilized, their forms to be changed and adjusted in the light of new circumstances and increased knowledge. Jefferson's view was a liberal one; thus, in regard to economic institutions he may fairly be called an agrarian only in the light of the age and circumstances in which he lived and his definition of the situations he observed about him. It is safe to say that in twentieth-century America he would not have been an agrarian in economics any more than he would have been an isolationist in foreign policy.

If America has not fulfilled the Jeffersonian dream of a pure agricultural democratic republic with liberty and equality for all at home and peace as a result of non-entangling alliances abroad—perhaps a dream that was nonutopian only in the simpler world of the eighteenth century—neither has it discarded the larger principles which motivated Jefferson's hopes and plans for America. A word of caution is in order: we must not forget that to Jefferson the products of human endeavors—even constitutions—were not sacrosanct. He believed in salvation by knowledge and science, and he repeatedly declared that new knowledge and new discoveries would enable man to improve his instruments for achieving the natural rights of freedom and equality. It is as unfair to Jefferson to freeze him at the knife edge of history known as the American Enlightenment as it is to disregard the motivating principles of his life and thought. Indeed, if the second error is avoided, so automatically will the first be.

5

On Political Institutions

Jefferson believed that man was a rational creature, endowed by nature with inalienable rights and with an innate sense of justice which could be strengthened by education. It is true that he considered men exploitative, but as he wrote Du Pont de Nemours, he also believed them "susceptible of much improvement," if they were free, secure, and educated. With Locke he agreed that man's capacity to reason enabled him to govern himself. And this, along with his Enlightenment faith that a science of society could be discovered, colored his view of politics and political institutions. "No experiment can be more interesting than that we are now trying," he wrote, "and which we trust will end in establishing the fact that man may be governed by reason and truth."[1] Above all he was committed to the primacy of human rights, a conviction he expressed well in a letter to James Madison regarding the Constitution: "A bill of rights is what the people are entitled to against every government on earth . . . and what no just government should refuse, or rest on inference."[2]

1. Thomas Jefferson, *The Writings of Thomas Jefferson*, ed. Andrew A. Lipscomb and Albert E. Bergh, 20 vols. (Washington: Thomas Jefferson Memorial Association, 1903), 11:33.
2. Thomas Jefferson, *The Writings of Thomas Jefferson*, ed. Paul Leicester Ford, 10 vols. (New York: G. P. Putnam's Sons, 1892–1899), 4:477.

Jefferson's political ideas were no doubt strongly influenced by the writers whom he had been reading with care and diligence ever since his student days. These included not only Locke, Montesquieu, Hobbes, Helvetius, Voltaire, and a number of constitutional historians, but also Lord Kames, Dalrymple, Sidney, and the ancients. Like many of his contemporaries of the American Enlightenment, Jefferson accepted the social contract doctrine that men had originally been in a state of nature where freedom of action prevailed; and that, to gain the advantages of corporate life, government was instituted among them by consent. As early as 1770, he declared publicly that under the law of nature all men are born free.[3]

Although he seldom referred to the time before which the social contract was supposed to have come into being, his references to contracts and compacts were frequent, and by these terms it is clear that he meant charters, constitutions, and historic formal agreements. His conviction that man was born free was in part a moral one. He was confident that force could not give "rights," nor could kings. These rights were "natural rights," deriving from the universal law of nature. "The God who gave us life gave us liberty at the same time,"[4] he declared.

Many of these ideas find parallels in the writings of John Locke, and there is no doubt that Jefferson was deeply influenced by the great Englishman. However, if special importance is attributed to the influence of Locke, this is because Locke was the most representative exponent of the thought of the Enlightenment. The ideas which Locke expressed—particularly those in his *Second Treatise on Civil Government*—were abroad in the Western world during the formative period of Jefferson's life, giving a distinctive character to the thought of Europe and America, and there is no doubt that Jefferson read

3. *Ibid.*, 1:380, 445.
4. *Ibid.*, 1:447.

Locke. But he also read others, whose works incorporated ideas similar to those of Locke. While Locke was probably the greatest single influence on his thinking—perhaps because Locke's ideas concurred with many of his own which had already taken shape—Jefferson synthesized many elements of thought into his own political philosophy, although he never developed this philosophy into a system and did not use his terms with the precision of an academician, often failing to define them.

Jefferson's progression from English citizen demanding English rights to avowed revolutionary and republican was, of course, not immediate or precipitous. As late as 1774 he made an unsuccessful appeal to the King in his *Summary View,* in which he declared that Parliament had no right to impose its arbitrary will upon the colonists in violation of their rights as Englishmen. "It is neither our wish nor our interest to separate from" Great Britain, he declared. "We are willing, on our part, to sacrifice everything which reason can ask to the restoration of . . . tranquillity."[5] Not until two years had passed and blood had been shed did he become an admitted republican. Within this brief period, however, he had surveyed the history of various European federative systems which might serve as models for the American experiment.[6] Since the days in which he had studied Montesquieu's *Esprit de Lois,* he had pondered the merits of a democratic republic, and throughout his life he recalled Montesquieu's avowal that the right of suffrage is the basis of such a government. Jefferson concluded that the people might exercise their sovereignty by means of their votes, a conclusion which is reflected in the Declaration of Independence and which made the chief concern of his life the attainment and preservation of liberty.

5. Saul K. Padover, *Jefferson* (New York: Mentor Books, 1963), p. 27.
6. Thomas Jefferson, *The Commonplace Book of Thomas Jefferson,* ed. Gilbert Chinard (Baltimore: The Johns Hopkins Press, 1926), pp. 24–28.

Jefferson's *Summary View,* having been printed in England as well as in America, established his reputation as both a superb writer and as a spokesman for the colonial cause. Thomas Paine's *Common Sense*—over which Washington, Jefferson, and others were enthusiastic—added many to the roster of those who felt the policies of the British government had at last become insufferable, and the spirit of independence was in the air at the meeting of the Congress in 1776. Richard Henry Lee's resolution that "these United Colonies are & of right ought to be free and independent states" brought forth an uproarious debate, resulting in the appointment of a committee of five to draw up a Declaration of Independence: Jefferson, John Adams, Franklin, Roger Sherman, and Robert Livingston.

Jefferson prepared the first draft, in which Franklin and Adams made a few revisions. But the work was almost entirely Jefferson's. He disavowed any claim to personal originality, however, stating that "all American whigs thought alike on these subjects. . . . Neither aiming at originality of principle or sentiment, nor yet copied from any particular and previous writing, it was intended to be expression of the American mind . . . harmonizing sentiments of the day . . . expressed in letters, printed essays . . . books of public right, as Aristotle, Cicero, Locke, Sidney."[7] The similarities to Locke were, of course, striking, but there were significant differences— such as Jefferson's substituting "the pursuit of happiness" for "property" in Locke's triplex of political values.[8] The political principles of natural rights and self-government were given immortal expression by Jefferson in a statement of remarkable compactness and simplicity, embracing in a few paragraphs a complete philosophy which set

7. Ford, *Writings,* 10:343.
8. George Mason had used the word "happiness" in the Virginia Declaration of Rights a month earlier. Padover, *Jefferson,* p. 35.

forth the reasons that justify the authority of the state and that define its fundamental rights and limitations; an ethical position which declared the aggregate happiness of individuals to be the supreme end of government; and a doctrine explaining the origins of nature and man. As revolutionary as it was in the light of the current political actualities, the document was based on the authority of the existing body of law as understood by the majority of the Congressional delegates,[9] and to Jefferson in particular, upon the supreme "laws of nature and of nature's God." The Declaration was an expression of consensus as well as a statement of principles.

The resounding phrases of the Declaration of Independence announced in majestic terms the basic political postulates of the new nation. In more specific terms, Jefferson in the *Notes on the State of Virginia* detailed his political philosophy in regard to the practical considerations of the governing of his own state. Herein he further revealed the foundations of the approach to political questions which he was to retain throughout his long and politically active life.

In the *Notes* Jefferson traced the structure of the Virginia government from its establishment in 1607 up to 1782. The original charter provided that the inhabitants were to enjoy "all the rights of natural subjects, as if born and abiding in England." Two councils were established, the Governor's Council, with members appointed by the Virginia Company and the governor, and the General Assembly, later to be known as the House of Burgesses, with members elected by the people. No orders of the Council in England were to be binding on the colony unless ratified by its General Assembly. When Virginia became a royal colony in 1624, the King assumed the power of government; and during the Crom-

9. Carl Becker, *The Declaration of Independence* (New York: Peter Smith, 1940), chapter 3.

well regime, Parliament took over these powers. The Assembly protested these and other violations of the charter. But further abuses followed, applicable to all the colonies, which Jefferson stated as follows: "The colonies were taxed internally and externally; their . . . legislatures suspended; charters annulled; trials by jury taken away; their persons subjected to transportation across the Atlantic, and to trials before foreign judicatories."[10] Therefore, the colonies declared themselves independent.

In Virginia, the new government was comprised of a governor and council of eight; a judiciary; and two elective legislative houses, the House of Delegates with members elected annually, and the Senate with members elected quadrennially. Concurrence of both houses was necessary for the passage of laws, and these legislative bodies appointed the governor and council. The constitution of the state "was formed when we were new and unexperienced in the science of government," Jefferson said, and contained "very capital defects."[11] The most serious shortcomings which Jefferson identified were those which denied liberty and freedom to the citizens and opened the door to future despotism and tyranny.

The first of these concerned the franchise. "The majority of the men in the state, who pay and fight for its support, are unrepresented in the legislature," he said, since freeholders entitled to vote did not number half those on the militia rolls.[12] He thus favored extending the franchise by decreasing property qualifications.

Furthermore, representation was unequal. He presented a statistical table to show that the number of

10. Lipscomb and Bergh, 2:158–59.
11. *Ibid.,* 2:160. Jefferson prepared a revision of the state constitution in 1783; however, his and Madison's efforts to secure enactment did not soon bear fruit. The constitution of 1776 was not repealed until 1830.
12. *Ibid.,* 2:160.

representatives in the legislature from the counties "below the falls of the rivers"—that is, in the eastern and Tide-water sections where the great planter elite was estab-lished—"possess half the senate, and want four members only of possessing a majority of the house of delegates." Thus, the nineteen thousand voters in Eastern Virginia "give law to upwards of thirty thousand" voters living in the rest of the state.[13] Jefferson considered redistrict-ing imperative.

To make matters worse, members of both the House and Senate were elected from the same class, as they had been in colonial times.[14] "The purpose of establishing different houses," Jefferson pointed out, "is to introduce the influence of different interests or different principles." He suggested that, as in some of the other states, one house might represent the interests of the people, the other the interests of property.[15]

Of even greater seriousness was the absence of checks and balances, a constitutional defect which invited despo-tism. All the power of government—executive, legislative, and judicial—was in the hands of the legislature (which elected the governor and appointed judges). Thus, there was a concentration of power in the hands of the one hundred and seventy-three legislators, and "one hundred and seventy-three despots would surely be as oppressive as one," as witness the despotism in the republic of Venice. "An *elective despotism*," he declared, "was not the gov-ernment we fought for."[16] The advantages of power and wealth would soon be discovered by the legislators, he said, and corruption would follow. Thus, revision of the constitution was urgent, in spite of the integrity of the present legislators. "The time to guard against corruption

13. *Ibid.*, 2:160–61.
14. See Charles S. Sydnor, *American Revolutionaries in the Making* (New York: The Free Press, 1965).
15. Lipscomb and Bergh, 2:162.
16. *Ibid.*, 2:163.

and tyranny, is before they shall have gotten hold on us."[17]

Another matter of serious import was the fact that the Virginia constitution had been enacted by the ordinary legislature at the time of the Revolution, having arrogated to itself the powers rightfully belonging only to an assembly upon which the people had conferred special powers to create a constitution. Furthermore, the legislators declared that the constitution they had enacted was unalterable, something Jefferson considered to be equivalent to one legislature passing acts which subsequent legislatures could not revoke. Clearly, any duly elected legislature may alter the acts of previous legislatures, as Coke had demonstrated. There was nothing sacred about the Virginia constitution: it could and should be revised. This the people desired, but must they now rise in rebellion to make their will known? Must the people's silence be construed as approval?

Perhaps most dangerous of all was the fact that the Assembly exercised the power of determining the quorum required for legislative action, following the precedent of the British Parliament. During the Revolution the House of Delegates voted that forty members would constitute a quorum, but even crisis did not justify such action—from forty they might reduce the quorum to four, and from four to one, thus introducing rule by oligarchy or monarchy. The people should accept only such laws as are passed by the action of the majority of their representatives and refuse to legitimize others enacted by a minority quorum.[18]

Answering the query of Barbé-Marbois regarding the state constitution gave Jefferson the opportunity to express other political ideas. He stated that during the Revolutionary upheaval of December 1776, "it was pro-

---

17. *Ibid.*, 2:165.
18. *Ibid.*, 2:165–71.

posed in the house of delegates to create a *dictator,* invested with every power . . . of life and death over our persons and properties; and, in June 1781 again . . . the same proposition was repeated, and wanted only a few votes of being passed."[19] This was a matter he discussed at great length.[20] The Virginia laws, he pointed out, contained no provision whereby elected representatives could abandon their posts and delegate their powers to others, without express permission from the people. The legislators could find no justification for their proposal in the crises which existed. "Necessities which dissolve a government, do not convey its authority to an oligarchy or a monarchy," he declared. "They throw back, into the hands of the people, the powers they had delegated."[21] Such were their "unalienable rights." The thought of creating a dictatorship "was treason against the people; was treason against mankind in general,"[22] for the American experiment was to hold implications for all humanity. The instigators of this proposal might look to Rome

19. *Ibid.,* 2:173-74.
20. It was obviously a subject of considerable importance to him, particularly since the latter proposal came at the end of his term as governor, at which time the Assembly voted to make an investigation of his conduct during the period of British armed assault. The move, supported by his enemies, came to nothing, and he was officially absolved of misconduct and tendered a vote of appreciation by the Assembly. Nevertheless, the experience wounded him deeply, perhaps more than any other experience in his life. Actually, Jefferson seems to have overemphasized the significance of the 1776 proposal of the House of Delegates that, in the face of imminent danger, the usual forms of government should be suspended for a limited time, although there may have been private talk of a dictatorship in the sense used by Jefferson, whose resentment toward Patrick Henry led him to believe that Henry was one of the instigators of the move. The 1781 incident, which resulted in the selection of General Thomas Nelson, Jr., the ranking Virginia militia officer, to succeed Jefferson as governor, he also attributed largely to Henry's activities. Adequate records to ascertain the validity of Jefferson's suspicions do not exist. Jefferson's bitterness in this regard can best be understood in the light of his fear that the proposed investigations of his conduct as wartime governor—which he also attributed to the efforts of Henry—would jeopardize his reputation as a public servant, a recurring spectre throughout his political career.
21. Lipscomb and Bergh, 2:175.
22. *Ibid.,* 2:176.

for justification; but the temporary tyrant elected there paved the way for permanent dictatorship. In Virginia, true consensus existed among the people, for they were united in their dedication to liberty, and calling upon the Roman precedent to exonerate legislators would not do. The world was full of precedents men might use to justify the *bellum omnium in omnia,* he declared, quoting Hobbes.

That the legislature could conduct itself in such a fashion pointed up the defects of the state constitution, with its failure to provide for the separation of powers; furthermore, the precedent of the legislature in fixing its own quorum added greatly to this danger. Such behavior under the color of legitimacy could but lead to tyranny and despotism at the hands of self-perpetuating elites—and at last to rebellion by the people.

To Jefferson constitutions, as we have seen, were not sacrosanct. But law as the foundation of democratic government was essential. In 1776, still in Philadelphia, he had written Thomas Nelson, Jr., in Virginia of his desire to participate in framing the new government of the Commonwealth. "It is a work of the most interesting nature and such as every individual would wish to have his voice in," he said. Liberty and independence were at stake, and providing a good government was now the most crucial of tasks: "for should a bad government be instituted for us, in future it had been as well to have accepted at first the bad one offered us from beyond the water without the risk and expense of contest."[23] It was his ardent desire to participate in the institutionalizing of government to secure "the blessings of liberty" to all, and to him all institutions were instruments to be used in the realization of the goals expressed in the Declaration of Independence. Constitutions providing for the structure of governments were therefore a ready

---

23. Ford, *Writings,* 2:1-2.

means of implementing programs to insure man's freedom and happiness. Later in life, he realized that many of the early American efforts had failed to penetrate "to the mother principle, that 'governments are republican only in proportion as they embody the will of the people and execute it.' "[24] His draft of a constitution for Virginia was itself conservative, but time could heal the defects in it (just as it could in the national constitution) via amendments, for no constitutions were legitimately perpetual. Although the Virginia convention failed to consider his draft, he was to play a decisive role in revising the laws of the state.

Jefferson was often described as "amiable," "agreeable," "soft-spoken," "gentle," by his contemporaries, and so his biographers speak of him today. In personal relationships and face-to-face associations, his amiability was no doubt a distinguishing mark of his personality; however, the expressions he set down in writing were often strong and sometimes extreme. Not only was this true of his denunciations of the British; his political opponents also felt the sting of his written attacks. For a man who hated controversy as much as he did, he was not infrequently violent in his criticisms of the Federalists and "the party of Hamilton," as he came to speak of them. But this can no doubt be understood by comprehending his definition of situations during the Federalist era.

In the early days of the Republic Jefferson, seeking unity and consensus among the people and among the leadership of the new nation, denounced political parties. "If I could not go to heaven but with a party," he declared, "I would not go there at all."[25] Jefferson had

---

24. *Ibid.,* 10:37.
25. Adrienne Koch and William Peden, eds., *The Life and Selected Writings of Thomas Jefferson* (New York: Random House, Inc., 1944), p. xxviii.

won undying fame as the author of the Declaration of Independence, and being a practical idealist in politics, he placed his early faith in an unstructured, almost automatic democracy, believing that an aroused public opinion was the most effective means of holding government to its proper course. This was especially true during his early days as a member of Washington's cabinet when his clashes with Hamilton first came to the fore. He became increasingly alarmed at the view of anti-democrats who appeared to long for the very system whose corruption he had found so repellant in Europe—a system of aristocratic privilege headed by a monarch, with no significant rights in the hands of the people. Although in nonofficial social relationships he and Hamilton maintained a friendly approach to each other, in the cabinet they clashed, as Jefferson said, like two fighting cocks.

Once during a visit to Jefferson's quarters, Hamilton observed three portraits on the wall, those of Bacon, Newton, and Locke. Not recognizing them, he inquired as to their identity. Jefferson replied that they were his "trinity of the three greatest men the world had ever produced." Hamilton responded emphatically, "The greatest man that ever lived was Julius Caesar."[26] To Jefferson this revealed Hamilton's political philosophy, one based on the belief that it was necessary to use either force or corruption to govern. He concluded that Hamilton was a monarchist who had no confidence in popular self-government, a dangerous man who relied on the moneyed class to provide support for the government. Thus, his and Hamilton's basic principles were fundamentally and irrevocably opposed. At last, opposition to Hamilton's policies grew among a number of Americans, but the early leadership of this opposition lay less in Jefferson's hands than it did in the hands of Madison

26. Ford, *Writings,* 9:296.

in particular.[27] Jefferson's hatred of controversy, among other things, led him to escape the conflict with Hamilton by resigning his post as Secretary of State and returning to Monticello in 1793. With the possible exception of Washington, Jefferson was the most sensitive major public figure of his era,[28] and he declared that he found "the pain of a little censure, even when it is unfounded, is more acute than the pleasure of much praise."[29]

But he could not sit out the controversy at Monticello. At last he was drawn into the thick of the fray and emerged as the leader of the opposition party, a leadership he pursued with such vigor that he must have surprised himself. The principles at stake overrode in importance his extreme distaste for controversy. The rights of man in America, he no doubt decided, were of far greater importance than his personal feelings and wishes.

Jefferson as a politician will be considered later in this study. Always the practical idealist, he at last became convinced that something more was needed to insure the rights of the people than an enlightened public opinion operating outside the structure of political parties. Indeed, in 1798, he declared:

> In every free and deliberating society there must, from the nature of man, be opposite parties and violent dissensions and discords; and one of these must for the most part prevail over the other for a longer or shorter time. Perhaps this party division is necessary to induce each to watch and relate to the people the proceedings of the other.[30]

Jefferson's emergence as party leader was thus the result of his view of political institutions, among which

27. William Nisbet Chambers, *Political Parties in a New Nation* (New York: Oxford University Press, 1963), p. 6.

28. Dumas Malone, *Jefferson and the Rights of Man* (Boston: Little, Brown and Company, 1951), p. xxiii.

29. Ford, *Writings,* 5:78.

30. Koch and Peden, pp. 714–15.

political parties themselves, he finally decided, were to play a vital role in the structure of democratic-republican government. The same ideals that motivated his early participation in the Revolutionary cause—indeed, which often led him to forge ahead of his compatriots in that cause—were at work in his later political endeavors. His analysis of political parties and of the basic differences he found between the Federalists and the Republicans is expressed with exceptional clarity in a letter he wrote in 1813 to John Melish, a Scotsman who had published a book regarding his travels in the United States.

> That each party endeavors to get into the administration of the government, and exclude the other from power, is true, and may be stated as a motive of action: but this is only secondary; the primary motive being a real and radical difference of political principle. . . . The question of preference between monarchy and republicanism, which has so long divided mankind elsewhere, threatens a permanent division here.[31]

The spectre of monarchy and oligarchy haunted Jefferson throughout his life, and the fear that his beloved Republic would at last embrace one of these institutions, with their despotism, tyranny, and denial of the rights of man, may correctly be seen as the single greatest motivating factor in his political endeavors. He could not forget Hamilton's expressed preference for the English constitution, his distrust of the people, his leadership of the moneyed class—what Jefferson liked to call the principles of "Anglomany and monarchy." Of all political institutions he unquestionably hated monarchy the most intensely, and along with it, a self-centered oligarchy of aristocracy which exploited a land and people for the benefit of the privileged class. In his last extant letter, written less than two weeks before his death, he spoke out with singular eloquence the principle that had moti-

31. Lipscomb and Bergh, 13:208-9.

vated so much of his life and thought, "that the mass of mankind has not been born with saddles on their backs, nor a favorite few booted and spurred, ready to ride them legitimately, by the grace of God."[32]

Legitimacy he believed should be based on constitutions to which the people gave their assent and approval in what Max Weber called a rational-legal system. Neither privilege of birth nor acquisition of power could provide true legitimacy: the rights of man were "unalienable." Political institutions, as instruments to be utilized in securing these natural rights, were to be controlled by the people, and he came to see that these instruments included political parties as well as constitutions and compacts of agreement. As Jefferson clearly understood, democracy is "a system of institutionalized opposition in which the people choose among alternative contenders for public office."[33] But democracy was still more: a structure of political institutions in which parties offered more than "alternative contenders for public office," which offered also to the people a clear choice of principles of government. And Jefferson saw the principles of the Federalists and those of the Republicans as standing in sharp and irreconcilable contrast.

Jefferson's entrance into the realm of party politics resulted, of course, from his growing fear of the policies of the Federalists, "an Anglican, monarchical, & aristocratic party . . . whose avowed object," he declared, "is to draw over us the substance as they have already done the forms of the British government."[34] In the famous Mazzei letter of 1792, he referred to "the apostates who have gone over to these heresies, men who were Samsons in the field & Solomons in the council, but who have had

---

32. *Ibid.*, 16:181.
33. Seymour Martin Lipset, *The United States—The First New Nation* (Berkeley, Calif.: Institute of International Studies, 1964), p. 326.
34. Thomas Jefferson, *The Works of Thomas Jefferson*, ed. Paul Leicester Ford, 12 vols. (New York: G. P. Putnam's Sons, 1904), 8:236.

their heads shorn by the harlot England,"[35] an accusation widely understood to refer to Washington himself. By 1798 Jefferson's alarm was so great that he secretly drew up the Kentucky Resolutions, in which he elaborated the theory of states' rights as an extension of the social contract doctrine, contending that the federal government was created by the states, that it was the agent of the states, and that it was therefore accountable for its actions to the states. He even suggested that the states might nullify unauthorized acts of the federal government, and if necessary, resort to rebellion to defeat the usurpation of their rights.

Jefferson's purpose herein was primarily to warn the Federalists that their assumption of undelegated and unconstitutional powers, as embodied in the Alien and Sedition Acts, would be resisted. He also hoped to compel them to undertake a reformation of their entire scheme of government. As the author of these Resolutions, he, the Vice-President of the United States, might conceivably have been charged with sedition and impeached for treason. However, he saw the course he followed as the only one open to him in combating the Federalists' attack on the fundamentals of democratic-republican government and freedom. This, along with his social contract orientation—one of the strongest elements in his philosophy—explains the views he expressed in the Kentucky Resolutions, which so many have incorrectly considered to be inconsistent with Jefferson's larger view.

It was in this sense that Jefferson believed his election in 1800 to be a revolution comparable to that of 1776. The impressive majority of votes received by the Republicans confirmed his faith in the people, who had rallied enthusiastically to a set of principles disavowing what he believed to be the dictatorial tendencies of even the

---

35. *Ibid.*

Adams Federalists. The Federalist vilification of Jefferson—perhaps unmatched in American political campaigns since—failed to mislead the people, who voted not only for candidates but also for principles. The Jeffersonian principles which had echoed resoundingly in the Declaration of Independence were heard again under the aegis of a political party. The principles were the same, and the choice of the people was clear and unequivocal.

The Federalists offered a program based upon policies antithetical to the interests of the people at large, and came increasingly to structure their policy to favor commercial groups alone. In a nation made up predominantly of farmers, this policy was suicidal. The "favored few" were to retain their positions of leadership under the Federalists, even under the moderate Adams Federalists. Jefferson's Republicans made their appeal more nearly universal. It was Jefferson himself who wrote the platform of his party, phrasing the noble ideals of the great American documents in practical terms the people could comprehend. The choice was thus one between programs and policies, not just between men. Adams the patriot and Jefferson the patriot were symbols; they were also spokesmen of principles.

When the Federalists surrendered power to the Republicans in 1801, this was the first peaceful, democratic transfer of power in modern politics, representing the first full acceptance of rational-legal patterns of democratic authority in modern times. As national consensus emerged during Jefferson's first administration, full acceptance of the rational legitimacy of the Constitution became a reality. Thus, the democratic values, which became part of the national ideology and the basis for the American authority structure, gained legitimacy as they proved effective. In more nearly Jeffersonian terms, tyranny and despotism were defeated and the rights of man reasserted. The political institutions of the American experiment had gained a stability which, under the watchful eye of an enlightened citizenry, held forth the opportunity for the realization of the "associated happiness of man." Thus, Jefferson saw the Republican victory as "the revolution of 1800," a victory of popular sovereignty which secured to the people their natural and inalienable rights of self-government. And this, to him, was the purpose of all political institutions.

Jefferson envisioned for the United States a diffused, decentralized government made up of subdivisions integrated into a total system, each part based upon republican principles, from the national to the local levels—a system also distinctively democratic in that it engaged the participation of all voting citizens. His general theory of government is well summarized in a letter he wrote in 1816 to Joseph C. Cabell, a state legislator who was his principal co-worker in establishing the University of Virginia. "The way to have a good and safe government," he wrote, "is not to trust it all to one, but to divide it among the many, distributing to every one exactly the functions he is competent to." These functions he outlines as follows:

> Let the national government be entrusted with the defense of the nation, and its foreign and federal relations; the State governments with the civil rights, laws, police, and administration of what concerns the State generally; the counties with the local concerns of the counties, and each ward direct the interests within itself. It is by dividing and subdividing these republics from the great national one down through all its subordinates, until it ends in the administration of every man's farm by himself; by placing under every one what his own eye may superintend, that all will be done for the best.[36]

In his ideal republic, Jefferson was strongly committed to the diffusion and decentralization of power. Any other

---

36. Lipscomb and Bergh, 14:421.

course was a fatal one, he believed, and this was the explanation of his dedication to the doctrine of states' rights which he had delineated in the Kentucky Resolutions. "What has destroyed liberty and the rights of man in every government which ever existed under the sun?" he asked. His answer was, "The generalizing and concentrating all cares and powers into one body. . . ." And, furthermore, in securing and protecting the freedom of man

> I do believe . . . that the secret will be found to be in the making himself the depository of the powers respecting himself, so far as he is competent to them, and delegating only what is beyond his competence by a synthetical process, to higher orders of functionaries, so as to trust fewer and fewer powers in proportion as the trustees become more and more oligarchical. The elementary republics of the wards, the county republics, the State republics, and the republic of the Union, would form a gradation of authorities, standing each on the basis of law, holding every one its delegated share of powers, and constituting truly a system of fundamental balances and checks for the government. Where every man is a sharer in the direction of his ward-republic, or of some of the higher ones, and feels that he is a participator in the government of affairs, not merely at an election one day in the year, but every day; when there shall not be a man in the State who will not be a member of some one of its councils, great or small, he will let the heart be torn out of his body sooner than his power be wrested from him by a Caesar or a Bonaparte.[37]

Jefferson's theory of government was a democratic one, providing the people the means of protecting themselves from tyranny and despotism. It had both idealistic and practical features, and was designed as a structure for organizing citizen participation at every level of government. Such a working system could well be called true self-government, with power ultimately in the hands of the people—at least, in the voting population of free

37. *Ibid.,* 14:421–22.

white males. He did not have universal suffrage in mind, of course; but, even so, his thinking was far in advance of that of most of his contemporaries. His system was also republican and rational-legal, with the trustees of the people holding power at the people's sufferance under a system of laws. Not only did he profoundly believe in separation of powers in a democratic republic; he outlined a plan by which he felt such a system could be implemented. It was the primacy of human rights which he saw as uppermost—indeed, the maintenance of such rights was the *raison d'être* of all government and of all political institutions. It is this which, among other things, makes Jefferson perennially and perhaps crucially relevant.

Jefferson's political philosophy was crystallized in the Declaration of Independence in words which have resounded throughout the world as a clarion call to all mankind to seek the rights of liberty and self-government. They have a universal impact, for, in the words of Lincoln, "the principles of Jefferson are the definitions and axioms of a free society."[38] He never doubted that the primary purpose of political institutions and activities was to secure and protect the rights of the people to freedom, and he was dedicated to the belief that the people were entitled to govern themselves. It must always be remembered that he made an enlightened citizenry the *sine qua non* of free society: "if a nation expects to be ignorant and free," he wrote, "it expects what never was and never will be."[39] Thus, there must first come "the diffusion of knowledge among the people," for "no other sure foundation can be devised, for the preservation of freedom and happiness."[40] Public education was therefore the indispensable precondition of liberty and self-

38. Philip S. Foner, ed., *Basic Writings of Thomas Jefferson* (New York: Willey Book Company, 1944), p. xiv.
39. *Ibid.*, p. xiii.
40. Thomas Jefferson, *The Papers of Thomas Jefferson*, ed. Julian P. Boyd (Princeton: Princeton University Press, 1950–   ), 10:244.

government, and an educated citizenry was always to be trusted as the best protector of its own rights. "I am not among those who fear the people," he said; "they are our dependence for continued freedom."[41] His faith in popular sovereignty was unwavering, and he constantly reiterated his belief that "the will of the people is the only legitimate foundation of any government."[42] Political structures and functions existed for one purpose only: to implement the people's will, and to secure and preserve to them their rights to freedom and happiness.

41. Foner, p. xiii.
42. *Ibid.*

6

On Legal Institutions

Jefferson had prepared himself to be a lawyer and he retained an abiding interest in the law throughout his life, particularly in the larger considerations of legal philosophy and the purposes of legislation, for he clearly understood that in advanced societies the institutionalized law incorporates and reinforces the cultural norms and thereby binds together the whole complex of social relationships so that a change in the law results in an alteration of the social system and vice versa.[1]

At first, Jefferson's interests in the law resulted in few consequences of far-reaching importance. For seven years he was a practicing lawyer, and his practice was fairly lucrative. However, he spent a great deal of his time overseeing the affairs of his plantation; he also began the construction of Monticello. During the second half of this period he had little need for income from his practice, for his marriage to Martha Wayles Skelton resulted shortly in the coming into his hands of a great deal of wealth. His father-in-law died about a year after Jefferson's marriage, leaving an estate of a dozen plantations and about four hundred slaves. Mrs. Jefferson inherited a third of the estate, 135 slaves and more than

---

1. Saul K. Padover, *Jefferson* (New York: Mentor Books, 1963), p. 38.

133

11,000 acres of land. Thus the Jeffersons found themselves among the greatest landholders in Virginia. Jefferson spoke of this inheritance as a "handsome fortune"
which "doubled the ease of our circumstances."[2]

Jefferson's legal practice was fairly extensive, both
before the county courts and the General Court in Williamsburg. He listed a total of nearly a thousand clients
in his records for the period, including many members
of the Virginia gentry as well as a number in humbler
circumstances—cases dealing with land ownership, debts,
the recovery of slaves, slander, and assault and battery.
From his records it appears that he collected only about
half the fees due him. He continued to read widely during this period and to make detailed notes on all the
things he encountered which fell within his wide range
of interests. These went far beyond the practice of law,
and his election to the House of Burgesses in 1768
opened the way for him to enter into the world of larger
considerations where he was soon to earn fame, particularly after the discontinuance of the county courts in
1774 ended his career as a practicing lawyer.

Jefferson appears never to have been especially happy
in the legal profession. He found the language of law

---

2. The Wayles estate was, however, to prove less of a blessing than
a curse, for Mr. Wayles was deeply indebted to English creditors—as
were many Virginia planters—and the repayment of a part of this debt
fell to Jefferson. He sold some five thousand acres of the Wayles land
and deposited the money in the state treasury for payment to the creditors after the Revolution. However, the depreciation following the war,
and other factors, meant that the debt was not paid, and for many
years it continued to trouble him. Those who owed him did not pay
him; during his years of public service he could not oversee his farming
operations; and after his retirement, a constant stream of visitors added
greatly to the financial burdens upon him. He continued to sell off his
lands and slaves, but he could never meet his obligations, and he died
deeply in debt. The Wayles inheritance had at first enriched, then
impoverished him. The experience of being involved in debts not of
his own making and unable to collect from those who owed him no
doubt helped give rise to his hostility to Hamilton's bank program and
his opposition to public debt.

and lawyers particularly repugnant; as a writer of innate literary artistry, he was constantly disgusted by the dry involved legal verbiage, and he jeered at such language as "lawyerish."[3] During his service with the Continental Congress, he often became impatient with the long-winded delegates belaboring legal points, but "how can it be otherwise," he asked in his *Autobiography*, "in a body to which the people send one hundred and fifty lawyers, whose trade it is to question everything, yield nothing, and talk by the hour? That one hundred and fifty lawyers should do business together, ought not to be expected."[4] These and similar statements of Jefferson were not, of course, devoid of dry humor, and his criticism of lawyers should be seen as coming from a man who was himself a member of the profession.

Of more significance is Jefferson's view that the "foundation of public happiness" lay "in wholesome laws."[5] His first important Revolutionary statement, the *Summary View* of 1774, was based on his premise that the British infringements were infringements of law. "Can his majesty . . . put down all law under his feet?" he asked. "Can he erect a power superior to that which erected himself?"[6] And in the Declaration of Independence, his indictments of the King began with the statement that "he has refused his assent to the laws most wholesome and necessary for the public good." It is true that Jefferson framed these statements in terms of his belief in the primacy of the natural law which insured human rights. It is also true that he sought to incorporate the principles of natural law and natural

---

3. Padover, *Jefferson,* p. 20.
4. Thomas Jefferson, *The Writings of Thomas Jefferson,* ed. Andrew A. Lipscomb and Albert E. Bergh, 20 vols. (Washington: Thomas Jefferson Memorial Association, 1903), 1:87.
5. Adrienne Koch and William Peden, eds., *The Life and Selected Writings of Thomas Jefferson* (New York: Random House, Inc., 1944), p. 342.
6. Padover, *Jefferson,* p. 27.

---

rights into the Virginia code of which he was a revisor. Thus, we again observe Jefferson as the practical idealist.

Much discussion has been given to the fact that in the Declaration of Independence Jefferson substituted the phrase "pursuit of happiness" for Locke's word "property," and some have taken this as an indication of his disregard of the importance of property rights and property laws.[7] However, Locke presupposed the pursuit of happiness, and Jefferson always assumed as basic the rights of an individual to hold property. It is true that such rights as freedom of mind, conscience, and person were the ones he valued most—the truly inalienable rights; but property was indispensable in the same sense that government was, a means to human happiness and not an end in itself. He therefore felt that all should have the opportunity of owning property, and that the division of property should be as nearly equal as practicable.[8]

In all his thoughts about the law, it was his dedication to the enjoyment of those rights he considered as deriving from natural law to which he gave primacy; and in a letter written in 1810 he identified these as rights of life, liberty, and property, which he equated with necessity, self-preservation, and the saving of one's endangered country. Statutory laws were indeed important, but natural laws were of first importance. Of this he wrote:

> A strict observance of the written law is doubtless *one* of the highest duties of a good citizen, but it is not *the highest.* The laws of necessity, self-preservation, of saving our country when in danger, are of higher obligation. To lose our country by a scrupulous adherence to written law, would be to lose the law itself, with life, liberty, property . . . thus absurdly sacrificing the end to the means.[9]

7. See Vernon L. Parrington, *Main Currents in American Thought* (New York: Harcourt, Brace and Company, Inc., 1930), 1:344.
8. Lipscomb and Bergh, 19:17–18.
9. *Ibid.,* 12:418.

This statement of Jefferson's summarizes his view of the law and indicates the importance he placed on property as well as on life and liberty—and especially his view that the law, like other human institutions, was in the final consideration but an instrument to be utilized in gaining for men the natural rights "to which the laws of nature and nature's God" entitle them.

Jefferson's draft of a constitution for Virginia made it unequivocally clear that he was not simply concerned with philosophical generalities but instead with a practical and definite legal program. Although his draft was not adopted, his preamble was, and his suggestions were drawn upon for purposes of amendment. Because of his interest in helping frame the legal institutions of Virginia, in 1776 he resigned as delegate to the Continental Congress and returned to his home state, where he became a member of the House of Delegates, retaining that office until he became governor in 1779. During this period he was a long-range political architect concerned with the future, not merely a short-range reformer.

Within four days after taking his seat, Jefferson astounded his more complacent colleagues by introducing his bill providing that tenants in tail should hold their lands in fee simple. This, in his opinion, would strike at the very root of aristocracy in Virginia.[10] He at the same time introduced a bill calling for a general revision of the laws. His primary objection to entail was that such a system was essentially irrational and unjust. The Virginia gentry had ruled well, but membership in the elite was based on inherited privilege, not on merit. He described his purposes in terms of natural philosophy which were basically democratic.

Earlier Jefferson had proposed that those who did not own land should be given 50 acres; he had also

---

10. *Ibid.,* 1:73.

proposed that irresponsible purchases of Indian lands by
land companies be prohibited. He objected to additional
large grants, which might become the bases of further
power and affluence to the already rich. Abolishing entail
seemed to him to be one means of preventing the perpetuation of the aristocracy. Entail was undesirable, he
felt, and so was primogeniture, which tended to create a
great number of dispossessed younger sons among the
gentry. Both of these had derived from what he considered that witches' cauldron of abuses, the Norman
conquest of England. Virginia had gone even beyond
English law in this respect, prohibiting the docking of
estates except by an Act of the Assembly and thus en-
abling even indolent and dissipated elder sons to hold
on to the great estates which they had inherited, regardless of the claims of creditors against them. The net
result was the perpetuation of wealth and property in
the hands of a few privileged families who formed, in
Jefferson's words, "a Patrician order, distinguished by
the splendor and luxury of their establishments."[11] For
his work in this area of law, Jefferson was called a traitor
to his class, as the abolition of entails and primogeniture
facilitated economic and social mobility at the same time
it restricted the power of the landed aristocracy. But the
fact that the legislature passed the bills promptly showed
that others shared his views of these relics of medieval-
ism.

Jefferson's attacks upon entail and primogeniture were
known in Virginia as the "Spirit of Leveling." However,
inheritance changes alone could not bring about the leveling Jefferson desired; free public education and the disestablishment of the Church were also needed, and to
these he later turned his attention. "I considered . . . these
bills as forming a system by which every fibre would be

---

11. *Ibid.,* 1:54.

eradicated of ancient or future aristocracy; and a foundation laid for a government truly republican,"[12] he said. He saw the system of entailing lands as the true cornerstone of aristocracy, by means of which the foresighted founder of a family could limit the distribution of his lands in perpetuity. In Virginia slaves too might be entailed and they and their descendants passed on from heir to heir. This system represented something that Jefferson abhorred, for he conceived of America as a land of boundless opportunity where merit and industry would bring just rewards.

Jefferson no doubt overemphasized the importance of abolishing primogeniture and entail if he indeed felt that doing so would eliminate aristocracy in Virginia, for there were other influences at work which helped maintain the rich and powerful in their privileged positions. At first glance it may appear that in this instance he permitted legalism to triumph over true reform, but it must be remembered that he alone could not effect a restructuring of the system of laws: here as elsewhere he had to practice the art of the possible. His penchant for overstatement and hyperbole may here as in other instances have misled many of his critics. In any event, few today would take at face value Jefferson's stated estimate of the importance of eliminating primogeniture and entail, even though these were necessary steps in the process of the democratization he sought to achieve.

Jefferson understood the purpose of legal institutions to be the protection of freedoms, not the support of special privileges which perpetuated a static aristocracy, for such an aristocracy was a threat to self-government. His hostility to artificial privilege of every sort was implacable, including the aristocracy of birth. In his *Autobiography,* he stated that his objective in offering

12. Thomas Jefferson, *The Works of Thomas Jefferson,* ed. Paul Leicester Ford, 12 vols. (New York: G. P. Putnam's Sons, 1904), 1:77.

the bill for the abolition of entail was to annul the effect of the unearned advantages of the gentry and, "instead of an aristocracy of wealth . . . to make an opening for an aristocracy of virtue and talent, which nature has wisely provided for the direction of the interests of society, and scattered with equal hand through all its conditions."[13]

Jefferson also performed other services in the interests of distributing land more widely, particularly among settlers in new territories, such as his support of the movement to establish Kentucky as a new county, and to provide for the protection of squatters on Virginia's western lands. His efforts in the latter instance were unsuccessful.[14]

Jefferson's greatest opportunity to correct the imperfections of the Virginia legal system came when his bill providing for a revision of the code—designed, he said, "with a single eye to reason, and the good of those for whose government it was framed"[15]—was passed by the Assembly. He was named first among the five revisors, the others being Edmund Pendleton, George Wythe, George Mason, and Thomas Ludwell Lee. The committee met in 1777, and Jefferson described the results as follows:

> At the first and only meeting of the whole committee, the question was discussed whether we would attempt to reduce the whole body of the law to a code, the text of which should become the law of the land? We decided against that, because every word and phrase in that text would become a new subject of criticism and litigation, until its sense should have been

13. Lipscomb and Bergh, 1:54.

14. In the Ordinance of 1784, drafted by Jefferson, he had included provisions for land distribution in the Northwest, as well as a ban on slavery which Congress rejected. However, the Ordinance of 1787 incorporated such a ban.

15. Thomas Jefferson, *The Writings of Thomas Jefferson*, ed. Paul Leicester Ford, 10 vols. (New York: G. P. Putnam's Sons, 1892–1899), 1:57–58.

settled by numerous decisions, and that, in the meantime, the rights of property would be in the air. We concluded not to meddle with the common law, i.e., the law preceding the existence of the statutes, further than to accommodate it to our new principles and circumstances; but to take up the whole body of statutes and Virginia laws, to leave out everything obsolete or improper, insert what was wanting, and reduce the whole within as moderate a compass as it would bear, and to the plain language of common sense, divested of the verbiage, the barbarous tautologies and redundancies which render the British statutes unintelligible.[16]

Jefferson's practical, matter-of-fact account of the committee's purposes hardly suggested the far-reaching purposes and philosophical principles he himself had in mind. The work was divided among the three members of the committee after Lee died and Mason had been relieved. Jefferson's assignment was to deal principally with the colonial statutes concerning crimes and punishments, religion, and descents (which his work in abolishing entail and primogeniture covered). He also considered the question of public education, though this matter was specifically assigned to Pendleton.

Settling down in earnest to his task, Jefferson determined to proceed with his work on the basis of the committee's decision to eliminate the verbosity and tautologies, or, as he said, the "involutions of a case within a case, and parenthesis within parenthesis, and their multiplied efforts at certainty by *saids* and *aforesaids*, by *ors* and *ands*."[17] Jefferson and Wythe worked conscientiously on the revision; however, Pendleton copied the Virginia acts verbatim, merely omitting what he disapproved. The other two committee members revised Pendleton's work and finally submitted 126 bills to the Assembly, of which approximately half were passed

16. Lipscomb and Bergh, 12:298-99.
17. *Ibid.*, 1:65.

within seven years and most of the others some years later, while Jefferson was Secretary of State. Most of the bills he proposed were local in nature; however, the three or four he considered of most importance were broadly philosophical and still, after a century and a half, intrigue the thoughtful. These dealt with citizenship, crime and punishment, religion, and education.

Among the bills Jefferson proposed was one to grant citizenship to immigrants after two years of residence and a declaration in court of their determination to remain within the state and abide by its laws.[18] His bills on education and religion will be discussed later.

He gave a great deal of attention to the unrevised Virginia criminal code, which he considered barbarous and savage, a code that was shockingly out of line with his views of a modern, progressive criminology. His bill for proportioning crimes to punishments was, however, bitterly opposed in the House of Delegates. It was not considered until the whole report was brought up, and when it was voted on a year later, it was defeated by a single vote. To Jefferson in France Madison wrote, "Our old bloody code is by this event fully restored."[19]

He had given more time to this bill than to all the rest together. The Virginia colonial code had called for some harsh punishments. Ducking was a commonly used punishment, especially for "brabling women," and whipping was the usual punishment for a multitude of offenses, the cat-of-nine-tails being commonly used. An adulteress might be dragged in a river behind a moving boat. Children of unmarried indentured servants were bound out until age 30, and the child of a servant mother

18. Claude G. Bowers, *The Young Jefferson, 1743-1789* (Boston: Houghton Mifflin Company, 1945), p. 192.

19. Dumas Malone, *Jefferson the Virginian* (Boston: Little, Brown and Company, 1948), p. 269.

and a slave father could be enslaved.[20] The colony, of course, followed the English system, in which there were approximately 350 capital crimes in the eighteenth century, from theft to treason.[21]

Jefferson spent over two years on the task of preparing his part of the revision of the code. His bill on crime and punishment, in particular, was notable for the care with which it was drawn up and for its studied simplicity.[22] In the spirit of the Enlightenment, his purpose was principally to relax the severity of punishments, making them at the same time more humane and more rational. This, as well as his understanding of the elements of social control, shows clearly in his preamble to the bill. The preamble also reveals how far in advance he was of the norms of his time.

> Whereas it frequently happens that wicked and dissolute men . . . commit violations on the lives, liberties and property of others; and the secure enjoyment of these having induced men to enter society, government would be defective . . . were it not to restrain such criminal acts by inflicting due punishments on those who perpetrate them, but it appears at the same time equally deducible from the purposes of society that a member thereof committing an inferior injury does not wholly forfeit the protection of his fellow citizens, but, after suffering a punishment in proportion to his offense, is entitled to their protection from all greater pain, so that it becomes a duty of the legislature to arrange in a proper scale the crimes which it may be necessary for them to repress, and . . . a corresponding gradation of punishments.

20. Harvey Wish, *Society and Thought in Early America* (New York: Longmans, Green and Company, 1950), pp. 79–80. Used by permission of David McKay Company, Inc.

21. Edwin H. Sutherland and Donald R. Cressey, *Principles of Criminology* (Philadelphia: J. B. Lippincott Company, 1960), p. 262.

22. This care was evident not only in the substance and style of the bill's provisions, but also in its physical appearance. Jefferson attached careful notes to the bill in Anglo-Saxon, Latin, Old French, and English, placing these notations in columns parallel to the text in a penmanship exhibiting unusual artistry.

And whereas the reformation of offenders is not affected at all by capital punishments, which exterminate instead of reforming, and should be the last melancholy recourse against those whose existence has become inconsistent with the safety of their fellow citizens; which also weakens the State by cutting off so many, who, if reformed, might be restored sound members of society, who even under a course of correction might be rendered useful in various labors for the public, and would be a living and long-continued spectacle to deter others from committing the like offenses.

And forasmuch as the experience of all ages and countries hath shown that cruel and sanguinary laws defeat their own purpose . . . when, if the punishment were only proportioned to the injury, men would feel it their inclination, as well as their duty, to see the laws observed . . . rendering crimes and punishments therefore more proportionate to each other.[23]

Jefferson's enlightened views were in part attributable to the work of Cesare Beccaria, an Italian mathematician and economist who in 1764 published his *Essay on Crimes and Punishment*. This book, which has been called the most important single work ever produced on criminal justice,[24] was read by Voltaire, and a French edition to which was appended an unsigned commentary by him was circulated among the leaders of the French Revolution.[25] Widespread reformations appeared on the continent of Europe following the publication of Beccaria's work.

Beccaria's suggested reforms were within the framework of the social contract approach, which saw the relationships between the state and the individual as mutually obligatory. In exchange for giving up some of his natural rights, the individual was entitled to protection from the state, for which purpose the state framed laws defining crimes and punishments. The purpose of

23. Ford, *Writings*, 2:203 f.
24. Richard R. Korn and Lloyd W. McCorkle, *Criminology and Penology* (New York: Holt, Rinehart and Winston, Inc., 1961), p. 403.
25. Carl Ludwig von Bar, *A History of Continental Criminal Law* (London: John Murray, 1916), p. 318.

punishment was to protect the state as well as the members of society from one another, not by exacting vengeance but by deterring the individual from committing crimes—a goal which could best be achieved by adjusting the degree of punishment to the crime in such a way that rational and responsible human beings would find the threat and unattractiveness of the penalty in excess of advantages to be gained from the illegal act.

Jefferson read the Italian edition of Beccaria and quoted at length from it in his *Commonplace Book*. Both in his *Autobiography* and in the notations he attached to the bill, he acknowledged his debt to Beccaria, who was especially vigorous in his contention that experience had demonstrated both the injustice and the inefficacy of the death penalty. Enlightened men were largely in favor of this view, and the committee of revisors agreed in advance that the death penalty should be limited to treason and murder, although the conservative Pendleton had warned Jefferson that if he intended doing away with capital punishment completely, he would have to "find a new race of men to be the subjects of it."[26] Jefferson was not so unrealistic, however, and in hopes of securing passage of the bill, he included many features approved by the committee which he himself found distasteful. To Wythe he wrote:

> I have strictly observed the scale of punishments settled by the Committee, without being entirely satisfied with it. The lex talionis, altho' a restitution of the Common law to the simplicity of which we have generally found so advantageous to return,[27] will be revolting to the humanized feelings of

26. Malone, *Jefferson the Virginian*, p. 270.
27. Jefferson also wrote Wythe that in his revision "I have aimed at accuracy, brevity & simplicity, preserving however the words of the established law, wherever their meaning has been sanctioned by judicial decisions, or rendered technical by usage." Nevertheless, he added, "I wished to exhibit a sample of reformation in the barbarous style into which modern statutes have degenerated from their ancient simplicity." Lipscomb and Bergh, 1:216.

modern times. An eye for an eye, and a hand for a hand will exhibit spectacles in execution whose moral effect will be questionable.[28]

Although he found the *lex talionis* shocking and distasteful, the judgment of his fellow revisors was respected. Nevertheless, his concern for sufficient approval to gain passage was not such that he incorporated all the legal provisions to which members of the House felt allegiance. His purpose was to effect a long-range reformation of the criminal law, and he felt it wiser simply not to mention some provisions he wished to discard. "I must pray you to be as watchful over what I have not said as what is said," he wrote Wythe, pointing out that "I have thought it better to drop in silence the laws we mean to discontinue."[29] This maneuver of Jefferson's, however, was not entirely successful. As a case in point, the following statute appeared among the proposals:

> Sect. XIV.   Whosoever shall be guilty of rape, or sodomy with man or woman, shall be punished, if a man, by castration, if a woman, by boring through the cartilage of her nose a hole of one half inch in diameter at the least.[30]

Indicative of his comprehension of the sociological elements in social control, he wished to leave the more unnatural sex crimes largely to public opinion. He divided "buggery" into sodomy and bestiality, and of the latter he said: "Bestiality can never make any progress; it cannot therefore be injurious to society in any great degree, which is the true measure of criminality in foro civilis, and will ever be punished, by universal derision."[31]

---

28. *Ibid.,* 1:217.
29. *Ibid.*
30. Malone, *Jefferson the Virginian,* 271.
31. Ford, *Writings,* 2:211n. The loss of social status following from knowledge of such unnatural acts would be sufficient to exert control over the individual. Cooley and other sociologists have indicated the

Jefferson's insights into the elements of a science of society were far in advance of those current in his day and anticipate the works of later students of society. In the *Notes on Virginia,* he pointed out that all laws "founded in force, and not in conscience" were not only arbitrary but also less likely to succeed.[32] He understood that the internalization of norms gave strength to laws and that effective socialization was a decisive feature of positive social control.

In his effort to make the criminal law more rational and humane, his revision provided the death penalty for only treason and murder. He bowed to the wishes of his colleagues regarding dismemberment, or *lex talionis,* which was retained as the penalty for rape or sodomy, as well as for maiming and disfiguring, the latter also involving the forfeiture to the victim of half the lands and goods of the offender. Crimes to be punished by hard labor plus reparation included manslaughter, counterfeiting, arson, robbery, burglary, larceny, and horse stealing. Suicide and heresy were "to be pitied, not punished." Pardon and privilege of clergy were to be abolished, as was attainder with corruption of blood and forfeiture of dower. Slaves guilty of offenses punishable in freemen by labor were to be "transported to Africa, or elsewhere . . . there to be continued in slavery." Those condemned to hard labor were to follow a "rigorous regimen."[33]

Although Jefferson's goal had been a wholesale revision of the law, he settled for considerably less. Perhaps he overemphasized the importance of the changes he secured in liberalizing, humanizing, and rationalizing the law; but the passage of his bills could not result from

sociopsychological elements at work in this process. See especially Richard L. LaPiere, *A Theory of Social Control* (New York: McGraw-Hill Book Company, Inc., 1954).

32. Lipscomb and Bergh, 2:199.

33. *Ibid.,* 2:202.

his efforts alone, and he no doubt compromised his goals in order to secure enactment of those particular laws he considered the most necessary. He cannot fairly be accused of having believed that he attained his original purposes, but neither can he be condemned for failing to propose changes which helped ameliorate the harsh criminal code he set out to revise.

Beccaria, in his positive approach, had designed a penal program to carry out his proposed reforms. The method used was to be imprisonment for a stated period of time. This he considered the most humane and flexible means of adjusting punishments to crimes, and Jefferson largely concurred. However, Jefferson felt that "hard labor on roads, canals, and other public works" might also be employed, a view shared by the revisors but not by the general public.[34] When tried elsewhere, especially in Pennsylvania, this experiment proved unsuccessful, and he afterwards concluded that the exhibition of criminals as public spectacles with shaven heads would produce in them loss of self-respect and thus lead to recidivism.[35] He became convinced that a better approach was that of confined labor such as was being tried in Europe (and later to be tried in Philadelphia). Thus, he promoted the plan for building a penitentiary in Virginia, he himself providing architectural sketches for the building while he was in Paris.

The majority of Jefferson's bills concerning crime and punishment were adopted in 1796, by which date the legislators were willing to limit capital punishment to treason and murder. However, they failed to distinguish between murder and manslaughter as he had done, but instead introduced a distinction between murder in the first and second degrees.

Jefferson also, as a part of his work in revising the

---

34. Bowers, pp. 187–88.
35. Ford, *Writings,* 1:63.

Virginia code, proposed the establishment of a new system of courts to replace the English system which had been disrupted by the Revolution. He advocated establishing Courts of Appeal, Chancery and Assize, as well as Admiralty and County Courts. The Admiralty Court bill was passed promptly, authorizing the capture and sale of British ships. However, it was over a year before his bills to establish regular courts were passed. The explanation of this delay may be found in the opposition of the planter class, since they were the chief debtors in the state and as a result of the lack of a market for tobacco, their chief crop, were without funds during this period to satisfy the demands of their creditors. So long as the establishment of regular courts could be postponed, they were relatively free from such claims.[36]

When the legislature refused to establish regular courts, Jefferson drafted a compromise proposal which would have suspended payment of debts whenever suitable security was given. However, even this was too much for the legislators. Persistent in his concern for justice, he then offered a bill providing that debtors to the British could deposit lawful money of the Commonwealth with the State, which would then be responsible for settling the accounts in question. This bill was passed. However, the post-Revolutionary Virginia currency proved, as he said, to be of no more value than oak leaves, and thus his bill failed to accomplish the purpose of making possible an honorable settlement of the claims of British firms against citizens of Virginia.[37]

In the *Notes on Virginia,* Jefferson summarized the alterations which the revisors had proposed in the Virginia laws. Pointing out that the English common law

---

36. Nathan Schachner, *Thomas Jefferson: A Biography,* 2 vols. (New York: Appleton-Century-Crofts, Inc., 1951), 1:145–46.
37. Jefferson himself suffered tremendous losses in the matter of his wife's estate as a result of this bill.

was retained as the basis of the revised code, he suggested that "the most remarkable alterations" which were made were the abolition of entail and primogeniture, the naturalization law, the revision of the criminal law, and the establishment of religious freedom. Several of these proposals will be considered in later sections of this study. He also included in his list the proposal of a general property tax to raise funds for the maintenance of the poor (a task formerly performed by the vestries), and for erecting bridges, courthouses, and other state and county buildings. Another of the bills to which he attached significance was that calling for the upkeep and repair of public roads and the compensation of property owners for lands taken over by the state or county for new roads. He also discussed his disappointment over the failure of the legislature to act favorably upon his proposals for the emancipation of slaves and for establishing a system of public education.

Jefferson's struggles with the federal judiciary demonstrate other vital aspects of his view of the role of law. He saw Adams's "midnight appointments" as an underhanded and illegal attempt to defeat the purposes of "the revolution of 1800" by means of retaining control of the judiciary via Federalist judges appointed for life. After securing repeal of the Judiciary Act, he called upon the House of Representatives to begin impeachment proceedings against the notorious John Pickering, who had appeared on the bench drunk, bullied witnesses, and generally comported himself in a disgraceful manner.

Before the Congress could act, Jefferson's cousin and enemy John Marshall, now Chief Justice, delivered the famous *Marbury* v. *Madison* decision, in which he declared, through a shrewd use of *obiter dicta,* an act of Congress unconstitutional and proclaimed the right of the Supreme Court to so decide. Jefferson was infuriated, for the author of the Kentucky Resolutions was profoundly convinced that it was the states which possessed the right of declaring an Act of Congress unconstitutional; now Marshall had arrogated that right to the Court.

When Congress took up the Pickering case, Jefferson followed the matter closely, and even before the guilty verdict was delivered, he requested that proceedings be started against the doctrinaire Federalist Samuel Chase, an attempt which ended in failure and which Jefferson considered a stunning blow to his efforts to relegate the judiciary to its proper place. Throughout the rest of his life he protested against the power of judges, which he considered always to be "seriously anti-republican, because for life,"[38] a power which deliberately defeated the will of the people and trampled down their rights. Courts in his view existed to insure the people's natural rights, and the fact that judges were appointed for life opened to them the means to usurp those rights and thus constituted a legal tyranny in bold contrast to the principles he held so dear.

The Burr treason trial further revealed Jefferson's bitterness toward the judiciary. Burr no longer represented a political threat to Jefferson, and some critics have interpreted his activity during the treason trial as a display of personal vindictiveness which, in the light of his usual behavior, appears to conflict with the generally accepted view of his character. But he appears to have been convinced of Burr's threat to the nation. He also probably saw this as another opportunity to clip the wings of the judiciary. Of Burr's ambitious scheme, he wrote: "This insurrection will probably show that the fault in our constitution is not that the Executive holds too little power, but that the Judiciary either has too much, or holds it under too little responsibility."[39] Jeffer-

---

38. Lipscomb and Bergh, 15:20.
39. Schachner, 2:851.

son's activities during the trial have provided a fertile source for his critics, some of whom contend that he instituted an unprecedented national dragnet seeking witnesses and affidavits from Louisiana to Maine, from Indiana to New Jersey, and appointing himself prosecutor-in-chief as he overrode the regular machinery of government, even seeking the suspension of habeas corpus in an effort to achieve his purposes.[40]

When Burr was acquitted, Jefferson worked unsuccessfully for a constitutional amendment to restrict the power of the judiciary. As a strict constructionist, he felt that such an amendment was necessary, but he failed in his effort to secure it.

Jefferson's conflict in principles between strict adherence to the constitution—which he in the Kentucky Resolutions had called the chains to bind rulers—and protection of the people's rights was finally resolved in favor of the primacy of the latter in the Louisiana Purchase. Throughout the rest of his life he questioned the propriety of his action in that instance, for the Constitution contained no provision for adding territory to the United States under such circumstances. Finally he appealed for justification to the people "for doing for them unauthorized, what we knew they would have done for themselves had they been in a situation to do it."[41] As dangerous as he might have found this doctrine to be in the hands of others, his view does point up the fact that to him constitutions were but instruments to insure the rights of the people, as indeed all laws were.

Jefferson viewed the law as a social institution. He understood that norms flow from those legal propositions which are enforced by the courts as well as from the traditional mores incorporated in customs and the com-

---

40. *Ibid.*, 2:852.
41. Lipscomb and Bergh, 10:411.

mon law;[42] thus, Jefferson was eager to establish a code based upon the most enlightened approach of his day. It is clear that he also understood along with Max Weber that "conduct oriented toward a custom . . . endowed with . . . legitimacy" contributes to social stability and consensus;[43] therefore, he chose to retain the common law basis in the Virginia code. But his proposals went far beyond what many of his contemporaries considered acceptable, although he was bound by the limits which society sets to planned legal change, one of the major sociological factors in the growth and development of law.

When Roscoe Pound stated that the purpose of law was "to achieve the maximum of human control over external nature and over internal nature for human purposes,"[44] he was expressing thoughts which had long before been Jefferson's. The conditions of society and the character of man were both considerations affecting Jefferson's concept of the role of law; to him political and legal questions were one and the same.[45] In his social contract orientation, the state existed to meet the needs of man, yet men owed obedience to the laws of the state in order that the rights of all might be protected. The contract was social and the obligations were mutual.

Jefferson, the practical idealist, sought to incorporate into the law those specific provisions which would benefit the members of society. Yet his final appeal was to the natural law, the higher moral law which acts normatively upon positive law in much the same way as positive law influences the customs or "living law" of the com-

---

42. Geoffrey Sawer, ed., *Studies in the Sociology of Law* (Canberra: The Australian National University, 1961), p. 27.

43. Max Rheinstein, ed., *Max Weber on Law in Economy and Society* (Cambridge, Mass.: Harvard University Press, 1954), pp. 3–4.

44. Sawer, p. 85.

45. Daniel J. Boorstin, *The Lost World of Thomas Jefferson* (Boston: Beacon Press, 1948), p. 202.

munity or group. To Jefferson the universal and ultimate principles of the natural law were self-evident, as were the rights deriving from such law. The sociological approach to law is concerned with the conditions and the forms in which law exists and is felt to be binding, as well as with the conditions under which it develops and changes in its dynamic interrelations with the varied elements and functional needs of social life. These were vital concerns of Jefferson, a reformer to whom legal and other social institutions were but means of securing and protecting these rights to which men by nature were entitled.

In a letter to Thomas Paine from Paris in 1789, Jefferson quoted a report of the French revolutionary committee which stated that "every government should have as its only end, the preservation of the rights of man. . . . Laws have as their object the general administration of the kingdom, the property and the actions of the citizens."[46] To this declaration he gave his enthusiastic approval. Yet to him both laws and constitutions were subject to change; they were not eternally binding. "It is the will of the nation which makes the law obligatory," he wrote; "it is their will which creates or annihilates."[47] The dead could not bind the living, even by the common law, which, to be legitimate, must be enacted by the people.[48] Indeed, the Jeffersonian approach was in conflict with the common-law theory that the binding force of legal institutions was roughly proportionate to their antiquity, as suggested by Blackstone. On the contrary, Jefferson viewed traditional law as a factor which perpetuated monarchy, tyranny, and despotism. He therefore warned men to remain aware that, although

---

46. Thomas Jefferson, *The Papers of Thomas Jefferson,* ed. Julian P. Boyd (Princeton: Princeton University Press, 1950–   ), 15:268.
47. Lipscomb and Bergh, 10:126.
48. *Ibid.,* 10:125–29.

it might be more convenient to treat ancient laws *as if* they had been reenacted, it was the obligation of legislatures to repeal them, "whenever a change of circumstances or of will calls for it," since "habit alone confounds what is civil practice with natural right."[49] Laws, like the constitutions which gave them the color of legitimacy, should not outlive the men who had authorized them, unless reenacted by legislatures; for "the earth belongs always to the living," and legal institutions were no more sacred than any others.

Perhaps the best illustration of Jefferson's approach to the law may be seen in his view of what he called "the inestimable institution of juries."[50] "The trial by jury," he said, "I consider . . . the only anchor ever yet imagined by man, by which a government can be held to the principles of its constitution."[51] So long as a constitution was in effect, approved by the people, the government should be forced to abide by it. It was the people, then, for whom constitutions and enacted laws existed. The law itself was the people's, inspired by them, enacted for them, supported by them—and the courts were to provide the opportunity for "trials by the people themselves, that is to say, by jury."[52] Jefferson often expressed his conviction that the people were the best guardians of their rights—the natural rights to which they were entitled by natural law. Rational men equipped with a moral sense and enlightened by education were competent to rule themselves within the framework of the social contract.

Jefferson's view of natural law was based on his Enlightenment faith in an orderly moral universe. As to enacted laws, situational considerations, as well as demo-

---

49. Boorstin, *The Lost World of Thomas Jefferson,* p. 210.
50. Koch and Peden, p. 330.
51. Boyd, 15:269.
52. *Ibid.,* 14:678.

graphic and ecological ones, were always important in determining their desirability and efficacy. Along with Montesquieu, he believed that human legal institutions no less than other constellations of norms should be reasonable and scientific, consciously designed to fit the realities of natural law and the needs of the people. As instruments of society, they should be freely and intelligently adjusted to the circumstances obtaining in each generation. The higher law of nature, of which they should be an expression, demanded only that they protect instead of violate the inalienable rights of man and promote his freedom, equality, and happiness.

If Jefferson failed to secure the enactment of such a system of laws, as in fact he did so fail, he did not alter his philosophy of either human or natural law or discard his conviction that the good life for man as a social being could come only by human fidelity to the law of nature.

7

On Educational Institutions

When Jefferson in his old age designed the marker for his grave, he specified that the inscription on the tombstone was to read: "Here was buried Thomas Jefferson, author of the Declaration of Independence, of the Statute of Virginia for religious freedom, & Father of the University of Virginia." He gave no reasons for his choice of these particular accomplishments—stating simply that "because of these, as testimonials that I have lived, I wish to be remembered"[1]—but it is obvious that they reflected his scheme of values.

Education clearly was a crucial part of his total plan for the United States. From Paris he wrote in 1786 to George Washington: "It is an axiom in my mind that our liberty can never be safe but in the hands of the people themselves, and that too of the people with a certain degree of instruction. This is the business of the state to effect, and on a general plan."[2] In his revision of the Virginia code, he had provided for the remodeling of the College of William and Mary so that it would

---

1. Nathan Schachner, *Thomas Jefferson: A Biography,* 2 vols. (New York: Appleton-Century-Crofts, Inc., 1951), 1:1008.
2. Thomas Jefferson, *The Papers of Thomas Jefferson,* ed. Julian P. Boyd (Princeton: Princeton University Press, 1950–   ), 9:150.

be a true university. However, his bill was not adopted, nor was his plan for free elementary schools.

Jefferson the educational innovator was the same man as Jefferson the revolutionary. Indeed, his plans for a public education system in Virginia, from elementary school through university, were no less revolutionary than were his political proposals. His original 1779 Act for the More General Diffusion of Knowledge failed of passage in the legislature, although it was called up on numerous occasions.[3] This bill was divided into several parts.[4] First, the bill called for free elementary schools for all. Next, more advanced free education was to be available for a selected group of poor boys, as well as for those able to pay tuition, in residential "grammar schools." Following this period of instruction, a university education was to be provided at public expense to a select few who would then be better able to serve the state—an education in a true university to be established by the state for the education of this "aristocracy of virtue and talents" as well as of those who could pay their own way.

Jefferson described the purpose of his bill in the *Notes on the State of Virginia*. It is clear that its provisions were a part of his efforts to make the Commonwealth of Virginia a model republic in which the scientific and rational goals of the Enlightenment might be realized, with implications for America as a whole. One "object of the revisal," he said, "is, to diffuse knowledge more

3. In 1786 Madison wrote him in Paris that "in order to obviate the objection of the inability of the County to bear the expense, it was proposed that it should be passed into a law, but its operation suspended for three or four years." Even in this form, however, Madison felt that the bill stood little chance of passage and expressed his opinion that "it will be best to let it lie over for the supplemental Revisors, who may perhaps be able to put it into some shape that will lessen the objection of expense." *Ibid.*, 10:575–76.

4. For the complete text of this bill, see Roy J. Honeywell, *The Educational Work of Thomas Jefferson* (Cambridge, Mass.: Harvard University Press, 1931), pp. 199–205; also Boyd, 2:526–43.

generally through the mass of the people. The bill proposes to lay off every county into small districts of five or six miles square, called hundreds," and in each "to establish a school for teaching reading, writing and arithmetic."[5] This was the elementary school. The teachers in these schools were "to be supported by the hundred, and every person in it entitled to send their children three years gratis, and as much longer as they please, paying for it." Beyond this level other factors were to be considered. Jefferson proceeded in the *Notes* to outline the system as follows:

> These schools to be under a visitor who is annually to choose the boy of best genius in the school, of those whose parents are too poor to give them further education, and to send him forward to one of the grammar schools, of which twenty are proposed to be erected in different parts of the country, for teaching Greek, Latin, Geography, and the higher branches of numerical arithmetic. Of the boys thus sent in one year, trial is to be made at the grammar schools one or two years, and the best genius of the whole selected, and continued six years, and the residue dismissed. By this means twenty of the best geniuses will be raked from the rubbish annually, and be instructed, at the public expense, so far as the grammar schools go. At the end of six years instruction, one-half are to be discontinued (from among whom the grammar schools will probably be supplied with future masters) ; and the other half, who are to be chosen for the superiority of their parts and disposition, are to be sent and continued three years in the study of such sciences as they shall choose, at William and Mary College, the plan of which is proposed to be enlarged, as will be hereafter explained, and extended to all the useful sciences. The ultimate result of the whole scheme of education would be the teaching all the children of the State reading, writing and common arithmetic; turning out ten annually of superior genius, well taught in Greek, Latin, Geography, and the higher branches of arithmetic; turning out ten others annually, of

5. Thomas Jefferson, *The Writings of Thomas Jefferson,* ed. Andrew A. Lipscomb and Albert E. Bergh, 20 vols. (Washington: Thomas Jefferson Memorial Association, 1903), 2:203.

still superior parts, who, to those branches of learning, shall have added such of the sciences as their genius shall have led them to; the furnishing to the wealthier part of the people convenient schools at which their children may be educated at their own expense. The general objects of this law are to provide an education adapted to the years, to the capacity, and the condition of everyone, and directed to their freedom and happiness.[6]

While Jefferson's proposal of three years of public education for all citizens seems modest enough, it was a radical one for the period in which he lived. Even more radical were his proposals to provide free public instruction for those selectively chosen, all the way through a university education—proposals too revolutionary for his fellow citizens and still not completely implemented. He detailed carefully the means whereby those "of the best and most promising genius and disposition" were to be chosen by the overseer in the presence of at least two of the three elected county officials (aldermen). The lower-level schools were to be within walking distance of the pupils' homes, but the "grammar schools" were to be boarding schools, with the payment of fees due from the selected poorer students to be made by the state. Those who were fortunate enough to be chosen for attendance at William and Mary were "there to be educated, boarded, and clothed, three years; the expense of which annually" shall be paid from public funds—a type of full scholarship which, Conant notes, is nonexistent today except on occasion for those of unusual athletic talent![7]

These radical proposals failed to gain popular support; and, indeed, it was not until the middle of the nineteenth century that taxpayers finally came to see the

---

6. *Ibid.,* 2:203–4.
7. James B. Conant, *Thomas Jefferson and The Development of American Public Education* (Berkeley: University of California Press, 1963) p. 7.

importance of free public elementary schools. Not until our own day did any promise of compromise between equality of status and the notion of equality of opportunity appear. It was many generations before Americans were willing to entertain the Jeffersonian ideal of educating one group at public expense for a longer period of time than others.[8]

Jefferson saw his selective system as making available to

the State . . . those talents which nature has sown as liberally among the poor as the rich, but which perish without use, if not sought for and cultivated. But of the views of this law none is more important, none more legitimate, than that of rendering the people the safe, as they are the ultimate, guardians of their own liberty.[9]

In this fashion he justified the necessary public expenditure and also revealed the role he assigned to education in a democratic republic.

For this purpose the reading in the first stage, where *they* will receive their whole education, is proposed . . . to be chiefly historical. History, by apprizing them of the past, will enable them to judge of the future; it will avail them of the experience of other times and other nations; it will qualify them as judges of the actions and designs of men; it will enable them to know ambition under every disguise it may assume; and, knowing it, to defeat its views. In every government on earth is some trace of human weakness, some germ of corruption and degeneracy, which cunning will discover, and wickedness insensibly open, cultivate and improve. Every government degenerates when trusted to the rulers of the people alone. The people themselves therefore are its only safe depositories. And to render even them safe, their minds must be improved to a certain degree.[10]

---

8. *Ibid.*
9. Lipscomb and Bergh, 2:206.
10. *Ibid.*, 2:206-7.

Jefferson follows this clear statement of the role and purposes of public education in a democratic republic with a plea for universal suffrage.

> An amendment to our constitution must . . . come in aid of the public education. The influence over government must be shared among all the people. If every individual which composes their mass participates of the ultimate authority, the government will be safe; because the corrupting the whole mass will exceed any private resources of wealth; and public ones cannot be provided but by levies on the people. In this case every man would have to pay his own price. The government of Great Britain has been corrupted, because but one man in ten has a right to vote for members of parliament. The sellers of the government, therefore, get nine-tenths of their price clear. It has been thought that corruption is restrained by confining the right of suffrage to a few of the wealthier of the people; but it would be more effectively restrained by an extension of that right to such numbers as would bid defiance to the means of corruption.[11]

Jefferson as an opponent of centralized government displayed considerable inconsistencies in his attitude toward the relation of the state to education. In 1817 he sent his friend Joseph Cabell a draft entitled "An Act for Establishing Public Schools," which provided:

> At this school shall be received and instructed gratis, every infant of competent age who has not already had three years' schooling. And it is declared and enacted, that no person unborn or under the age of twelve years at the passing of this

---

11. *Ibid.*, 2:207–8. Boorstin sees these statements as indicating that when Jefferson professed faith in the "good sense" of the masses, he simply meant that the cost of bribing them would be too great for any one or several men to carry through; and that it was in this sense that the people were the only "safe depositories" of government and the best guardians of their own rights. Daniel J. Boorstin, *The Lost World of Thomas Jefferson* (Boston: Beacon Press, 1948), pp. 191–92. As President, Jefferson pointed the way to the extension of suffrage to all free male adults, as well as the development of a more democratic climate of opinion, which in turn influenced the attitude of people toward education. Conant, p. 10.

act, and who is *compos mentis,* shall, after the age of fifteen years, be a citizen of this commonwealth until he or she can read readily in some tongue, native or acquired.[12]

In a footnote, Jefferson gave his views of the "rights and duties of society toward its members, infant and adult," as follows:

> It is better to tolerate the rare instances of a parent refusing to let his child be educated, than to shock the common feelings and ideas by the public asportation and education of the infant against the will of the father. What is proposed here is to remove the objection of expense, by offering education gratis, and to strengthen parental excitement by disfranchisement of his child while uneducated. . . . If we do not force instruction, let us at least strengthen the motives to receive it when offered.[13]

In the *Notes on Virginia* he had said nothing about compulsory school attendance, though this is certainly implied. However, almost 40 years later, after the experience of leading the Republican party in the overthrow of the Federalists, Jefferson appeared clearly unwilling to use the power of the state to enforce compulsory school attendance. The relationship he saw existing between education and political structure is demonstrated in his famous letter to John Adams in 1813. Referring to his success in securing the abolishing of entails and primogeniture, he said:

> These laws . . . laid the axe to the roots of Pseudo-aristocracy. And had another which I prepared been adopted by the legislature, our work would have been complete. It was a Bill for the more general diffusion of learning. . . . Worth and genius would thus have been sought out from every condition of life, and completely prepared by education for defeating the competition of wealth and birth for public trusts. . . . Although

12. See Honeywell, pp. 233–43.
13. *Ibid.*

this law has not yet been acted on . . . I have great hope that some patriotic spirit will, at a favorable moment, call it up, and make it the keystone of the arch of our government.[14]

It has been pointed out that one of the great inconsistencies of Jefferson's life and career was that, in the position of President, he did nothing to make his educational scheme a reality—during the period of his greatest political power he failed to use his influence to promote his proposals for public education, either in Virginia or in any other state,[15] in spite of the fact that he was still loyal to his plan in 1813, as the above letter shows. Jefferson's letter to Adams clearly reveals the important sociological and political implications of his plan; therefore, it is not surprising that he made a second attempt in 1817 to reform Virginia education. No doubt he failed to use his influence as President to advance his plan because he felt that public education should be a local concern and that pressure or even inspiration from the White House would fly in the face of his political philosophy.

In any event, his reentry into the concerns of education in Virginia was signaled by his election to the board of trustees of Albemarle Academy, a private school, in 1814. It was in this same year that he wrote a long letter to Peter Carr, his nephew, setting forth his views on education in general, after long years of inquiry and reflection. Perhaps the most remarkable thing is that his ideas regarding education had changed so little since he first drew up the Virginia bill in 1779. In the letter to Carr, he repeats his earlier proposals for elementary schools, but he drops the term "grammar schools" in favor of the term "general schools," which he discusses as follows:

14. Lester J. Cappon, ed., *Adams-Jefferson Letters* (Chapel Hill: University of North Carolina Press, 1959), 2:387–92.
15. Conant, p. 12.

At the discharging of the pupils from the elementary schools, the two classes separate—those destined for labor will engage in the business of agriculture, or enter into apprenticeships to such handicraft art as may be their choice; their companions, destined to the pursuits of science, will proceed to the college, which will consist, 1st of general schools; and 2d, of professional schools. The general schools will constitute the second grade of education.

The learned class may still be subdivided into two sections: 1. Those who are destined for learned professions as means of livelihood; and 2. The wealthy, who, possessing independent fortunes, may aspire to share in conducting the affairs of the nation, or to live with usefulness and respect in the private ranks of life. Both of these sections will require instruction in all the higher branches of science; the wealthy to qualify them for either public or private life; the professional section will need those branches, especially, which are the basis of their future profession, and a general knowledge of the others, as auxiliary to that, and necessary to their standing and association with the scientific class. All the branches, then, of useful science, ought to be taught in the general schools, to a competent degree, in the first instance. These sciences may be arranged into three departments, not rigorously scientific, indeed, but sufficiently so for our purposes. These are I, Language; II, Mathematics; III, Philosophy.[16]

Thus, the former "grammar schools" had been transformed into general schools or colleges, and in the draft which he sent Cabell in 1817, Jefferson entitled one provision "A Bill for the Establishment of District Colleges and University," to be combined with the "Act for Establishing Elementary Schools" into a proposal under the title "A Bill for Establishing a System of Public Education." The state was to be divided into nine collegiate districts, each with a board of visitors, and instruction was to be given in modern languages as well as in Greek and Latin, along with English grammar, geography, "the higher branches of numerical arithmetic, the

---

16. Lipscomb and Bergh, 19:214–15.

mensuration of land, the use of globes, and the ordinary elements of navigation."

The provisions for selecting poor boys for scholarships were less rigorous than those in the 1779 bill. This new draft provided that the visitors of the elementary schools

> after the most diligent and impartial observation and enquiry of the boys who have been three years . . . and whose parents are too poor to give them a collegiate education, shall select from among them some one of the most promising and sound understanding, who shall be sent to the first meeting of the Visitors of their collegiate district, with such proofs as the case requires and admits, for the examination and information of that Board; who, from among the candidates so offered from the several counties of their district, shall select two . . . who shall be admitted to their College, and there maintained and educated five years at the public expense.[17]

This proposed bill further provided that one of those thus selected should be chosen to proceed to the university for three additional years at public expense. The object of this bill, Jefferson said, was "to bring into action that mass of talents which lies buried in poverty in every country, for want of means of development, and thus give activity to a mass of mind, which, in proportion to our population, shall be the double or treble of what it is in most countries."[18]

Jefferson's educational plans acknowledged the fact that, as he said, "the mass of our citizens may be divided into two classes, the laboring, & the learned." The learned could also be divided into two classes, as we have seen—those who required a profession as a means of livelihood, and the wealthy of independent fortune "who may aspire to share in conducting the affairs of the na-

---

17. Conant, p. 15. The number of students to receive scholarships under this plan was far fewer than under the 1779 plan. See Honeywell, p. 30.
18. Lipscomb and Bergh, 15:153.

tion." He insisted upon practical knowledge as being of primary importance, and he probably believed that the administration of public affairs should not be the means of a livelihood. The corollary of this belief is obvious, that public offices should be filled primarily by those of independent means, as in the colonial period during which he grew up.

It is clear that he also believed that education was the *sine qua non* if the people were to be truly competent in self-government, able to exercise their reason and ascertain the truth. The fact that he wished to provide means whereby the "natural aristocracy of virtue and talents" might achieve an education "at public expense, for the care of the public concerns" is convincing evidence of his desire to open the doors to leadership to those of ability, irrespective of family status or economic class. The fact that his plan admitted only a few to these opportunities bears witness to his being a practical idealist ready to practice "the art of the possible"; for he found it necessary to offer compromises when his plan of 1817 met no greater success than the one he had offered in 1779. But even the 1817 proposal for public education from elementary school through college was too extreme for his contemporaries and the total plan was never implemented.

Jefferson's claim to fame as an educational innovator derives largely and properly from his bill of 1779 and his *Notes on Virginia,* in which he expressed his radical ideas concerning the role of education in a democratic republic. Interestingly enough, his views may have been derived in part from John Knox's *Book of Discipline of 1561,* a copy of which was in his library and which perhaps came to him through Dr. William Small while he was a student at William and Mary. In any event, Knox outlined a system of education in many respects similar to that proposed by Jefferson in 1779. Indeed, Knox's scheme went considerably beyond Jefferson's, emphasizing that no student of ability was to be barred because of poverty from achieving higher education. Knox proposed to cover the expenses of such students from funds obtained by the confiscation of Catholic properties. In his theocracy, as in Jefferson's republic, advanced education was to serve the state. Jefferson, of course, hated tyranny, especially religious tyranny. Yet his mind was always open. Thus, if the plan he proposed was adapted from one designed to perpetuate the tyranny of a religious state, through Jefferson's genius it became an implement to be utilized in securing religious freedom and personal liberty in a democratic republic.[19]

Whatever their source, Jefferson's bold educational ideas did not bear fruit in his lifetime, except for the establishment of the state university. In 1779, he had proposed that William and Mary be remodeled into a true university. As late as 1800, he found it lacking in those qualities which he felt should characterize an institution of higher learning. In that year he wrote Joseph Priestley of his alma mater:

> We have . . . a College just well enough endowed to draw out the miserable existence to which a miserable constitution has doomed it. It is moreover eccentric in its position, exposed to all bilious diseases as all the lower country is. . . . We wish to establish in the upper country, and more centrally for the State, an University so broad and liberal and *modern,* as to be worth patronizing with the public support, and be a temptation to the youth of other States to come and drink of the cup of knowledge and fraternize with us.[20]

Jefferson's original opposition to William and Mary seems to have stemmed from his strong objection to the clerical tyranny he observed there as a student. The

---

19. Conant, p. 19.
20. Lipscomb and Bergh, 10:140.

Revolution provided an opportunity to revamp the college, and he proposed in his bill that the legislature should "aid and improve the seminary, in which those who are to be the future guardians of the rights and liberties of their country may be endowed with science and virtue."[21] His bill provided that the new Board of Visitors "shall not be restrained" by "the canons or the constitution of the English Church"[22]—in other words, that this former seat of Anglicanism in Virginia be secularized. This the conservatives opposed.

Jefferson's other proposals for William and Mary were hardly revolutionary. He recommended that the number of professors be increased from six to eight, one each for the following subjects: one of moral philosophy, the laws of nature and nations, and the fine arts; one of law and police; one of mathematics; one of history, civil and ecclesiastical; one of natural philosophy and natural history; one of anatomy and medicine; one of ancient languages; and one of modern languages. The professorship of theology was to be abolished. He also proposed that a missionary be sent to the Indian tribes to study their "laws, customs, religions, traditions and more particularly their languages, constructing grammars thereof" —a lifelong concern of Jefferson's and one indicative of his interests in anthropology and linguistics.

In the letter to Priestley, he suggested the following courses for his proposed state university: botany, chemistry, zoology, anatomy, surgery, medicine, natural philosophy, agriculture, mathematics, astronomy, geography, politics, commerce, history, ethics, law, arts, and fine arts. A second letter followed, apologizing for his oversight in omitting languages.

While serving as President, Jefferson proposed, in his sixth annual message of 1806, an amendment to the Con-

---

21. Conant, p. 22.
22. *Ibid.,* p. 23.

stitution to provide federal support for a national university. "Education," he pointed out is

> among the articles of public care, not that it would be proposed to take its ordinary branches out of the hands of private enterprise, which manages so much better all the concerns to which it is equal; but a public institution can alone supply those sciences which, though rarely called for, are yet necessary to complete the circle, all the parts of which contribute to the improvement of the country, and some of them to its preservation.[23]

Nothing came of this recommendation; the bill for a national university died in committee, and Jefferson seems not to have pushed his proposal very hard. It is interesting to observe that, for political reasons or otherwise, he expressed his willingness to leave to private institutions the ordinary branches of education. His position, however, does not appear inconsistent since in his 1779 plan the "grammar schools" were to be supported largely by tuition. Jefferson was not only a supporter of public education but of private as well.

Some attribute his plans for a national university to the influence of Du Pont de Nemours, whom he had known in Paris and who came to New York in 1800. Before arriving in New York Du Pont de Nemours had drawn up a complete plan for a system of national education in the United States. The city of Washington was to be the site of four *grandes écoles*—of medicine, mining, legislation, and mathematics—the capstone to a system which included common schools and intermediate colleges. It is entirely possible that his plan helped inspire Jefferson's proposal for a national university.

When Jefferson retired to Monticello after his second presidential term, his interest in Virginia education was

---

23. Saul K. Padover, ed., *The Complete Jefferson* (New York: Duell, Sloan and Pierce, 1943), p. 425.

reawakened. By 1814 his ideas regarding higher education had progressed far beyond those he expressed in his plans to revamp William and Mary. In his old age he appears to have become increasingly interested in higher education, particularly after his second plan for the establishment of elementary schools failed. More and more he gave his thoughts and efforts to the question of building the state university which he envisioned. He proposed a greatly expanded list of subjects to be taught at this highest level, and his efforts resulted in the establishment of eight separate schools at the new university, each with a wide range of subjects and each school under a separate professor. Thus, a student could study in one school only, if he desired, making Jefferson the originator of the elective system.[24] This system he described to Professor Ticknor of Harvard in 1823.

> I am not fully aware of the practices at Harvard, but there is one from which we shall certainly vary, although it has been copied, I believe, by nearly every college and academy in the United States. That is, the holding the students all to one prescribed course of readings, and disallowing exclusive application to those branches only which are to qualify them for the particular vocations to which they are destined. We shall, on the contrary, allow them uncontrolled choice in the lectures they shall choose to attend.[25]

The establishment of the University of Virginia became Jefferson's chief interest outside his family after his retirement from the presidency. It is "the last object," he said, "for which I shall obtrude myself on the public observation."[26] And obtrude himself he did, never tiring in his efforts to bring to fulfillment the dream of his old age, never letting the legislators rest until they

---

24. Conant, p. 25.
25. Lipscomb and Bergh, 15:455.
26. Albert Jay Nock, *Jefferson* (New York: Hill and Wang, 1963), p. 191.

had carried through the plans he had made for the people of his state and the welfare of the commonwealth. It was a long and arduous battle, bedeviled by many a delay and untold frustrations; but on the whole, considering the fate of his bills to establish elementary and "common schools," it went better than might have been expected.

The beginnings of the state university might properly be said to be found in the incorporation of Central College in Charlottesville in 1816 by an act of the legislature, largely a result of Jefferson's endeavors and those of his nephew Peter Carr, President of the Board of Trustees, and of Joseph Cabell, a member of the legislature. In 1814 Jefferson had become a trustee of Albemarle Academy in Charlottesville, and it was this institution which became Central College, with a Board of Visitors including Jefferson, Madison, and Monroe.

In 1814 Jefferson had written Cabell that the future of the Republic depended upon dividing the counties into wards or "hundreds" and establishing in each a system of public education. The future would hang, he was convinced, on "those two hooks,"[27] since reason was the "only oracle God has given us" and people must be educated to protect their rights in a republican form of government. Cabell was an enlightened man who had traveled widely in Europe. He fell in enthusiastically with Jefferson's educational schemes, and in 1809, at Jefferson's request, introduced in the legislature a bill to establish a "Literary Fund" from forfeitures, escheats, and fines. The debt paid by the federal government to Virginia in 1816 was added to this fund, making a total of over a million dollars. The Literary Fund had originally been envisioned as a source of support for ele-

---

27. Thomas Jefferson, *The Writings of Thomas Jefferson*, ed. Paul Leicester Ford, 10 vols. (New York: G. P. Putnam's Sons, 1892–1899), 11:382.

mentary schools; however, when the legislature failed to pass Jefferson's second general education bill, as we have seen, Central College became the chief beneficiary of these moneys.

When Jefferson drew up his plans for a state university, he offered two alternatives: that the university be established at a location the legislature might decide, or that it take over Central College. He strongly preferred the second alternative, as he had been deeply concerned with the erection of Central College; however, he knew that William and Mary opposed this plan, as did other sections of the state. The legislators felt that the cost of the university should be covered entirely by moneys available from the Literary Fund, without additional tax burdens upon the people of the state. Many, too, questioned the desirability of locating the university in Charlottesville. Alternative plans were offered by various legislators, some even suggesting that the Literary Fund moneys should be used in part to support charity schools with the balance utilized to retire the state debts. Jefferson called upon Monroe to give support to his plan and bombarded Cabell with requests for information on the progress of the bill. "It is a bantling of 40. years birth & nursing," he wrote, "& if I can once see it on its legs, I will sing with sincerity and pleasure my nunc dimittas."[28]

Cabell suggested to him that, as a matter of practical politics, it would be well to leave out Jefferson's prohibitions involving ministers of religion and religious instruction, to which he replied, "There are fanatics both in religion and politics who without knowing me personally have long been taught to consider me as a rawhead & bloody bones."[29] He, of course, accepted Cabell's advice. At last in 1818, when the legislature acted upon the bill,

---

28. Schachner, 2:956.
29. *Ibid.,* 2:957.

rejecting Jefferson's plans as a whole, it provided $45,000 a year for the education of the poor and $15,000 for a university.

The location and other matters were left undetermined. The act required the governor to appoint a commission of 24 members to select the site and to determine the plan of organization and the curriculum. The commission met at Rockfish Gap on August 1, 1818, with Jefferson serving as chairman and with Monroe, Madison, and Cabell among the members. Three sites were debated: Staunton, Washington College at Lexington, and Central College in Charlottesville. Jefferson, of course, had given his best efforts to Central College for some time, secretly intending it to be the nucleus of the proposed state university. He had drawn up detailed papers showing that Charlottesville was the demographic and geographical center of the state; he had also brought to the meeting completed plans for buildings, for curriculum, and even a system of rules for student governance. Jefferson won his case, by a vote of 16 to five, a complete victory for a master politician.

Jefferson's report was submitted to the legislature and, in spite of considerable opposition to the location, was overwhelmingly approved in January, 1819. He was appointed one of the visitors, and shortly thereafter, the rector of the Board. At 75, he threw himself energetically into the project of establishing the university of which he proudly called himself father.

While awaiting the final decision of the legislature Jefferson had worked constantly on his architectural plans for the University. Almost immediately he personally staked out the grounds, surveyed them, and proposed the prompt erection of a pavilion to house the professorship in languages. Already he was drafting plans for a whole range of buildings. His exact and precise plans for cornices, frieze, architrave, columns, and shafts mingled the Doric, Corinthian, and Tuscan styles, and incorporated features from such classical buildings as the Theatre of Marcellus, the Fortuna Virilis, the Baths of Diocletian, and the Temple of Trajan, using as his source of information the work of Palladio. He was, of course, no mere copyist, and modified and transmuted elements of the classical models to gain new effects. His enthusiasm was almost boundless. The library he designed would be a rotunda, the inner concave ceiling of which would be painted "sky-blue and spangled with gilt stars in their position and magnitude copied exactly from any selected hemisphere of our latitude,"[30] constituting a planetarium with an ingenious movable seat so that an operator might shift the positions of the constellations for the instruction of the assembled students.

He sought the advice and aid of the nation's best architects, William Thornton and Benjamin Latrobe, to whom he explained his purposes in detail.

> Instead of building a magnificent house which would exhaust all our funds, we propose to lay off a square, or rather 3. sides of a square about 7. or 800 f. wide, leaving it open on one end to be extended indefinitely. On the closed end, and on the two sides we propose to arrange separate pavilions for each professor and his school. Each pavilion is to have a school-room below, and 2. rooms for the Professor above; and between pavilion and pavilion a range of Dormitories for the students, one story high, giving each a room 10 f. wide & 14 f. deep. The Pavilions about 36 f. wide in front, & 24 f. in depth. . . . The whole of the pavilions and dormitories to be united by a colonade in front, of the height of the lower story of the pavilions & about 8 f. wide under which they may go dry from school to school. The top of the dormitories to be flat. . . . Now what we wish is that these pavilions . . . should be models of taste and correct architecture, and of a variety of appearance, no two alike, so as to serve as specimens of . . . orders for the architectural lectures.[31]

30. *Ibid.*, 2:959-60.
31. *Ibid.*, 2:960.

The care which Jefferson lavished on the architecture of the University was no greater than that he expended on the educational aspects of the undertaking. He avowed that the professors would be "of the first order. . . . Ours shall be second to none on the continent."[32] However, he wrote Cabell,

> Of all things the most important, is the completion of the buildings. . . . The great object of our aim from the beginning, has been to make the establishment the most eminent in the United States, in order to draw to it the youth of every state, but especially of the south and west. We have proposed, therefore, to call to it characters of the first order of science from Europe, as well as our own country; and, not only by the salaries and the comforts of their situations, but by the distinguished scale of its structure and preparation. . . . Had we built a barn for a college, and log huts for accommodations, should we ever have had the assurance to propose to an European professor of that character to come to it? . . . To stop where we are, is to abandon our high hopes, and become suitors to Yale and Harvard for their secondary characters to become our first. . . . The report of Rockfish Gap, sanctioned by the Legislature, authorized us to aim at much higher things. . . . The opening of the institution in a half-state of readiness, would be the most fatal step which could be adopted.[33]

Jefferson had good cause for his pleas to Cabell, who acted as his legislative agent. Cabell dutifully reported to Jefferson the legislative difficulties encountered, difficulties which demonstrate the fact that political maneuvering in regard to educational matters was very much the same in Jefferson's time as today.[34] A number of legislators felt that the University should receive only the interest from the Literary Fund moneys and none of the capital—much too small an amount with which to begin

---

32. *Ibid.*
33. Conant, pp. 27–28.
34. *Ibid.*, p. 27.

construction. Cabell at last saw the bill through the political labyrinth and the first funds to begin construction were appropriated in 1822. But Jefferson's troubles were far from over.

One source of trouble was the growing animosity of the religious bodies to the idea of a secular institution. His hatred of doctrinal theology led him to write that dogmas "have been the bane and ruin of the Christian church, its own fatal invention, which, thro' so many ages, made of Christendom a slaughter house, and at this day divides it into castes of inextinguishable hatred to one another. Witness the present internecine rage of all other sects against the Unitarians," who were being attacked because they had no creed.[35] His incautious remark that the older denominations "may well be afraid of the progress of the Unitarians to the South" spread like wildfire through the state and antagonized many. Cabell advised him that these comments had raised additional difficulties in the legislature, angering some to the extent that they refused to vote additional funds for the University. "Would it be believed in future times," Jefferson wrote in despair, "that such efforts are necessary to carry such a bill, for such an object!"[36]

Not only did he have to face religious opposition; political influences were also at work. One source of difficulty was the opposition of the people of Richmond to the Rotunda, for they feared that such a magnificent building might inspire people to insist that the capital be moved to Charlottesville. Even a member of the Board of Visitors shared this feeling and agreed with the legislative leader who vowed he "would never vote another Dollar to the University but on condition that it should not be applied to that building."[37]

35. Schachner, 2:982–83.
36. *Ibid.*, 2:983.
37. *Ibid.*

Progress was slow in securing funds for the building program; however, by 1822 loans of approximately $200,000 had been authorized, with still another $50,000 needed. It was this additional amount at which the legislature balked, and the Rotunda was still lacking. Difficulties with workmen added to Jefferson's problems. Furthermore, he thought he saw the Presbyterians again sowing mischief among the legislators. His patience worn thin, he cried out against them in bitter words.

> This is rather the most numerous of our present sects, and the most ambitious, the most intolerant & tyrannical of all our sects. They wish to see no instruction of which they have not the exclusive direction. Their present aim is ascendancy only, their next exclusive possession and establishment. They dread the light which this University is to shed on the public mind, and its obstruction to their ambition. But there is a breeze advancing from the North, which will put them down. Unitarianism has not yet reached us; but our citizens are ready to receive reason from any quarter. The Unity of a supreme being is so much more intelligible than the triune arithmetic of the counterfeit Christians that it will kindle here like a wildfire.[38]

Fortunately, it was time for a newly elected legislature to assume its duties. Aid to the University had been the chief issue in the election, and the people spoke out unequivocally, electing many friends of the University to both the House and the Senate. Cabell saw his bill for the Rotunda through, and in 1823 a loan of $60,000 was authorized. At last the needed funds to complete Jefferson's building program were at hand. It had been a long, hard fight, one in which Jefferson's optimism had only occasionally given way to discouragement. His indomitable will and enthusiasm overcame all difficulties, and with Cabell's untiring assistance, victory had been won, even for the controversial Rotunda and library.

---

38. *Ibid.,* 2:984.

But, warned Cabell, "we must never come here again for money to erect buildings."[39]

The victory was a crucial one to Jefferson, for education was essential if the republic was to survive. Just before the final victory in the legislature, he had written:

> I look to the diffusion of light and education as the resource most to be relied on for ameliorating the condition, promoting the virtue and advancing the happiness of man. That every man shall be made virtuous, by any process whatever, is indeed no more to be expected, than that every tree be made to bear fruit, and every plant nourishment. The briar and the bramble can never become the vine and the olive; but their asperities may be softened by culture, and their properties improved to usefulness in the order and economy of the world. And I do hope, in the present spirit of extending to the great mass of mankind the blessing of instruction, I see a prospect of great advancement in the happiness of the human race; and that this may proceed to an indefinite, tho' not to an infinite degree.[40]

Jefferson, the practical idealist, uttered his testament of dedication to education with due regard for the realities of human life, but his expression of hope would serve to inspire many who followed him. His dedication was not one of words only. Daily the old gentleman rode down from Monticello to supervise the construction of his University, usually on Eagle, his favorite horse. The round-trip distance was approximately ten miles, but even at 80 he rode down and back alone; and when he was not on the site supervising the work, he carefully watched through his telescope the progress being made. No detail was too small to escape his attention. A visitor in 1822 told of seeing Jefferson take a chisel from one of the Italian sculptors he had brought over to fashion the columns and marble work, and then proceed to demon-

---

39. *Ibid.,* 2:985.
40. *Ibid.,* 2:986.

strate to the artisan how to carve a particular design he wanted. The visitor reported that the old gentleman walked with "an elastic step" and extended his greeting with a "sweet, winning smile."[41]

By 1824 Jefferson had high hopes of seeing his "academical village" open its doors within a few months. He had dispatched young Francis Gilmer to England and Scotland to seek professors, but Gilmer reported that well-known educators there were accustomed to higher salaries than the University could pay, whereupon Jefferson advised him to get younger men of ability. "I consider," Jefferson wrote Madison, "that his return without any professors will compleatly quash every hope."[42] Jefferson was also agitated over other problems. William and Mary had proposed to move from Williamsburg to Richmond to compete with the University. But matters improved; the legislature refused William and Mary's petition, and Gilmer returned with his professors in tow.

The original faculty was an excellent one—six men from abroad and one American, John Tayloe Lomax, the professor of law. Among the Europeans were four Englishmen—George Long of Cambridge, professor of ancient languages; Thomas Hewitt Key, professor of mathematics; Charles Bonnycastle, professor of natural philosophy; and Robley Dunglison, professor of anatomy and medicine. George Blaettermann of Germany, professor of modern languages, and George Tucker of Bermuda, professor of moral philosophy, completed the faculty. They were paid $1,500 per year, plus a fee of 20 dollars from each student, and given rent-free living quarters.[43]

---

41. Saul K. Padover, *Jefferson* (New York: Mentor Books, 1963), p. 171.
42. Schachner, 2:996.
43. Padover, *Jefferson*, p. 173.

Jefferson had also engaged Thomas Cooper, a liberal-minded scientist, for the faculty. However, the clergy raised what Jefferson called a "hue and cry" against Cooper and forced the Board of Visitors to cancel his appointment. Jefferson was furious at the Presbyterians —whom he blamed for this "Holy Inquisition," as he called it—but since the University was tax-supported, he could do nothing.[44]

At long last all difficulties had been surmounted, and on March 7, 1825, the University was officially opened. Jefferson continued his active role in its development, and as rector he proved a rigid disciplinarian, for all his talk of treating the students as mature young men. He permitted only one vacation a year, from December 15 to January 31; and when students asked for an additional ten days beginning July 4, he refused. The students also petitioned that dancing and the use of small swords be taught. "Dancing," he commented, "is generally, and justly, I think, considered among *innocent* accomplishments; while we cannot so consider the art of stabbing and pistolling our friends."[45]

Growing restive perhaps under his strict hand, a group of students got uproariously drunk and, when two professors attempted to quell the disturbance, greeted them with insults and brickbats. The professors sought to resign, but the Board refused to accept their resignations and the culprits were expelled. Preparing for further disturbances, he indicated his intention of calling in "the civil authority in the first instance of disorder, and to quell it on the spot by imprisonment and the same legal coercions provided against disorder generally committed by other citizens," since he did not feel that University

44. *Ibid.*
45. Schachner, 2:1001. In August 1825 he wrote his granddaughter: "We have passed the limit of 100 students. . . . We treat them as men and gentlemen, under the guidance mainly of their own discretion." Lipscomb and Bergh, 18:341.

students should, as young adults, be insulated from the provisions of the law. Jefferson was not all strictness and discipline with the young men, however; he invited them to dinner at Monticello, especially on Sundays, and took great pleasure in their company. He thought them "a very fine parcel of young men" to enjoy the University program, which, he said in the spring of 1825, "comprehends every branch of useful knowledge, and our Professors are of the first order of science, so that I hope it will prove a great blessing to my country."[46]

Some of the students were inadequately prepared for university work. Jefferson realized that the lower-level schools in Virginia were poor—so poor, in fact, that he doubted if the teachers would have been able to qualify as sophomores at Eton and Westminster. Part of this could be attributed, of course, to the failure of either his 1779 bill or his 1818 bill for a public education system to gain passage in the legislature; and in the latter year even he himself was willing to let this plan drop in order to secure passage of the bill to establish the University, for he understood that he could not have both.

In 1817 Charles Fenton Mercer, a Federalist, had offered a public school bill in the Virginia legislature rather similar to Jefferson's except that it placed a great deal of power in the hands of a state board of education, something to which Jefferson was unalterably opposed. His fear of centralized state authority may have been greater than his desire for a public education system. In any event, Cabell, unable to secure an amendment to the Mercer bill placing the state university in Charlottesville, appears to have lent his influence (and therefore indirectly that of Jefferson) to the bill's defeat, although it passed the House and was tied in the Senate. Unques-

---

46. *Ibid.*, 2:1001. See also Honeywell, p. 138.

tionably this, along with Jefferson's insistence on an extremely decentralized school system, retarded primary school legislation and development in Virginia. The fact remains, however, that the passage of such a bill would have meant the failure of the University bill; and, even if both had been passed, an insufficient amount of money to develop either satisfactorily. Jefferson opted for the University, promising that later he would do his best to secure the establishment of a public school system, something he did not live long enough to accomplish. Indeed, almost all his attentions outside his family were centered on the University the last seven years of his life. Perhaps his position regarding public education was inconsistent. It is certainly ironically true that it was Jefferson's insistence upon the establishment of schools publicly managed and free for all which marks him as a great educational statesman and which was the doctrine that Americans accepted 50 years after his death.[47]

To the higher education of young men he gave his best and most careful thought. However, "a plan of female education," he confessed, "has never been a subject of systematic contemplation with me."[48] One of the obstacles to the education of women he found to be their "inordinate passion for novels," from which resulted "a bloated imagination, sickly judgment and disgust toward all real business of life."[49] French, English, music, drawing, and dancing were the subjects he decreed that his daughters should study, and apparently this was the extent of his interest in the subject of education for women.

Jefferson believed that one of his most valuable contributions to his countrymen was his role in the founding of the University of Virginia. In exhorting Cabell to

47. See Conant, pp. 29–40.
48. Schachner, 2:962.
49. Nock, pp. 58–59.

continue his efforts in the promotion of this project, he asked:

> What service can we ever render equal to this? What object of our lives can we propose so important? What interest of our own which ought not to be postponed to this? Health, time, labor, on what in the single life which nature has given us, can these be better bestowed than on this immortal boon to our country?[50]

And as time passed, he became increasingly convinced of the paramount worth of this project, not only to enrich the lives of his fellow Virginians and to offer an example to the nation at large, but even to protect the young men of the South from the "lessons of anti-Missourianism."[51]

The University stood as a monument to Jefferson's genius in more ways than one. Its architecture, which is unique in classical beauty among American educational complexes, is a tribute to one aspect of his genius.[52] But

50. Schachner, 2:979. Jefferson's deep concern for the University is reflected in a letter he wrote Madison less than five months before his death. "If I remove beyond the reach of attentions to the University, or beyond the bourne of life itself, as soon I must, it is a comfort to leave that institution under your care." And to his old friend and loyal co-worker, he added: "To myself you have been a pillar of support through life. Take care of me when dead, and be assured that I shall leave with you my last affections." Adrienne Koch and William Peden, eds., *The Life and Selected Writings of Thomas Jefferson* (New York: Random House, Inc., 1944), p. 728.

51. Lipscomb and Bergh, 15:310-13.

52. Examples of Jefferson's architecture may be found in several sections of the state. In addition to the University buildings, he designed the Capitol in Richmond and numerous homes for friends in the Charlottesville area. He is widely considered one of the finest architects America has produced. See Padover, *Jefferson*, p. 161; Merrill D. Peterson, *The Jefferson Image in the American Mind* (New York: Oxford University Press, 1962), pp. 380-401; Dumas Malone, *Jefferson the Virginian* (Boston: Little, Brown and Company, 1948), pp. 143-50; Karl Lehmann, *Thomas Jefferson: American Humanist* (New York: The Macmillan Company, 1947), pp. 156-88; Claude G. Bowers, *The Young Jefferson, 1743-1789* (Boston: Houghton Mifflin Co., 1945), pp. 218-22, 372-74; and especially Fiske Kimball's privately printed *Thomas Jefferson, Architect* (Boston: n. p., 1916). Jefferson was also vitally interested

it was in other ways that his contribution was to be even more impressive, for it was here that his educational theories were tested. The University represented the most radical experiment in early American education: it called for no standardized entrance requirements and required no fixed period of residence, instead allowing a student to graduate when he had satisfactorily completed his work. The elective system originated at the University and was widely adopted throughout the nation. Although nine public institutions were founded before it was, in the period between 1825 and 1860, it was

> one of the few which endeavored to be a university in the European sense of that word. Furthermore, it set the tone for other universities . . . . Not only was the University of Virginia's influence throughout the South enormous in these years, but the example of what a publicly financed and publicly managed institution could accomplish must have affected policy in many of the newer states . . . . One could almost say that the shape of higher education in the West . . . was largely fashioned in Virginia.[53]

Of it, Jefferson himself wrote: "This institution will be based on the illimitable freedom of the human mind. For here we are not afraid to follow truth wherever it may lead, nor to tolerate any error so long as reason is free to combat it."[54] This eloquent statement might well be considered a declaration of independence for higher education. It reflects one of Jefferson's most famous statements: "I have sworn upon the altar of God, eternal hostility against every form of tyranny over the mind of man."[55]

---

in the fine arts, and his revision of the Virginia code included provisions for establishing a state art gallery as well as a state library. Thomas Jefferson, *Notes on the State of Virginia,* ed. Thomas Perkins Abernethy (New York: Harper and Row, Publishers, 1964), p. 143.

53. Conant, p. 29.
54. Honeywell, p. 99.
55. Lipscomb and Bergh, 10:175.

The impact of Jefferson's ideas on American education has been far-reaching. It is clear that Jefferson, in spite of his revolutionary principles, was thinking largely in terms of the agrarian society in which he lived, with its essentially hierarchical structure. What he wished to introduce by his scholarship system was a higher degree of social mobility. He obviously assumed that men in positions of public leadership must be well educated; he could not have foreseen that commerce and industry instead of education would provide the avenues of upward mobility in the nineteenth and early twentieth centuries, that even the spoils system of Jacksonian democracy would decrease the need for education as a vehicle to carry the talented upward.[56]

But significant changes had occurred by the middle of the twentieth century. The relation of the new technology to modern society and modern industry demands men and women highly educated in the social sciences and the humanities, and education has indeed become a prerequisite for leadership and public service—just as scholarships based on a selective system have become a part of the educational approach. Jefferson's assumption that only university graduates would fill positions of public leadership proved false for a century and a half. The wheel has now come almost full circle. Today, in somewhat different form and for entirely different reasons, Jefferson's view has proven valid—along with the sociological and political considerations which motivated him to formulate his educational proposals. The United States has already accepted his first two proposals, those for the establishment of state universities and of universal free subcollegiate education. Through a growing scholarship system and free public colleges, we have also begun to offer American youth of all socioeconomic levels

---

56. Conant, pp. 58–60.

the opportunities to prepare for the professions and those positions demanding high levels of education. As we continue to expand this approach our educational practices will become completely Jeffersonian.[57]

Such are the results of Jefferson's plans to enlighten the minds of his countrymen and to provide opportunities for all, a labor to which he gave some of the best efforts of his life and which entitle him to be called one of the most innovative educational statesmen in the history of the world.[58]

---

57. *Ibid.,* pp. 61–63.
58. *Ibid.,* p. 29.

8

On Religious Institutions

Of the various bills Jefferson presented as a revisor of the Virginia code, he considered the bill for establishing religious freedom his greatest contribution; and of all the contests in which he engaged during his long life, he considered his championship of religious freedom the one from which he suffered most.[1] Nevertheless, he probably gained more friends than he lost in his struggle to overthrow religious authoritarianism, for the dissenting sects were grateful for his efforts. Most of the attacks from which he suffered in later life he regarded as coming from the clergy, especially from those whose churches were closely associated with state governments or who were otherwise moved by political considerations. The intensity and duration of the religious controversy gave him reason to consider it severe, for this controversy persisted throughout his life, and indeed pursued him beyond the grave.

His Act for Establishing Religious Freedom, offered to the Assembly in 1779 but not passed until 1786, is an eloquent statement of his views of religion and religious institutions. The preamble to the bill declares

---

1. Thomas Jefferson, *The Writings of Thomas Jefferson,* ed. Paul Leicester Ford, 10 vols. (New York: G. P. Putnam's Sons, 1892–1899), 1:53.

"that Almighty God hath created the mind free," then proceeds to state that since God did not coerce His creatures to follow Him, no "legislators or rulers, civil as well as ecclesiastical . . . setting up their own opinions and modes of thinking as the only true and infallible," had a right to force performance of religious observances, including the support of clergy, by means of "temporal punishments or burdens, or by civil incapacitations." To do so was to deny man his "natural rights"; and "to allow the civil magistrate to intrude his power into the field of opinion" was "a dangerous fallacy, which . . . destroys all religious liberty . . . and finally, that truth is great and will prevail if left to herself . . . unless disarmed of her natural weapons, free argument and debate . . . ."

Therefore, "no man shall be compelled to frequent or support any religious worship, place or ministry whatsoever," nor shall any be "enforced, restrained, or burthened . . . on account of his religious opinions . . . the rights hereby asserted are the natural rights of mankind," and any law holding otherwise is "an infringement of natural right."[2]

Jefferson became the symbol of complete religious liberty as a result of this legislative endeavor. To some he was a prophet; to others he was a dangerous freethinker; and to still others he was a despicable infidel. He himself regarded religion as a strictly private affair, and although he retained throughout life a profound belief in the moral foundations of the universe, he had no patience with man-made ecclesiasticism and dogmas. He felt that every man had a right to his own judgment in matters of religion, and that this was no concern of others, as most assuredly it was no concern of the state.

---

2. Thomas Jefferson, *The Writings of Thomas Jefferson,* ed. Andrew A. Lipscomb and Albert E. Bergh, 20 vols. (Washington: Thomas Jefferson Memorial Association, 1903), 2:300–3.

It cannot be doubted that Jefferson's greatest objective was to free men from oppression, whether from kings or tyrants or priests, and in all that he wrote on the subject of religion, this concern for freedom and independence is apparent. "I never will, by my word or act, bow to the shrine of intolerance, or admit a right of inquiry into the religious opinions of others," he wrote. "On the contrary, we are bound, you, I, and everyone, to make common cause, even with error itself, to maintain the common right of freedom of conscience."[3]

Jefferson was extremely reticent about his own beliefs. "I never told my own religion," he wrote, "nor scrutinized that of another. I never attempted to make a convert, nor wished to change another's creed."[4] He seemed determined not to influence others by his thinking on this subject, including members of his own household. His grandson reported that if a member of the family asked his opinion on any religious subject, Jefferson always replied that "it was a subject which each was bound to study assiduously for himself . . . that it was a matter solely of conscience . . . that the expression of his opinion might influence theirs, and he would not give it!"[5] As time went on and as he was drawn more and more into controversy, he began to express his ideas on matters of religion from time to time, particularly in his private letters; and these expressions, taken as a whole, provide insight into his concepts of religion and religious institutions. That he was a free-thinker is obvious; however, he was also a devout follower of those precepts which he believed to be of the essence of Christianity.

Jefferson's position—that religion was a private matter and that the state should neither support nor oppose

---

3. *Ibid.*, 10:378.
4. *Ibid.*, 15:60.
5. Henry S. Randall, *The Life of Thomas Jefferson*, 3 vols. (New York: Derby and Jackson, 1858), 3:672.

any particular church or doctrine—in the course of time became the official American position. But in his own day, the battle had not been completely won, in Virginia or elsewhere. Without the rise of the dissenting sects— Presbyterians, Baptists, and Methodists—Jefferson's bill for establishing religious freedom could not have passed the legislature. These sects complained that the Established Church restricted their activities, and that the Anglican clergy were cold, formal, and often unfaithful. This latter charge did not impress Jefferson, a man whose high moral code was recognized by all who knew him; the alleged infidelity of the Anglican clergy did not alarm a disciple of the Enlightenment who refused even to admit the validity of the term.

It was other matters that bothered Jefferson about the Established Church, and these were matters of freedom of conscience and belief. The history of religious persecution in Virginia went back to the earliest days of the colony. Under the brutal and bloody Dale Code of early colonial times, a blasphemer was thrust through the tongue with a bodkin; a person who failed to observe the Sabbath was whipped; those who expressed doubts about the Trinity were put to death. When the dissenting sects first appeared, they were prohibited from following their faith and forms of worship. Those who failed to attend the Established Church on Sunday could be fined 50 pounds; and in every parish the people, regardless of their faith, were required to furnish a house and 200 acres of glebe land to the Anglican clergyman in charge of the parish. The self-perpetuating parish vestries held autocratic powers, the vestrymen being members of the same oligarchy who controlled the state.

Although the state was often lax in enforcing the rules requiring attendance at the services of the Established Church and there was a somewhat cavalier attitude toward the various laws regarding religion in general, they were still laws. And persecution of the Presbyterians and Baptists was a reality. The gentry did not take lightly the challenge to their power by the dissenters, and the arrest and imprisonment of Baptists, in particular, were far from infrequent. James Madison, as a student at home on vacation from Princeton, wrote a friend there:

> I want again to breathe your free air. I have, indeed, as good an atmosphere at home as the climate will allow, but have nothing to brag of as to the state of liberty in my country . . . . That diabolical, hell-conceived principle of persecution rages among some; and, to their eternal infamy, the clergy can furnish their quota of imps for such purposes.[6]

Jefferson himself no doubt witnessed some of these persecutions and was undoubtedly aware that his fellow revisor, Edmund Pendleton, as magistrate of Caroline County, had cast six Baptist ministers into jail for preaching without a license and disturbing the peace—a quite common practice during this period.

Jefferson's interests in religion went back to his student days. In his *Commonplace Book* he copied numerous passages on the subject from Locke, Bolingbroke, and Montesquieu. He was particularly impressed by Montesquieu's contention that "no church is bound by the duty of toleration to retain within her bosom obstinate offenders against her laws," yet "we have no right to prejudice another in his civil enjoyment because he is of another church."[7] Jefferson's chief objection to Montesquieu was based on the latter's advocacy of the Established Church in England as "government by a presbytery which resembles republican government."[8] He saw this as leading to religious persecution and tyranny, and

6. Claude G. Bowers, *The Young Jefferson, 1743–1789* (Boston: Houghton Mifflin Company, 1945), p. 198.

7. *Ibid.,* p. 200.

8. *Ibid.,* p. 199.

noted that religion is a matter of faith and that each man must be free to choose his own.

After Jefferson took his seat in the House of Burgesses and emerged as a leader in the movement for independence from England, his interests in religious freedom became a compelling concern, and he began to work for the disestablishment of the Anglican Church. In this he was supported by the dissenters, who forwarded numerous petitions to the legislature, demanding that independence be extended to religious matters. Those on the frontier, in particular, were vocal and insistent in their demands, especially the Presbyterians and Baptists. But in the legislature these petitions ran up against the stone wall of opposition by the gentry. Slowly, however, Jefferson drew supporters to his side—notably James Madison and George Mason, whose Virginia Declaration of Rights calling in general terms for religious toleration and freedom had won passage in the legislature. When at last, however, Jefferson presented his Act for Establishing Religious Freedom, he found that the legislators still resisted, and it was seven years before the battle was won—a battle that Jefferson called the most bitter of his life.

In the *Notes on Virginia,* he clearly indicated the importance he placed on complete religious freedom. Surveying the historical background, he pointed out that Quakers coming to Virginia in search of civil and religious freedom found that it existed only for members of "the reigning sect," which had made it a penal offense for parents to refuse to have their children baptized; had prohibited Quakers from assembling; and had made it a crime for shipmasters to bring Quakers into the state. The law also provided that Quakers already in Virginia might be imprisoned until they agreed to leave, and that if they returned, they should be punished—by death for the third such offense.

Yet the numbers of dissenters continued to grow, and by the outbreak of the Revolution they constituted two-thirds of the population of the state. Finally, in 1776 the legislature repealed all acts of Parliament which made independent opinion in matters of religion a criminal offense, including the common law provision that heresy was a capital crime punishable by burning at the stake. Yet those laws which had been passed by the legislature remained unchanged. They provided that denial of the Trinity was a crime punishable on the first offense by incapacity to hold any office or employment, civil, ecclesiastical, or military; on the second offense, by disability to sue, receive a gift or legacy, be a guardian, executor, or administrator, and by three years' imprisonment without bail.

These, Jefferson declared, were unjust extensions of the rights of government, whose legitimate powers extended only "to such acts as are injurious to others. But it does me no injury for my neighbor to say there are twenty gods, or no god. It neither picks my pocket nor breaks my leg."[9] Therefore, private religious beliefs should be of no concern to the law or the state, and even the requirement of a profession of religion from witnesses in legal cases should be abolished; for "if it be said" their testimony "cannot be relied on, reject it then . . . . Constraint may make" a man "worse by making him a hypocrite, but it will never make him a truer man."[10] Reason and free inquiry alone are the effective agents against error, not government. Was it not the government which forced Galileo to recant? Reason had established "the Newtonian principles of gravitation" far more effectively than government fiat could have, declared Jefferson, the Enlightenment spokesman of deistic convictions. "It is error alone which needs

9. Lipscomb and Bergh, 2:221.
10. *Ibid.*

the support of government. Truth can stand by itself."[11]
If opinion is to be subjected to coercion, who will
be the inquisitors? All men are fallible. "And why subject it to coercion? To produce uniformity. But is uniformity of opinion desirable?"[12] Perfect consensus Jefferson believed to be neither desirable nor possible.

> Millions of innocent men, women, and children, since the
> introduction of Christianity, have been burnt, tortured, fined,
> imprisoned; yet we have not advanced one inch toward uniformity . . . . Let us reflect that the earth is inhabited by a
> thousand millions of people. That these profess probably a
> thousand different systems of religion. That ours is but one
> of that thousand.[13]

And if our religion is the true one, free inquiry will
confirm it. Religious disputes lead to dissensus and
weaken a society; the way to silence such disputes "is to
take no notice of them" by eliminating religious matters
completely from the concerns of the law.

While it was true, Jefferson said, that in his day the
people of Virginia would not "suffer an execution for
heresy, or three years' imprisonment for not comprehending the Trinity," the people might not always so
restrain the government. The spirit of the times might
alter, indeed it would alter. "Our rulers will become
corrupt, our people careless . . . . From the conclusion
of this war we shall be going down hill." When the
threat of war has been removed, the unity and integration of society will weaken. People "will forget themselves, but in the sole faculty of making money." Therefore, "the time for fixing every essential right on a
legal basis is while our rulers are honest, and ourselves
united . . . . The shackles . . . which shall not be knocked

11. *Ibid.*, 2:222.
12. *Ibid.*, 2:223.
13. *Ibid.*

off at the conclusion of this war, will remain with us long."[14]

It is clear from these comments in the *Notes on Virginia* that Jefferson's greatest concern was for liberty and freedom, in religion as in all other forms of institutional behavior. And, finally, when his bill for religious freedom was passed, he felt great pride in the results of his long and arduous efforts. To Madison he wrote from Paris in 1786 after the bill had become law:

> The Virginia act for religious freedom has been received with infinite approbation in Europe and propagated with enthusiasm. I do not mean by the governments, but by the individuals which compose them. It has been translated into French and Italian, has been sent to most of the courts of Europe, and has been the best evidence of the falsehood of those reports which stated us to be in anarchy. It is inserted in the new Encyclopedia, and is appearing in most of the publications respecting America. In fact it is comfortable to see the standard of reason at length erected, after so many ages during which the human mind has been held in vassalage by kings, priests and nobles: and it is honorable for us to have produced the first legislature who had the courage to declare that the reason of man may be trusted with the formation of his own opinions.[15]

The attention which this statute received abroad was in part the result of Jefferson's own efforts; he had it printed and circulated as widely as possible. It must not be forgotten that he ranked this achievement next in importance to the Declaration of Independence, for he believed that in both he had spoken for all humanity. The Virginia bill was a proclamation of both intellectual and religious independence for the individual, and as such perhaps deserves the importance Jefferson attributed

14. *Ibid.*, 2:224–25.
15. Thomas Jefferson, *The Papers of Thomas Jefferson*, ed. Julian P. Boyd (Princeton: Princeton University Press, 1950–   ), 10:603–4.

to it. It was, furthermore, an expression of the values most dear to him, for, as Charles Beard says, "over and above, through, in, and under all of Mr. Jefferson's thought . . . was his faith in liberty of inquiry, thought and expression."[16] And the impact of this bill was felt not only in America, but its influence was of monumental proportions in the prerevolutionary movement in France, as well as in Europe generally.[17] It is perhaps not surprising that Jefferson considered his efforts to achieve religious freedom for mankind of like importance to his efforts in securing political liberty, for the first was a corollary of the second. In his view political freedom without liberty of thought and conscience was impossible. Thus, he chose to rest his reputation upon his endeavors to free man from the tyranny of governments, of churches, and of ignorance.

His own personal religious beliefs were largely consistent with the deistic tenets of the Enlightenment. He attempted to reconcile what he believed to be the Christianity of Jesus with his own scientific outlook and social philosophy. Thus, he rejected revelation as a source of religious knowledge, for he considered "reason and free inquiry the only effectual agents" for discovering truth; they would "support the true religion by bringing every false one to their tribunal, to the test of their investigation."[18] His epistemology was positivistic and empirical; he therefore rejected all "organs of information" except his senses, ridding himself of "the pyrrhonisms with which an indulgence in speculations hyperphysical and antiphysical, so uselessly occupy the mind." The senses reveal enough realities

---

16. "Thomas Jefferson: A Civilized Man," *The Mississippi Valley Historical Review* 30 (September, 1943): 168.
17. Gilbert Chinard, "Jefferson's Influence Abroad," *The Mississippi Valley Historical Review* 30 (September, 1943): 175.
18. Lipscomb and Bergh, 2:221.

for all the purposes of life, without plunging into the fathomless abyss of dreams and phantasms. I am satisfied, and sufficiently occupied with the things which are, without tormenting or troubling myself about those which indeed may be but of which I have no evidence.[19]

What Jefferson called his "materialistic philosophy" demanded valid scientific evidence via the senses as a basis of knowledge and belief, and if "a single sense may sometimes be deceived . . . all our senses together, with their faculty of reasoning"[20] may never be, unless we close our eyes to the evidence available to us. And among those things for which adequate evidence did not exist and which the senses could not perceive nor the reason comprehend was the specific attributes of God. Even Jesus himself "has told us only that God is good and perfect, but has not defined him. I am, therefore of his theology, believing that we have neither words nor ideas adequate to that definition."[21] Since Jefferson suffered his faith to go no farther than his facts, he said that he never permitted himself to "meditate a specified creed."[22]

This is not to say, of course, that he considered religion unimportant, for indeed he did not. "The relations which exist between man and his Maker, and the duties resulting from those relations," he said, "are the most interesting and important to every human being and the most incumbent on his study and investigation."[23] He was indeed unorthodox, but it is clear that he arrived at his own religious beliefs only after rigorous investigation and examination. No doubt an insight into his search for religious truth may be gleaned from the letter he

19. *Ibid.,* 15:275–76.
20. *Ibid.,* 15:276.
21. *Ibid.,* 15:203.
22. *Ibid.,* 15:373.
23. *Ibid.,* 19:414.

wrote his nephew, Peter Carr, in 1787 from Paris regarding religion.

Your reason is now mature enough to examine this object. In the first place, divest yourself of all bias in favor of novelty or singularity of opinion . . . . On the other hand, shake off all the fears and servile prejudices, under which weak minds are servilely crouched. Fix reason firmly in her seat, and call to her tribunal every fact, every opinion. Question even the existence of a God; because, if there be one, he must more approve of the homage of reason, than that of blindfolded fear . . . . Read the Bible . . . as you would Livy or Tacitus. The facts which are within the ordinary course of nature, you will believe on the authority of the writer, as you do those of the same kind in Livy and Tacitus . . . . But those facts in the Bible which contradict the laws of nature must be examined with more care . . . . Here you must recur to the pretensions of the writer to inspiration from God. Examine upon what evidence his pretensions are founded, and whether that evidence is so strong, as that its falsehood would be more improbable than a change in the laws of nature, in the case he relates. For example, in the book of Joshua, we are told, the sun stood still for several hours. Were we to read that fact in Livy or Tacitus, we should class it with their showers of blood, speaking of statues, beasts, etc. . . . You will next read the New Testament. It is the history of a personage called Jesus. Keep in your eye the opposite pretensions: 1, of those who say he was begotten by God, born of a virgin, suspended and reversed the laws of nature at will, and ascended bodily into heaven; and 2, of those who say he was a man of illegitimate birth, of a benevolent heart, enthusiastic mind, who set out without pretensions to divinity, ended in believing them, and was punished capitally for sedition . . . .
Do not be frightened from this inquiry by any fears of its consequences. If it ends in a belief that there is no God, you will find incitements to virtue in the comfort and pleasantness you will feel in its exercise, and the love of others which it will procure you. If you find reason to believe there is a God, a consciousness that you are acting under his eye, and that he approved you, will be a vast additional incitement; if that there be a future state, the hope of a happy existence in that increases the appetite to deserve it; if that Jesus was

also a God, you will be comforted by a belief of his aid and love. In fine, I repeat, you must lay aside all prejudices on both sides, and neither believe nor reject anything, because any other persons, or description of persons, have rejected or believed it. Your own reason is the only oracle given you by heaven, and you are answerable, not for the rightness, but unrightness of the decision.[24]

It is clear that Jefferson was a free-thinker and that he must have applied to his own investigations those tests he suggested to his nephew. His own reason led him to a view of Christianity which he felt "ought to displease neither the rational Christian nor the Deists, and would reconcile many to a character they had too hastily rejected."[25] It was his conclusion that Christianity, "when divested of the rags" or obscurantist accretions in which priests and ministers "have enveloped it, and brought to the original purity and simplicity of its benevolent institutor, is a religion of all others most friendly to liberty, science, and the freest expansion of the human mind."[26] Indeed, he believed it to be "the most sublime and benevolent, but most perverted system that ever shone on man."[27]

So believing, Jefferson made a careful investigation of the New Testament, of the life and teachings of Jesus, and of the early Church. From this he prepared what came to be known as the Jefferson Bible—a collection of passages from the gospel writers which met his test of reason. Of this project he wrote John Adams that in order to reveal the "pure principles" of Christianity "we would have to strip off the artificial vestments in which they have been muffled by priests who have travestied them into various forms, as instruments of riches and power to themselves," and retain "the very words

24. Boyd, 12:15–17.
25. Lipscomb and Bergh, 10:174.
26. *Ibid.,* 10:237.
27. *Ibid.,* 10:228.

only of Jesus," which he himself had done, with the same verses cut from Greek, Latin, French, and English texts, pasted neatly in parallel columns in an octavo volume bound in red morocco, which he entitled "The Life and Morals of Jesus of Nazareth." This, he said, "is a document in proof that I am a *real Christian,* that is to say, a disciple of the doctrines of Jesus."[28]

In his effort to humanize Jesus—for he was convinced that Jesus was a man and not "the son of God, physically speaking"—Jefferson attempted to explain the cultural and social bases of "the great reformer of the Jewish religion." He found that at the time of Jesus the Jews followed an ethical code "often irreconcilable with the sound dictates of reason and morality," and one which was "repulsive and anti-social, as respecting other nations." Of Jesus himself, he pointed out that his parentage "was obscure; his condition poor; his education null; his natural endowments great; his life correct and innocent: he was meek, benevolent, patient, firm, disinterested, and of the sublimest eloquence." His message was offered under numerous disadvantages: he wrote nothing of himself; the elite of his country, "entrenched in power and riches," strongly opposed him; and "unlettered and ignorant men," writing long after the events had taken place, provide our only sources of information about him. His death at 33, before he had attained the height of his reasoning power, was a result of the conspiracy between "the altar and the throne." Only fragments of his teachings survived, "mutilated, misstated, and often unintelligible," and even these were handed down in a form showing the results of priestly

---

28. Merrill D. Peterson, *The Jefferson Image in the American Mind* (New York: Oxford University Press, 1962), pp. 301-2. As was his custom in religious matters, he kept this syllabus to himself. Even his grandchildren did not know of its existence until after his death. However, there is evidence that he read from this volume nightly before going to sleep. *Ibid.*

. . . engrafting on them the mysticisms of a Grecian sophist,[29] frittering them into subtleties, and obscuring them with jargon until they have caused good men to reject the whole in disgust . . . . He corrected the Deism of the Jews, confirming them in their belief of the one only God, and giving them juster notions of his attributes and government. His moral doctrines . . . were more pure and perfect than those of the most correct of the philosophers . . . inculcating universal philanthropy . . . . He pushed his scrutinies into the heart of man; erected his tribunal in the region of his thoughts, and purified the waters at the fountainhead. He taught, emphatically, the doctrine of a future state . . . and wielded it with efficacy, as an important incentive, supplementary to the other motives to moral conduct.[30]

Jefferson felt that the test of reason would distinguish the "spurious" from the "genuine" doctrines of Jesus, which in their pure form he believed to constitute "the most sublime and benevolent code of morals" ever offered to man. Jefferson's humanitarian spirit and advocacy of social reforms found a strong counterpart in the teachings of Jesus, for he understood them to emphasize both inward motive and intention as well as overt behavior. To Jefferson man was a social creature, and he saw it as the genius of Jesus that the latter's doctrines inspired sympathetic impulses toward others plus a code of behavior that epitomized social morality. This even the great Epicurean and Stoic philosophers he had so long admired failed to do, for they emphasized a morality based upon individual self-interest which Jefferson came to consider inadequate for man as a social creature.[31] Although he called himself an Epicurean, he clearly recognized himself as ultimately and irrevocably committed to the consummate social idealism of Jesus—for Jefferson the scientist, statesman and philosopher was also, in

---

29. Jefferson had reference here to Plato.
30. Lipscomb and Bergh, 10:379–85.
31. *Ibid.,* 10:381–82, and 15:220. See also Adrienne Koch, *The Philosophy of Thomas Jefferson* (Chicago: Quadrangle Books, 1964), p. 31.

the profoundest depths of his being, Jefferson the social reformer.

Jefferson pointed out that he read the doctrines of Jesus "as I do those of other ancient and modern moralists, with a mixture of approbation and dissent. . . . I am a Materialist; he takes the side of Spiritualism;[32] he preaches the efficacy of repentence toward the forgiveness of sin; I require a counterpoise of good works to redeem it, etc."[33] Yet Jefferson called himself a Christian "in the only sense in which he wished any one to be; sincerely attached to his doctrines, in preference to all others; ascribing to himself every *human* excellence; and believing he never claimed any other."[34] Jefferson found the essential doctrines of Jesus to be

> simple, and tend all to the happiness of man. 1. That there is one only God, and He all perfect. 2. That there is a future state of rewards and punishments. 3. That to love God with all thy heart and thy neighbor as thyself, is the sum of religion.[35]

The Christianity of which Jefferson considered himself a follower was obviously something quite different from orthodox Catholicism or Protestantism. It was a primitive Christianity devoid of the scheming perversions of a priesthood which had "compounded from the heathen

32. Jefferson's materialism was really empiricism or sensationalist positivism, which demanded evidence as the basis of knowledge and belief. He seemed to reserve the term spiritualist for those who followed anti-scientific transcendental metaphysics. Koch, p. 100.

33. Lipscomb and Bergh, 15:244–45.

34. *Ibid.,* 14:385.

35. *Ibid.,* 15:383–84. These phrases may be compared with those used by Jefferson in his First Inaugural Address, in which he spoke of America as "enlightened by a benign religion, professed, indeed, and practiced in various forms, yet all of them including honesty, truth, temperance, gratitude, and the love of man: acknowledging and adoring an overruling Providence, which by all its dispensations proves that it delights in the happiness of man here and his greater happiness hereafter." *Ibid.,* 3:320.

mysteries a system beyond the comprehension of man, of which the great Reformer . . . were He to return on earth, would not recognize one feature."[36] The "mild and simple principles of the Christian philosophy would produce too much calm, too much regularity of good, to extract from its disciples a support for a numerous priesthood, were they not to sophisticate it, ramify it, split it into hairs, and twist its texts till they cover the divine morality of its author with mysteries, and require a priesthood to explain them."[37] Jefferson's harsh criticisms of the priesthood were largely those of the *Philosophes*: that the clergy had perverted the teachings of Jesus into "an engine for enslaving mankind, and aggrandizing their oppressors in Church and State: that the purest system of morals ever before preached to man has been adulterated and sophisticated by artificial constructions, into a mere contrivance to filch wealth and power to themselves."[38]

Among the doctrines so used by the clergy was the dogma of the Trinity—"these metaphysical heads" which usurp "the judgment seat of God" and condemn as His enemies "all who cannot perceive the Geometrical logic of Euclid in the demonstrations of St. Athanasius, that three are one, and one is three; and yet that the one is not three nor the three one."[39] St. Paul was "the first corruptor of the doctrines of Jesus,"[40] followed by Platonists, Plotinists, Stagyrites, Gamalielites, Eclectics, Gnostics, and Scholastics with "their essences and emanations, their Logos and Demiurgos, Aeons and Daemons, male and female, with a long train of etc., etc., etc., or shall I say at once, of nonsense."[41] He declared that the

36. *Ibid.*, 14:386.
37. *Ibid.*, 10:254.
38. *Ibid.*, 15:60.
39. *Ibid.*, 13:378.
40. *Ibid.*, 15:245.
41. *Ibid.*, 13:389.

Christian priesthood had found "in the mysticism of Plato materials with which" to "build up an artificial system, which might from its indistinctness, admit everlasting controversy, give employment for their order, and introduce it to profit, power and preeminence."[42]

To Jefferson the crowning achievement of the clergy in its quest for power was the union of church and state. He traced the incorporation of Christianity into common law, naming opinions dating from 1458 to 1767. Of this usurpation by priests, he commented: "What a conspiracy this, between Church and State! Sing Tantarara, rogues all, rogues all, Sing Tantarara, rogues all!"[43]

Jefferson's faith in progress led him later in life to believe that Christianity in the United States, where freedom of religious opinion and separation of church and state prevailed, would undergo a reformation, keeping pace with "the other improvements of the human mind," although he felt that it would come "too late for me to witness it."[44] He looked for the triumph of rational Christianity, and the Unitarian movement seemed to him to offer the greatest promise. In his old age he expressed his hope that there was "not a *young man* now living in the United States who will not die a Unitarian."[45] The greatest obstacle in the way of such a development was opposition from the Presbyterians, for "the blasphemy and absurdity of the five points of Calvin, and the impossibility of defending them, render their advocates impatient of reasoning, irritable, and prone to denunciation." Their "ambition and tyranny would tol-

---

42. *Ibid.,* 14:149-50. "It is fortunate for us," Jefferson added, "that Platonic republicanism has not obtained the same favor as Platonic Christianity; or we should now have been all living, men, women and children, pell mell together, like beasts of the field or forest."
43. *Ibid.,* 16:48-51.
44. *Ibid.,* 15:288.
45. *Ibid.,* 15:405.

erate no rival if they had the power."[46] He hoped that the Unitarians would follow the example of the Quakers and remain creedless. "Be this the wisdom of the Unitarians, this the holy mantle which shall cover with its charitable circumference all who believe in one God, and who love their neighbor!"[47]

Jefferson continuously declared his belief in God. However, as a rationalist and empiricist, he did not believe in mysteries, miracles, incomprehensible "logomachies," the divinity of Jesus, nor the doctrine of the atonement. "Jesus did not mean to impose Himself on mankind as the Son of God," he said, although "He might conscientiously believe Himself inspired from above. . . . Elevated by the enthusiasm of a warm and pure heart, conscious of the high strains of an eloquence which had not been taught Him, He might readily mistake the coruscations of His own fine genius for inspirations of a higher order."[48] However, he admitted that Jesus sometimes spoke in "eastern hyperbolisms."[49]

Jefferson rejected Judaism, which "supposes the God of infinite justice to punish the sins of the fathers upon their children, unto the third and fourth generation."[50]

---

46. *Ibid.*, 15:403–4. Jefferson summarized the five points of Calvinism as follows: "1. That there are three Gods. 2. That good works, or love of our neighbor, are nothing. 3. That faith is everything, and the more incomprehensible the proposition, the more merit in its faith. 4. That reason in religion is of unlawful use. 5. That God, from the beginning elected certain individuals to be saved, and certain others to be damned; and that no crimes of the former can damn them; no virtues of the latter save." Jefferson described Calvin as "indeed an atheist, which I could never be . . . . If ever a man worshipped a false God, he did . . . not the God whom you and I acknowledge and adore, the Creator and benevolent Governor of the world; but a daemon of malignant spirit." *Ibid.*, 15:425.
47. *Ibid.*, 15:385.
48. *Ibid.*, 15:261. To John Adams he wrote, "And the day will come, when the mystical generation of Jesus, by the Supreme Being as His Father, in the womb of a virgin, will be classed with the fable of the generation of Minerva in the brain of Jupiter." *Ibid.*, 15:430.
49. *Ibid.*, 15:245.
50. *Ibid.*, 15:203.

He also rejected atheism, for he held the rational and deistic belief

> that when we take a view of the universe in its parts, general or particular, it is impossible for the human mind not to perceive and feel a conviction of design, consummate skill, and indefinite power in every atom of its composition. The movements of the heavenly bodies, so exactly held in their course by the balance of centrifugal and centripetal forces; the structure of our earth itself, with its distribution of lands, waters and atmosphere; animal and vegetable bodies, examined in all their minutest particles; insects, mere atoms of life, yet as perfectly organized as man or mammoth; the mineral substances, their generation and uses; it is impossible, I say, for the human mind not to believe, that there is in all this, design cause and effect, up to an ultimate cause, a Fabricator of all things from matter and motion, their Preserver and Regulator while permitted to exist in their present forms, and their regeneration into new and other forms. We see, too, evident proofs of the necessity of a superintending power, to maintain the universe in its course and order. . . . So irresistible are these evidences of an intelligent and powerful Agent, that, of the infinite number of men who have existed through all time, they have believed, in the proportion of a million at least to a unit, in the hypothesis of an eternal pre-existence of a Creator, rather than in that of a self-existent universe. Surely this unanimous sentiment renders this more probable, than that of the few of the other hypothesis.[51]

Jefferson recognized the universality of religious beliefs and institutions. Even so, he was unable to give a definitive answer to the problem of the specific nature of the Divinity. He could only conclude that

> on the basis of sensation, of matter and motion, we may erect the fabric of all the certainties we can have or need. . . . To talk of *immaterial* existences is to talk of *nothings*. To say that human souls, angels, God, are immaterial, is to say, they are *nothings,* or that there is no God, no angels, no soul. . . . "In

---

51. *Ibid.,* 15:426–28.

the beginning God existed, and reason (or mind) was with God, and that mind was God. This was in the beginning with God. All things were created by it. . . ." The world was created by the Supreme, Intelligent Being.[52]

"I cannot reason otherwise," he said, "but I believe that I am supported in my creed of materialism by the Lockes, the Tracys, and the Stewarts."[53] Jefferson's positivistic epistemology found support in his conviction that Locke, in particular, as well as the church fathers of the first three centuries, maintained the materiality of the soul;[54] he especially found the works of Dugald Stewart on the uniform operation of human mental faculties a strong support for his views. It will be recalled that Jefferson saw thinking itself as "a form of action," and he supported his view by reference to the works of such men as Cabanis and Flourens, who demonstrated that thought has a physiological basis in that it occurs "in the cerebrum and cerebellum" and that damage to the cerebrum destroys the senses and the ability to think.[55]

If mind or thought was therefore material and God was reason or mind, as Jefferson believed, then God was material, and so were souls, the essence of which he believed to be thought. Jefferson felt that his social science required the "materialist" point of view.

To his nephew Peter Carr he wrote: "Give up money, give up fame, give up science, give up the earth itself and all it contains, rather than do an immoral act."[56] In all his thinking about religion he placed chief emphasis upon morality, and in his old age concluded that the "interests of society require the observation of those moral precepts only in which all religions agree, (for all

---

52. *Ibid.*, 15:273–75.
53. *Ibid.*, 15:274.
54. *Ibid.*, 15:266.
55. *Ibid.*, 16:90–92. See also Koch, pp. 97–102.
56. Boyd, 8:406.

forbid us to murder, steal, plunder, or bear false witness,)."[57] Jefferson understood the necessity of moral norms as the basis of social life, and he was firmly committed to the view that the universe itself was a moral one. He concluded that the love of God and of one's fellowman were the foundations of morality and that "nature hath implanted in our breasts a love of others, a sense of duty to them, a moral instinct . . . nature has constituted *utility* to man" as the standard of virtue.[58] Social life was possible for men because of the moral norms and of men's predispositions to abide by them. Those who follow the universal moral standard "will never be questioned, at the gates of heaven," he said, "as to the dogmas in which they all differ."[59]

Jefferson believed the test of religion to be faith in God plus a rigorous personal and social morality, and he sought to fulfill what he thought to be his religious and moral duties. He was consistently vocal and eloquent in his testimony of belief in a Divine Creator, Preserver, and Protector. His personal moral code was of the highest order and his humane social morality inspired him to spend the greater part of his life in efforts to improve the welfare of his countrymen—indeed, to help bring the blessings of liberty and happiness to mankind. Religion and the moral behavior it inspired he considered essential to man and society. But he never changed his view that religion must remain a personal matter between the individual and his God.

His crusade against religious tyranny and intolerance elicited some of the best efforts of his life; and the separation of church and state, which came to be the official doctrine of the nation, owes much to Jefferson. Religious pluralism demanded that the course he suggested be im-

57. Lipscomb and Bergh, 12:315.
58. *Ibid.,* 14:138–44.
59. *Ibid.,* 13:377.

plemented, if unity and integration were to be realized in the nation. It therefore can be said that his contribution to the welfare of his countrymen was in this area commensurate with the results of his endeavors in politics, law, and education.

His dream of a rational Christianity was, however, another matter, and his influence upon the internal structure of the various religious bodies may be said to have been minimal. Believing that no true religion was possible without absolute freedom of mind and conscience, he could hardly have been expected to exert a revolutionary influence on religious bodies whose very existence was justified by their dogmas. Leaders of orthodox bodies continued long after his death to excoriate him as a "howling infidel." The Unitarians, however, acclaimed him as a saint; and as the years have passed and Jefferson has become more and more the symbol of America's search for the image of itself, he has also become a hero to more and more religious bodies and their leadership. By the middle of the twentieth century, clergymen of various denominations were praising him as a man of faith and drawing lessons from his life and thought. Indeed, in recent years his religion has been second only to his political ideas as the subject of articles published about him, the great majority of which have depicted him as a Christian of some type.[60] It would appear that no area of American life has been unaffected by Jefferson, the hero of democracy.

Jefferson's religious views were, of course, in part the product of his own day, of the Enlightenment with its emphasis upon reason and science, in which nature was seen as a work of art from the Creator's hand. The "variety of minds" was a divinely designed division of labor to make possible the fulfilling of human needs in

---

60. Peterson, p. 303.

society, and utility was thus the test of morality. In the kind of primitive communities whose cohesion was based upon what Durkheim called mechanical solidarity, difference of opinion was lacking—but to Jefferson "difference of opinion leads to inquiry, and inquiry to truth" in religion and science.[61] Freedom of thought, inquiry, and conscience were therefore essential elements in the Divine plan, and Jefferson's thoughts about religion were grounded in this conviction. The well-being and happiness of mankind could never be realized when such freedom was restricted. Thus, religious institutions—no less than political, educational, and other social institutions—were but instruments to be utilized in securing to man his natural and inalienable rights. Only by abstraction can we analyze the role of separate social institutions in Jefferson's thought. All were integrated in an approach based upon his essential assumption of a moral universe designed by an all-wise and benevolent Creator for the happiness of man as a social creature. Jefferson was anticlerical for the same reason that he was anti-authoritarian in every area of life. And if belief in a divine Creator and concern for one's fellowmen is of the essence of religion, as Jefferson believed them to be, it may be said unequivocally that he was indeed a religious man.

---

61. Lipscomb and Bergh, 14:283.

9

On Differentiation, Social Stratification, and Racial Minorities

Jefferson identified the Virginia class structure of his day in this interesting typology: at the top were the "aristocrats, composed of the great land-holders who had seated themselves below tide water on the main rivers, and lived in a style of luxury and extravagance, insupportable by the other inhabitants, and which, indeed, ended, in several instances, in the ruin of their own fortunes." Next were "the younger sons and daughters of the aristocrats, who inherited the pride of their ancestors, without their wealth." In the next stratum were "the pretenders, men who from vanity, or the impulse of growing wealth, or from that enterprize which is natural to talents, sought to detach themselves from the plebeian ranks, to which they properly belonged, and imitated, at some distance, the manners and habits of the great." And then, "next to these, were a solid and independent yeomanry, looking askance at those above, yet not venturing to jostle them."[1] Jefferson might also have added that next came the poorer, landless whites, and after them Indians and Negro slaves. His charac-

---

1. Thomas Jefferson, *The Writings of Thomas Jefferson,* ed. Paul Leicester Ford, 10 vols. (New York: G. P. Putnam's Sons, 1892–1899), 9:472–74.

terization of social classes includes the variables of both economic standing and prestige rank, as is clearly indicated in his reference to the younger sons and daughters of the gentry and to the "pretenders."

There is no doubt that Jefferson, by virtue of family and wealth, was born to the top rank, though perhaps not to the very top.[2] It is true that he often lashed out at the aristocracy of which he was a member; however, he was no alien to the society in which he was born. His closest friends and associates were of the gentry, and he was obviously most at ease in their company. His dedication to democracy is not to be understood as the result of alienation from his social class, nor as the product of the frontier, as Turner maintained.[3] His belief

---

2. As we have seen, his mother's family were of the aristocracy and his father's of the local county oligarchy. He inherited considerable wealth from his father as well as from his father-in-law. However, his financial position was often precarious after the Revolution, and in his old age his debts far outstripped the value of his possessions. Nevertheless, his fame and distinction by that time placed him at the top in prestige.

3. Turner, postulating that American democracy was a product of the frontier, declared that "Jefferson was the first prophet of American democracy, and when we analyse the essential features of his gospel, it is clear that the Western influence was the dominant element." Frederick Jackson Turner, *The Frontier in American History* (New York: Henry Holt and Company, 1958), p. 250. However, Turner admitted that "Jefferson was the John the Baptist of democracy, not its Moses." *Ibid.,* p. 251. Even Turner saw Jefferson as highly cultivated, refined, and educated—the "civilized man" par excellence so well depicted by Albert Jay Nock. Contemporary historians attribute little validity to the Turner thesis, which Boorstin points out was once accepted as "a dogma to be applied rather than a hypothesis to be tested." Daniel J. Boorstin, *The Americans: The National Experience* (New York: Random House, 1965), p. 435. See also Lee Benson, *Turner and Beard: American Historical Writings Reconsidered* (New York: The Free Press, 1960), pp. 41-91. The frontier no doubt had its influence on Jefferson's thinking; he was, however, in no sense the same sort of frontiersman as was Andrew Jackson, and the Albemarle County of his day had little in common with the backwoods of the Carolina-Tennessee-Kentucky mountains of Jackson's day. In Jefferson's time even those who were building fortunes beyond the Blue Ridge in the Shenandoah Valley of Virginia were often of the same families as the Tidewater gentry; and in the Piedmont—in Albemarle County, in particular —the leading families were descendants of the aristocracy whose social

in democracy instead derived from the fact that he internalized the natural rights and natural law values of the Enlightenment more fully than most of his contemporaries, and that his own original and innovative mind led him to conclusions which were more liberal than even those of the Enlightenment. Furthermore, he was an activist whose beliefs inspired him to efforts at reformation and amelioration.

His objection to the continuation of the powers of an entrenched aristocracy were twofold: first, that they were likely to become tyrannical and lead to monarchy; secondly, that they prevented the discovery of the "natural aristocracy of virtue and talents" to be found in all classes of society. He nevertheless recognized the differences in the social classes of his day and believed that public office and leadership were the responsibility of the educated and dedicated few.[4] His objection was less to aristocracy as such—with its corollary of inferior ranks—than to hereditary aristocracy. Not only was a hereditary aristocracy founded on irrational and unjust principles, but it provided a ready-made avenue to despotic privilege which denied the mass of men their natural rights. What he sought was to broaden the base of leadership and power, and to enable the people to hold a rigorous rein on the ambitions of their leaders.

His early objections to a hereditary aristocracy were reinforced by what he observed in France. To George

and economic position was based upon land ownership, slaves, and the other elements of the Tidewater way of life. Charles S. Sydnor, *American Revolutionaries in the Making* (New York: The Free Press, 1965), p. 95. See also Carl Bridenbaugh, *Myths and Realities: Societies of the Colonial South* (New York: Atheneum, 1965), pp. 1, 39, 120.

4. He was clearly aware of his own superior status and early sought to prove himself worthy of the privileges which were his by virtue of birth and wealth. He sought unsuccessfully to secure a copy of the ancestral Jefferson coat of arms, referring to it half-humorously; nevertheless, he obviously approved some of the symbols of aristocracy. When no such coat of arms could be located, he adopted a seal bearing the motto, "Rebellion to Tyrants is Obedience to God."

Wythe he wrote, "If anybody thinks that kings, nobles, or priests are good conservators of the public happiness, send him here." For in France, the nation "with the finest soil on earth, the finest climate under heaven, and a people of the most benevolent, the most gay and amiable character of which the human form is susceptible," the evidences of an authoritarian and rapacious aristocracy were widespread. And to this letter he added his famous injunction: "Preach, my dear Sir, a crusade against ignorance; establish and improve the law for educating the common people," that they might protect themselves from such tyrants.[5]

Perhaps his fear of the growth of the aristocratic spirit in his own country—a strong element in his ardent objection to the Federalists—can best be illustrated by his comments on the Society of the Cincinnati. Of his fellow Americans, he said, "Of distinction by birth or badge they had no more idea than they had of the mode of existence in the moon or planets." It was in Europe that the miseries attendant upon hereditary social stratification could best be observed, "where the dignity of man is lost in arbitrary distinctions, where the human species is classed into several stages of degradation, where the many are crushed under the weight of the few," a melancholy situation which suggested to Jefferson the image of "God almighty and his angels trampling under foot the hosts of the damned."[6]

To Washington Jefferson wrote that the Society of the Cincinnati was a real threat to American government, for it would eventually produce such a hereditary aristocracy. He approved aristocratic virtues but not aristocratic privileges, as he made clear to Lafayette regarding

5. Thomas Jefferson, *The Writings of Thomas Jefferson,* ed. Andrew A. Lipscomb and Albert E. Bergh, 20 vols. (Washington: Thomas Jefferson Memorial Association, 1903), 5:396–97.
6. Ford, *Writings,* 4:175.

the latter's proposal of a limited monarchy in France. Jefferson's distinctive contribution was in opening the doors of high position to all who belonged there because of their abilities, regardless of their family or origin— the "aristocracy of virtue and talents." Any other basis for membership in the leadership elite was an artificial one—whether of wealth, birth, or other accidental condition.[7] And furthermore, as governments existed only to insure the rights of the people, an educated citizenry was necessary in order to hold the leadership elite in check, since temptation and opportunity for personal aggrandizement were always available to what he called the *aristoi*. The essential rights were not those of the aristocracy, whether of birth or of talent, for they were in a position to protect themselves; it was the rights of the people which must come first; it was the sheep which must be protected from the wolves, as he phrased it. As has been noted, he was opposed to all forms of political, military, intellectual, and religious tyranny, wherever and in whatever form they might be found.

Jefferson showed great concern for the protection of the rights of minorities. The two racial minorities which were a part of the Virginia population, Indians and Negroes, engaged his attention and his interest. He wrote much about them which is of sociological relevance and import.

His fascination with Indians and deep sympathy for them went back to the days of his childhood when many of them, en route to petition the governor or legislature in Williamsburg, stopped overnight at Shadwell. As a

---

7. Many have pointed out his democratic social practices as President, including his replacing the rectangular table in the White House with a round one so that the protocol of seating in order of precedence at official receptions might be avoided—an act reflecting his belief that rank and authority were but the accidental attributes of man. Seymour Martin Lipset and Reinhard Bendix, *Social Mobility in Industrial Society* (Berkeley: University of California Press, 1959), p. 78.

student at William and Mary, he was deeply impressed by the farewell oration of a chief of the Cherokees who was about to sail for England. Ontassete, as Jefferson knew him (others called him Ostenaco, Oconasta or Outacity), had been a guest once at Shadwell, and Jefferson visited his camp at Williamsburg, where he with 165 members of his tribe had journeyed to seek permission to visit the Great King in England. Jefferson was deeply moved by the eloquence of the chief's farewell oration to his people, although the young man understood nothing that was said. It was an experience that Jefferson never forgot. Many years later, as governor and President, he was to receive visits from the Indians and to smoke the peace pipe with them. He had a profound anthropological interest in the Indians and all his life was a student of their languages and customs.

In the *Notes on Virginia* he listed the tribes of Indians with a completeness and precision rare for his time, indicating their territories, chief towns, and the number of their warriors. The three chief tribes in Virginia were the Powhatans, the Mannahoacs, and the Monacans, each with numerous subtribes. Jefferson reported in some detail their customs and means of social control. Since they had never submitted themselves to laws or government, "their only controls," he pointed out, "are their manners, and that moral sense of right and wrong, which, like the sense of tasting and feeling in every man, makes a part of his nature. An offense against these is punished by contempt, by exclusion from society, or, where the case is serious, as that of murder, by the individual whom it concerns." Jefferson herein displayed an exceptional perceptiveness for matters of sociological significance, reporting further that "crimes are very rare among them; insomuch that were it made a question, whether no law, as among the savage Americans, or too much law, as among the civilized Europeans, submits man to the greatest evil, one who has seen both conditions of existence would pronounce it to be the last; and that the sheep are happier of themselves, than under the care of the wolves." However, since large "societies cannot exist without government," the Indians divide themselves into small groups and subtribes.[8]

Captain John Smith in 1607 reported that the Powhatan confederacy consisted of about eight thousand members, "which was one for every square mile," Jefferson adds, and with "the proportion of warriors to their whole inhabitants . . . three to ten." By 1669 the census revealed that their numbers had been reduced to about one-third. "Spiritous liquors, the small-pox, war, and an abridgement of territory to a people who lived principally on the spontaneous productions of nature, had committed terrible havoc among them." But "that the lands of this country were taken from them by conquest, is not so general a truth as is supposed. I find in our historians and records, repeated proofs of purchase."[9]

With these losses, social changes followed, including the annihilation of several subtribes and the near disappearance of others. "There remain of the *Mattaponies* three or four men only, and have more negro than Indian blood in them. They have lost their language, have reduced themselves, by voluntary sales, to about fifty acres of land." The condition of "the *Pamunkies*" was almost as bad. Only ten or twelve of them survived. "The older ones among them preserve their language in a small degree, which are the last vestiges on earth, as far as we know, of the Powhatan language."[10]

Jefferson then describes some of the customs of the Virginia Indians. "I know of no such thing existing as an Indian monument," he says, "for I would not honor with

8. Lipscomb and Bergh, 2:129.
9. *Ibid.,* 2:129–31.
10. *Ibid.,* 2:132.

that name arrow points, stone hatchets, stone pipes, and half-shapen images . . . unless indeed it would be the barrows, of which many are to be found all over this country." He then gives a detailed description of Indian burial customs and his investigation of a burial site near Monticello. Of these barrows or mounds he says, "They are of different sizes, some of them constructed of earth, and some of loose stones." The mound which he excavated contained bones "lying in the utmost confusion, some vertical, some oblique, some horizontal."[11] He therefore concluded that, in order to establish whether the mound contained the bones of only those fallen in battle or was a village sepulchre, he should cut perpendicularly through the mound and investigate the condition of the bones found at the different strata.

This he proceeded to do, conducting his investigation as if he were a physical anthropologist, and also taking due note of archaeological considerations. He found four layers of bones, each divided by strata of stones and earth. The bones nearest the surface were least decayed. Thus, he decided that the barrow contained the remains of those who had died both of natural causes and in battle; and that these remains were collected from time to time and interred in the barrow. The fact that the bones were found in distinct layers and that they were of both adults and children led him to reason in this fashion.[12] His approach was scientific and his reasoning logical.

Jefferson then posed the question of the origin of the American Indians. Anticipating the theory later accepted by scientists, he pointed out that the Indians resembled Orientals and were probably descendants of wanderers from Asia who crossed over to the American continent, for "the late discoveries of Captain Cook, coasting from

11. *Ibid.,* 2:135.
12. *Ibid.,* 2:137–38.

Kamschatka to California, have proved that if the two continents . . . be separated at all, it is only by a narrow strait." To establish the Indian lineage, "a knowledge of their several languages would be the most certain evidence. . . . In fact, it is the best proof of the affinity which can ever be referred to." The English, Dutch, German, Swiss, and Scandinavians had long been separated, but their common origin can be demonstrated philologically. "It is to be lamented, very much lamented," he said, "that we have suffered so many of the Indian tribes already to extinguish, without our having previously collected and deposited in the records of literature, the general rudiments at least of the languages they spoke." If the vocabularies of different tribes in North and South America were available, with "their appelations of the most common objects of nature, of those which must be present to every nation barbarous or civilized, with the inflections of their nouns and verbs," this would enable "those skilled in the languages of the old world to compare them" with those in the new world in order to trace the derivations of the various Indian tribes.[13] Jefferson's scientific interest in this matter remained with him throughout life, and from time to time, as circumstances permitted, he continued his efforts to collect the various Indian dialects and vocabularies. His interests in the Indians were sociological, anthropological, and philological.

His concern for the Indian was also humanitarian, and it is probably true that this blurred his scientific vision to some degree. His enthusiasm for Indian eloquence led him to relate a story which got him into considerable difficulties in later years. He told of how the family of a Mingo chief named Logan, a friend of the whites, had been murdered by one Colonel Michael Cre-

---

13. *Ibid.,* 2:139–41.

sap, a story he had either heard in Williamsburg or read in the *Virginia Gazette*. Logan was said to have made an eloquent appeal to Lord Dunmore, the governor, absolving himself of blame for the tragedy and pointing out his long-standing friendship for the white man. Jefferson was touched by the appeal when he learned of it, and he used it as evidence of the Indians' oratorical powers, one of his rebuttals to Buffon's contention that Indians were inferior creatures. Luther Martin, a strong Federalist and Cresap's son-in-law, took up the latter's defense in the Baltimore newspapers, whereupon Jefferson appealed to those who were familiar with the incident to come to his support. Evidence was offered that Jefferson's story was incorrect in naming Cresap the murderer; however, he did not withdraw his accusation, and a confused controversy with partisan political overtones developed, out of all proportion to Jefferson's reporting of the incident as he had heard it related.[14]

As we have seen, Jefferson used the *Notes on Virginia* to refute Buffon's contention that "quoique le sauvage du noveau monde soit à peu près de même stature que l'homme de notre monde, cela ne suffit pas pour qu'il puisse faire une exception au fait général du répétissement de la nature vivante dans tout ce continent; le sauvage est foible et petit par les organes de la generation; il n'a ni poil, ni barbe, et nulle ardeur pour sa femelle."[15] Jefferson avers that from what he has seen of man, the Indian is "neither more defective in ardor, nor more

---

14. See Thomas Jefferson, *Notes on the State of Virginia,* ed. William Peden (Chapel Hill: University of North Carolina Press, 1955), pp. 226–58, in which Jefferson presents the lengthy evidence he collected regarding this matter.

15. Lipscomb and Bergh, 2:80–81. "Although the savage of the new world is about the same height as man in our world, this does not suffice for him to constitute an exception to the general fact that all living nature has become smaller on that continent. The savage is feeble and has small organs of generation; he has neither hair nor beard, and no ardor whatever for his female." Peden, p. 58.

impotent with his female, than the white reduced to the same diet and exercise." Furthermore, the Indian has highly admirable qualities: he is brave; he chooses death rather than surrender; he endures tortures stoically; he is an affectionate and indulgent parent; he is tender-hearted; his mental capacity is equal to that of the whites. It is true, Jefferson points out, that Indian women are submitted to unjust drudgery, but this, he says, is the case "with every barbarous people. . . . It is civilization alone which replaces women in the enjoyment of their natural equality." It is also true that Indians raise fewer children than whites, but the explanation of this is to be found in the circumstances in which they live.[16]

Jefferson's approach to the question of the Indian was comparative and situational, always taking into account sociological factors. In the matter of family size, he pointed out, birth control played a part, for "they have learned the practice of abortion by use of some vegetable; and . . . it even extends to prevent conception for a considerable time after." Furthermore, diet was also a consideration. Famines were common among them, and during these periods, reproduction rates were low, but Indian women married to white traders and provided with an adequate diet produced as many children as white women.

His sympathy and admiration for the Indian led Jefferson to emphasize the extenuating environmental circumstances which he took to be explanatory of their culture and abilities. "To form a just estimate of their mental powers," he stated, "great allowance must be made for those circumstances of their situation which call for a display of particular talents only." Since their culture prohibits the use of force and compulsion in maintaining conformity, "they are to be led to duty and to

---

16. Lipscomb and Bergh, 2:81–85.

enterprise by personal influence and persuasion. Hence, eloquence in council, bravery and address in war, become the foundation of all consequence with them," and are important ingredients in effecting social control. Furthermore, it would be unfair to judge Indian intelligence by the standards of the whites because "letters have not yet been introduced among them."[17]

Jefferson was a serious student of Indian society and a meticulous observer of the normative structure of that society. If he was not always utterly objective in his appraisal of this group and their culture, it was because of his profound sympathy for them and his humanitarian desire to see their lot improved. He was here, as in some other instances, both the scientist and the reformer, and if he erred by a lack of scientific detachment, it was because of his human sympathy and commiseration. And, in the *Notes on Virginia,* it may perhaps also have been because he was determined to refute Buffon's insufferable canard on America. Here he attempted to defend human nature and challenge the doctrine of human inequality, and in so doing, scientific observation and his social philosophy converged. He declared that any apparent inferiority on the part of the Indian could be explained by environmental conditions and historical facts.

Although Jefferson was convinced of the natural equality of the Indian to the white, he took a very different view of the Negro. The comparison was indeed invidious. It is perhaps significant that in the *Notes on Virginia* he did not discuss the Negro in the natural history section but rather under the administration of justice. He pointed out that one of the objectives of revising the Virginia code was to emancipate all slaves born after the passing of such an act. He had proposed the prohibition of the slave trade as early as 1776, and such a bill was passed

17. *Ibid.,* 2:85–90.

by the Virginia legislature in 1778. But emancipation
was another matter. His proposal was that slaves born
after the act was passed—for only they were to be emancipated—"should continue with their parents to a certain
age, then be brought up at the public expense, to tillage,
arts, or sciences, according to their geniuses," until the
males were 21 and the females 18, at which time they
were to be "colonized to such place as the circumstances
of the time should render most proper." They were to
be provided with "arms, implements of household and
the handicraft arts, seeds," work animals, and whatever
else they would need to establish themselves in their new
location outside the United States. They were to be declared "a free and independent people" and provided
American protection until such a time as they were strong
enough to defend themselves.[18]

This provision was to be offered as an amendment to
the emancipation act; but if emancipation was difficult,
this provision was impossible. The emancipation bill
failed, of course, and so the amendment was never offered. But its second provision is interesting as an insight
into Jefferson's thinking, for the amendment was also to
provide that vessels were "at the same time" to be sent
"to other parts of the world for an equal number of
white inhabitants" to be brought back as immigrants to
replace the emancipated slaves.

> It will probably be asked, why not retain and incorporate the
> blacks into the State, and thus save the expense of supplying
> by importation of white settlers the vacancies they will leave?
> Deep-rooted prejudices entertained by the whites; ten thousand
> recollections by the blacks, of the injuries they have sustained;
> new provocations; the real distinctions which nature has made;
> and many other circumstances, will divide us into parties, and
> produce convulsions, which will probably never end but in the
> extermination of the one or the other race.[19]

18. *Ibid.*, 2:191–92.
19. *Ibid.*, 2:192. Jefferson consistently referred to Negroes as "blacks,"

It may hardly seem possible at first glance that what follows in the *Notes* came from the pen of the same enlightened liberal who wrote the Declaration of Independence.[20] However, Jefferson was a product of eighteenth-century Virginia and shared many of the norms of the society in which he was socialized. Consideration of this fact should lead us to see his comments not only as an index of local opinion and customs, but also to grasp the fact that he was far more enlightened than most of his Southern contemporaries. His line of reasoning is nevertheless startling.

In addition to the political objections to assimilation, Jefferson indicated that there were other objections which were "physical and moral." The first of these was color. Reflecting the ethnocentrism and value judgments of his day, he declared that color is a determinant of beauty. "Are not the fine mixtures of red and white . . . preferable," he asks, "to that eternal monotony . . . that immovable veil of black which covers the emotions?" Furthermore, whites were superior in beauty by virtue of their "flowing hair" and their "elegant symmetry of form." Indeed, the Negro himself concurred in this judgment, as is evidenced by his own preference for the white woman, a situation analogous to "the preference of the Oranootan for the black woman over those of his own species."[21] If superior beauty is a matter for consideration "in the propagation of horses, dogs, and

and to members of his own race as "whites." He obviously felt that this usage was desirable.

20. Jefferson's draft of the Declaration of Independence included a strong condemnation of slavery, which was eliminated by Congress.

21. This highly ethnocentric remark of Jefferson's led his critics to accuse him of comparing the Negro to the orangutan, or orangoutang, or even of saying that the Negro was descended from this creature. William Lloyd Garrison charged that Jefferson was the first to broach the vulgar opinion that "the negro is a distinct genus, inferior to the human race, and nearly allied to the *simia* species." Merrill D. Peterson, *The Jefferson Image in the American Mind* (New York: Oxford University Press, 1962), p. 176.

other domestic animals, why not in that of" human beings?

There were still other unattractive features of the Negro which would make assimilation undesirable. "They secrete less by the kidneys, and more by the skin, which gives them a very strong and disagreeable odor." Physically, they are stronger than whites and require less sleep. "A black after hard labor through the day will be induced by the slightest amusements to sit up until midnight, or later, though knowing he must be out with the first dawn of the morning." They appear to be at least as brave as whites, but this may "proceed from a want of forethought, which prevents their seeing danger till it be present." Their sexual drive is stronger, and the males are "more ardent after their female; but love with them seems to be more an eager desire, than a tender delicate mixture of sentiment and sensation." They feel less deeply and their griefs are transient. They give little serious thought to their problems or to matters of serious import, and "to this must be ascribed their disposition to sleep when abstracted from their diversions, and unemployed in labor."[22]

If ever Jefferson seemed to belong to the lost world of the eighteenth century, it is in this section of the *Notes on Virginia*. If ever he sounded parochial and ethnocentric, it was here. His assessment of the characteristics of the Negro no doubt reflected the prevailing Virginia biases. In addition to the other deficiencies of the Negro, Jefferson also considers those of a mental or intellectual nature. "Comparing them by their faculties of memory, reason, and imagination," he says, "it appears that in memory they are the equal of whites; in reason much inferior . . . ; and in imagination . . . dull, tasteless and anomalous."

---

22. Lipscomb and Bergh, 2:192–94.

Perhaps recalling that he had explained the seeming inferiority of Indians on the basis of the circumstances of their life, Jefferson considers briefly the circumstances under which Negroes lived in America, declaring that it would be unfair "to follow them to Africa" for this purpose. "We will consider them here, on the same stage with the whites, and where the facts are not apocryphal on which a judgment is to be formed." And it will be only fair "to make great allowances for the differences of condition, of education, of conversation, of the sphere in which they move." But, even so, "many have been so situated, that they might have availed themselves of the conversation of their masters; many . . . have always been associated with the whites. Some have been liberally educated," yet none known to Jefferson had ever presented any evidence of intelligence and ability remotely equal to that of the whites. Indians, with none of the above advantages, often displayed evidence to "prove their reason and sentiment strong, their imagination glowing and elevated." But not so the Negro. "Never yet could I find that a black had uttered a thought above plain narration; never saw even an elementary trait of painting or sculpture." Yet the Negro was not utterly without talents. "In music they are more generally gifted than the whites . . . and have been found capable of imagining a small catch." But their artistic creations were minimal if indeed they could be said to exist at all. "Misery is often the parent of . . . poetry," for instance; "among the blacks is misery enough, God knows, but no poetry."[23]

Here in the *Notes* Jefferson refers to two Negro writers, Phyllis Wheatley and Ignatius Sancho; however, he finds them deficient compared to white authors, and even suggests the possibility that the works published under

---

23. *Ibid.*, 2:194–96.

their names may have been written by whites. He then adds that "the improvement of the blacks in body and mind, in the first instance of their mixture with the whites, has been observed by every one, and proves that their inferiority is not the effect merely of their condition of life." Comparing American Negro slaves with the white slaves of Rome, he points out that Negro slaves enjoyed more rights than Roman slaves. The latters' owners were allowed to kill them if they so pleased, while in America this practice "would be punished capitally." The Romans secured evidence from their slaves by means of torture, but in America the testimony of slaves was not sought in legal cases, though proof against them when accused of crime was required to be as "precise" as that "required against . . . a freeman." Roman slaves often excelled in science and the arts. "But they were of the race of whites. It is not their condition, then, but nature, which has produced the distinction"[24] between white and Negro slaves, as between whites and Negroes generally. The Negroes' shortcomings could not be explained on the basis of the circumstances under which they lived, although the Indians' seeming deficiencies could be so explained.

But Jefferson's characterization of the Negro was not entirely unfavorable. He closes his discussion in the *Notes* by modifying his earlier comments and with more attention to the scientific questions involved in the matter of racial superiority and inferiority, and he comes to admit the possibility that the Negro may prove himself equal to the white—but only the possibility that he may do so.

Jefferson's most eloquent defense of the Negro is in the area of morality. Even if nature has been less bountiful to Negroes "in the endowments of the head, I believe

---

24. *Ibid.*, 2:196-99.

that in those of the heart she will be found to have done them justice."[25] Their propensity to theft, for instance, is to be "ascribed to their situation, and not to any depravity of the moral sense. The man in whose favor no laws of property exist, probably feels himself less bound to respect those made in favor of others." Surely, Jefferson feels, the slave may "justifiably take a little from one who has taken all from him." Jefferson's perception of the sociological considerations involved is clearly revealed in his statement that "a change in the relations in which a man is placed should change his moral ideas of right and wrong." Among the Negroes, there are "numerous instances of the most rigid integrity, and as many as among their better instructed masters, of benevolence, gratitude, and unshaken fidelity." Jefferson's remarks may sound patronizing by present-day standards, but they were obviously sincere. His recognition of these virtues in the Negro no doubt represented a view far more advanced than that of many of his slave-owning contemporaries.

Furthermore, Jefferson as scientist admits that his view of the Negro may be incorrect, and that "the opinion that they are inferior in the faculties of reason and imagination must be hazarded with great diffidence. To justify a general conclusion, requires many observations"; therefore, he wishes to leave the question open for further evidence, thus admitting the possibility that the Negro may yet prove himself the white man's equal. Jefferson the humanitarian further adds, "as a circumstance of great tenderness," that branding the Negro irrevocably as an inferior creature "would degrade a whole race of men from the rank in the scale of beings which their Creator has perhaps given them." He does not wish to be unfair; he has stated his opinions frankly,

25. *Ibid.*, 2:199.

but, no doubt unlike many of his contemporaries, he refuses to close the door utterly. In fairness, he admits that the evidence he has offered of Negro inferiority is not perfectly conclusive, and declares that he advances it "as a suspicion only, that the blacks, whether originally a distinct race, or made distinct by time and circumstance, are inferior to the whites in the endowments of both mind and body." This may seem like a grudging concession in the light of his extensive cataloguing of the Negro's shortcomings; the significant fact, however, is that Jefferson was fair enough to admit the possibility of Negro equality at a time and in a place where such an admission must have seemed like radical heresy to most of the members of the dominant race.

In any event, questions of superiority and inferiority aside, Negro slavery, Jefferson was profoundly convinced, must be abolished—although he insisted that emancipation must be accompanied by expatriation. Unlike the white Roman slaves who, when freed, might intermarry with their former owners "without staining the blood" of the latter, Negroes when freed must immediately "be removed beyond the reach of mixture."[26] It would no doubt be unrealistic to expect Jefferson the eighteenth-century Virginian to entertain a view which would approve of eventual Negro-white amalgamation. He clearly felt that racial intermarriage would indeed "stain the blood" of the whites. Protestations to the contrary, Jefferson obviously considered the Negro at least biologically inferior to the white.

Many of his enemies pounced upon Jefferson's comments in the *Notes,* often wrenching them from context, to prove that he was anti-Negro or pro-Negro, as the case might be, to serve their purpose. The battle raged on, long after his death, gaining particular virulence in

---

26. *Ibid.,* 2:199–201.

the fateful days before the Civil War. Some gave credence to the whispered story of his relations with "Black Sal" Hemings, one of the slaves he inherited from his wife's estate and who accompanied his youngest daughter Polly to France in 1787. The story was originally circulated in print in 1802 by a disappointed and vindictive political associate, James T. Callender, although it had been whispered first by the Federalists in the bitter campaign of 1800. William Cullen Bryant and John Quincy Adams wrote verses on the subject, and abolitionists revived and retold it. They gave less attention to Jefferson's "African brothel," as they called it, than to his alleged mulatto offspring, one abolitionist reporting that he had heard a Southern gentleman declare that the latter had seen the daughter of Thomas Jefferson sold in New Orleans for one thousand dollars.[27]

No serious student of Jefferson has declared his belief in these stories, but several writers, such as W. E. B. DuBois, have recorded them as true or probably true, and a number of newspaper and magazine accounts have appeared from time to time (including the November, 1954, issue of *Ebony*) on Jefferson's Negro descendants. One account states that "in four generations, these proud Negro descendants . . . have made the long and improbable journey from the white marbled splendor of Monticello to the 'Negro ghetto' in the democracy their

27. Peterson, pp. 181–82. The writer is acquainted with several elderly people in Charlottesville (where Jefferson is still known and almost universally spoken of as "Mr. Jefferson") who refer freely and matter-of-factly to his mulatto offspring. Reference is sometimes made to one Henry Martin, said to have been Jefferson's grandson, who rang the bells at the University of Virginia from about 1868 to 1909. Older Virginians used to say that "the best blood of Virginia flows in Negro veins," and stories of miscegenation have been widely told, particularly by elderly ladies and gentlemen of the upper class. One might well judge that not all such accounts are apocryphal. The story of Jefferson's alleged mulatto daughters is told in some detail in Raymond Leopold Bruckberger, *Image of America* (New York: Viking Press, 1959).

forebear helped to found."[28] The rise and progress of the miscegenation legend is probably attributable to three principal factors: political circumstances, including the hatred some Federalists felt for Jefferson; the sometimes bitter and extreme statements of abolitionists; and the fact that Jefferson never remarried after his wife's death in 1782 when he was thirty-nine.[29]

In any event, Jefferson was not unaware of the temptations and evils inherent in slavery, and in the *Notes on Virginia,* he made the indictment of slavery which is most often quoted as evidence of his deep humanity and honest belief in freedom for all. It also reveals his comprehension of the process of socialization, as well as the profundity of his commitment to the solving of this urgent social problem.

The existence of slavery Jefferson saw as producing "an unhappy influence on the manners" of the whites.

---

28. Peterson, p. 186.

29. This was not the only scandal to touch Jefferson. John Walker, a close friend of his youth and early manhood, accused him of having engaged in attempts from 1764 to 1779 to seduce his wife. Walker contended that his wife did not report these attempts to him until after Jefferson had gone to France. Jefferson admitted that "when I was young and single I offered love" to Mrs. Walker, and it is accepted that he made such improper advances to his friend's wife, later giving Walker a statement exculpating the lady from blame. Political enemies saw that the scandal attained wide circulation, but in a grossly exaggerated form. Malone says that Jefferson was guilty of "an unmoral, not an immoral act." Later in life he and the Walkers were partially reconciled, and Walker probably realized that the story, grown to inflated proportions, had undeservedly damaged both Jefferson and himself—that the extent of Jefferson's offense had been not more than one or two improper advances to his wife. See Dumas Malone, *Jefferson the Virginian,* (Boston: Little, Brown and Company, 1948), Appendix II, pp. 447-51.

The other great romantic attachment of his life was to Maria Cosway, a talented English painter and musician of whom he had become enamoured in Paris. It was to her that he wrote his famous "my head and my heart" letter. His head won, although Jefferson's profound attraction to this married woman was one of the strongest emotional experiences of his life. There was no suggestion, however, that any serious improprieties had taken place between them. See Helen Duprey Bullock, *My Head and My Heart: A Little Chronicle of Thomas Jefferson and Maria Cosway* (New York: Putnam's, 1945).

"The whole commerce between master and slave is a perpetual exercise of the most boisterous passions," he said, "the most unremitting despotism on the one part, and degrading submissions on the other." This is observed by the children, "who learn to imitate it; for man is an imitative animal." Then, in their relationship with slave children, the children of the masters display the same characteristics. "Thus nursed, educated, and daily exercised in tyranny," they "cannot but be stamped by it with odious peculiarities." The individual socialized in such an environment "must be a prodigy" if his manners and morals are undepraved thereby.

Slavery, by "permitting one-half the citizens . . . to trample the rights of the other, transforms" the slave-owners into despots and the slaves into their enemies, Jefferson declared. It destroys the morals of the slave-owners as well as their industry, "for in a warm climate, no man will labour for himself who can make another labour for him."

Jefferson foresaw the direst consequences for America if slavery were not abolished. He anticipated slave rebellions and revolutions, as well as the destruction of the nation's liberties. "I tremble for my country when I reflect that God is just, that his justice cannot sleep forever," he cried. "The Almighty has no attribute which can take sides with" slave-owners. But Jefferson thought that he saw a change coming as a result of the Revolution, with "the spirit of the master abating, that of the slave rising from the dust . . . the way I hope preparing . . . for a total emancipation."[30] It was a hope that of course was realized only as the result of a bloody war, which in his old age he foresaw and which he profoundly dreaded.

By modern standards, Jefferson's attitude toward the

---

30. Lipscomb and Bergh, 2:225–28.

Negro seems illiberal and unenlightened, but it was definitely an advanced attitude for eighteenth-century Virginia. From his earliest days he considered slavery a moral wrong and an outrage to humanity. In his *Autobiography* he tells of making an effort in the House of Burgesses in 1769, during his first session as a member, "for the permission of the emancipation of slaves, which was rejected."[31] Thereafter, he grasped every opportunity to strike at the "infamous practice" of slavery. In the *Summary View* he castigated the Crown for "shameful abuse of power" in defeating colonial efforts to prohibit the external slave trade; in his draft of the Declaration of Independence he made the same charge; and in his 1784 proposed plan of government for the Western Territory, he stipulated that no slavery should exist there after 1800.[32]

In 1791 a Negro mathematician and surveyor named Benjamin Banneker sent Jefferson a copy of an almanac he had compiled. In acknowledging it, Jefferson wrote:

> Nobody wishes more than I do to see such proofs as you exhibit, that nature has given our black brethren, talents equal to those of the other colours of men, and that the appearance of a want of them is owing merely to the degraded condition of their existence, both in Africa and America. . . . I have taken the liberty of sending your Almanac to Monsieur de Condorcet, Secretary of the Academy of Sciences in Paris . . . because I considered it as a document which your whole colour had a right for their justification against the doubts which have been entertained against them.[33]

Although Jefferson attempted to remain open-minded

---

31. Ford, *Writings*, 1:5. See also Ford, *Writings*, 9:477; and Randall, 1:58.

32. Boyd, 1:130, 318; Boyd, 6:608. Early efforts to abolish the slave trade bore fruit at last, of course, in the Act of Congress in 1808 ending this infamous traffic. See Oscar Handlin, *The Americans* (Boston: Little, Brown and Company, 1963), p. 200.

33. Lipscomb and Bergh, 8:241–42.

on this critical question, as time went on he became discouraged over the possibility of voluntary abolition. "Nothing is more certainly written in the book of fate," he declared in his *Autobiography*, "than that these people are to be free."[34] Yet in his old age he realized that the younger generation—from whom he had expected so much because they had received "their early impressions after the flame of liberty had been kindled in every breast"—had failed to make progress against the evils of slavery.[35] As long as he lived, some continued to look to him as the logical leader of an emancipation movement, but calling upon him to take the lead "in this salutary but arduous work," he said, was "like bidding old Priam to buckle the armour of Hector," adding:

> My opinion has ever been that, until more can be done for them, we should endeavor, with those whom fortune has thrown in our hands, to feed and clothe them well, protect them from ill usage, require such reasonable labor only as is performed voluntarily by freemen, and be led by no repugnancies to abdicate them, and our duties to them.[36]

In the last year of his life, he expressed his conclusion that abolition would not come in his lifetime. "The revolution in public opinion which this case requires is not to be expected in a day, or perhaps in an age," he said. He felt that he had done all that he could: "My sentiments have been forty years before the public. Had I repeated them forty times, they would only have become more stale and threadbare. Although I shall not live to see them consummated, they will not die with me. But, living

---

34. Thomas Jefferson, *The Works of Thomas Jefferson,* ed. Paul Leicester Ford, 12 vols. (New York: G. P. Putnam's Sons, 1904), 1:68.
35. Adrienne Koch and William Peden, eds., *The Life and Selected Writings of Thomas Jefferson* (New York: Random House, Inc., 1944), p. 642.
36. Ford, *Works,* 1:77.

or dying, they will ever be in my most fervent prayers."[37]

It was his considered opinion that until abolition and emancipation could be effected, it was the duty of the slave-owner to maintain his slaves in the best circumstances possible, not to free them wholesale into a world which held no welcome for them and in which they could not be expected to make their way. This opinion was unavoidable to Jefferson the practical idealist.

In his old age, Jefferson took an adamant stand against the proposed settlement of the Missouri question which called for prohibiting the further introduction of slaves into Missouri and for providing for the gradual emancipation of those already there. He has been criticized for this stand, as it appears to be in direct opposition to his view of 1784 expressed in the plan of government he proposed for the Western Territory. However, he saw in the suggested Missouri settlement implications for the future of the nation other than the question of slavery. To Lafayette he wrote: "On the eclipse of federalism [the Federalists] with us, although not its extinction, its leaders got up the Missouri question, under the false front of lessening the measure of slavery, but with the real view of producing a geographical division of parties, which might insure them the next President."[38] Jefferson's profound fears for the future of the Republic rushed to the fore: the Federalists were called from the past, threatening to divide the Union, and perhaps destroy it, in which event the question of slavery might well become an academic one. Therefore, he decided that more was at stake than the matter of slavery: the survival of the nation itself hung in the balance. The Missouri question, "like a fire-bell in the night," he wrote

---

37. Edward Dumbauld, ed., *The Political Writings of Thomas Jefferson* ed. Edward Dumbauld (Copyright, 1955, by the Liberal Arts Press, Inc.), p. 62. Reprinted by permission of The Liberal Arts Press Division of the Bobbs-Merrill Company, Inc.
38. Lipscomb and Bergh, 15:492.

"awakened and filled me with terror. I considered it at once as the knell of the Union." He seems convinced that the Union itself would eventually be destroyed if the proposed plan were followed, that "a geographical line, coinciding with a marked principle, moral and political, once conceived and held up to the angry passions of men" would lead to a division of the nation into two opposing camps, and of course he was right. The question to him, therefore, was not one of slavery as such.

"I can say, with conscious truth," he declared, "that there is not a man on earth who would sacrifice more than I would to relieve us of this heavy reproach, in any *practicable* way." The economic aspect of emancipation was "a mere bagatelle which would not cost me a second thought, if, in that way, a general emancipation and *expatriation* could be effected." The solution must be a practical one, and this he was convinced the Missouri Compromise was not. He seemed to be sure that the passage of slaves from one state to another "would not make a slave of a single human being who would not be so without it," just as the diffusion of slavery over a greater territory would hasten emancipation by distributing the "burden" of slavery to a greater number of owners.[39] He was convinced that the onus of slave ownership would become increasingly unpleasant and indefensible; thus, the greater the number of slave owners, the greater would be the forces seeking emancipation. His thinking here was no doubt unrealistic, for not all men found the ownership of slaves beset with the profound moral implications which deeply perturbed Jefferson throughout his life. He was quite certain that the essential matter involved in the Missouri question was not really slavery but instead the encroaching and suffocating power of the federal government in violation of the Con-

---

39. *Ibid.*, 15:249–50.

stitutional guarantee to the states of their rights to exercise their just powers. This, of course, was the same fear
which gave rise to the Kentucky Resolutions, for Jefferson was unquestionably and profoundly convinced that
the very survival of the Union depended upon the preservation of the rights of the states to control their own
local affairs, which included the regulation of slavery.

It is clear beyond doubt that he ardently desired the
abolition of slavery—with expatriation[40]—but he desired
even more strongly the preservation of the Union. It is
also clear that he was strongly convinced that the solution to the slavery problem was rightfully a local one.
The rights of the states must be preserved, he felt, else
there would be no liberty, no democracy, no Union. As
a Southerner, he believed that the Southern states had
rights as inviolable as those of the Northern states, and
in spite of his abhorrence of slavery, it was the right of
the Southern states to settle the problem without federal
coercion. On such, he believed, hinged the fate of the
Union.

From time to time Jefferson freed several of his slaves,
but to have emancipated them all, thus depriving himself
of his entire labor force and a significant portion of his
property, would have been less than practicable, just as
turning them loose in an inhospitable world would not
have been humane. "To give liberty to, or rather, to
abandon persons whose habits have been formed in slavery is like abandoning children,"[41] he said, and in the

---

40. Jefferson did not participate in the founding of the American
Colonization Society. Peterson, pp. 177-78. However, he did suggest
that both free Negroes and slaves convicted of crimes might be exported
to Africa, perhaps to Sierra Leone. Nathan Schachner, *Thomas Jefferson:
A Biography*, 2 vols. (New York: Appleton-Century-Crofts, Inc., 1951),
2:704. As he stated repeatedly, he felt that any plan of emancipation
should include provisions for expatriation.

41. Saul K. Padover, ed., *Thomas Jefferson on Democracy* (New York:
Mentor Books, 1954), p. 100. At one time, Jefferson had 55 house
servants at Monticello—testimony, no doubt, to the complexities of run-
ning a large house and entertaining many guests.

circumstances of his times he was no doubt right. Periodically, he also sold off slaves he had inherited from the Wayles estate, particularly those on his Poplar Forest plantation, always in an effort to pay off the old Wayles debt and always with careful stipulations that families were not to be broken up and that those sold were to be treated kindly. There can be no doubt that he detested this traffic in human beings, and that he undertook such sales with the greatest reluctance and under the pressure of dire economic necessity.

At his death he emancipated several of his favorite slaves, as was the custom among Virginia gentlemen. Perhaps he would have given their freedom to more had his financial position not been so desperate. In any event, it cannot be denied that he abhorred slavery and both wished and worked for its abolition. Here again, however, he was the practical idealist; and in his day the time never arrived when it was practicable or even possible to eradicate this great evil. He had worked arduously to see this "enormity" destroyed; but he could not go beyond the possible.

Jefferson's abhorrence of slavery was based on moral, humanitarian, philosophical, and political grounds. He viewed slavery as a clear violation of natural rights, and he worked more energetically to abolish it than did other national political leaders of the Revolutionary and post-Revolutionary periods. He ardently hoped for eventual emancipation and abolition, even though he apparently could not bring himself to consider Negroes the equals of whites. In this particular respect, he was the product of his environment, and his ideas were largely consistent with those of most of his educated Southern contemporaries. Washington, John Marshall, George Wythe, and the majority of the Virginia elite maintained objections to slavery similar to those of Jefferson. Yet they did not free their slaves either. "Would anyone believe that I am Master of Slaves of my own purchase," Patrick Henry asked, as a case in point. "I am drawn along by the general inconvenience of living without them," he continued. Even so, he looked forward to the time "when an opportunity will be offered to abolish this lamentable Evil."[42] Like Jefferson, Washington, and others, he considered slavery a moral wrong. Indeed, practically every Southern gentleman looked upon slavery as an evil, but a necessary one, during this period, particularly in Virginia, Maryland, and South Carolina.

Jefferson's objections to slavery were far more profound than those of his contemporaries, and it is important to remember that he, unlike them, worked actively to destroy this great evil. He found, however, that his proposals for emancipation were something "the public mind would not . . . bear."[43] From 1769 on, he continued his struggle against the legalized bondage of human beings, while many others with more conservative views extolled the virtues of emancipation but did nothing to bring it about. At last, even this traditional upper-class lip service to the cause disappeared, and a new view was voiced by a new Southern leadership. In the last year of Jefferson's life, Thomas Cooper, president of South Carolina College, published his well-known pamphlet presenting the view that slavery was a "positive good" instead of the evil an earlier generation of Southern leaders had felt it to be. Cooper's efforts were followed by those of Thomas R. Dew of William and Mary College, and then by George Fitzhugh's influential *Sociology for the South.* Finally, the political and moral justification of slavery reached its zenith in the efforts of John C. Calhoun.[44] The hardening of attitudes which

---

42. Samuel Eliot Morrison and Henry Steele Commager, *The Growth of the American Republic,* 2 vols. (New York: Oxford University Press, 1962), 1:246.
43. Ford, *Works,* 1:77.
44. Morrison and Commager, 1:537.

Jefferson had foreseen meant at last that war alone could rid the nation of the enormity which he abhorred.

Jefferson's philosophical and theoretical dedication to human liberty was complete; thus, his objections to slavery were implacable. Yet, as the practical idealist, he remained a slave-owner throughout life. And even though he believed that all men, black, red, and white, should be free, he was an eighteenth-century Southerner: he was not so impervious to the influences of environment and the prevailing climate of opinion as to believe that Negroes were in actuality the equals of whites in endowments and abilities. His experience in the America of his day perhaps made such a conclusion inevitable, for it must be remembered that Jefferson was a positivist and an empiricist, suffering his faith to go no farther than his facts, as he said. It is certainly not surprising that the facts of Negro life under the deplorable conditions of slavery presented no real opportunities for the Negro to display his talents and abilities. No group of people living under such circumstances could offer the kind of empirical evidence of their equality that Jefferson, the scientist and the Southern slave owner, may have demanded, particularly in view of the fact that his concepts of the Negro were derived largely from observations of uneducated plantation slaves. Even though he later in life had the opportunity to observe Negroes living under more favorable circumstances, it is perhaps not surprising that his early experiences in rural Virginia had predisposed him to view the Negro largely in the image of the plantation slave stereotype. This Jefferson freely admitted. His doubts regarding the Negro's intellectual abilities were, he said, "the result of personal observation in the limited sphere of my own State, where the opportunities for the development of their genius were not favorable, and those of exercising it still less so." And then he added significantly, "But whatever be their degree of talent it is no measure of their rights."[45]

Can it be seriously maintained that Jefferson believed the doctrine he so eloquently promulgated—that all men were by nature born equal as well as free? In a philosophical sense, yes; in practice, he unquestionably believed that all should be free, but he evidently believed in equality only in the sense that this element of the American ideology (for which he was in part responsible) is now believed: that men, whatever their color, creed, or condition, should be equal before the law. The view that all men are equal in talents and abilities has found few supporters in any age.

Free Negroes were unquestionably among those of whom he said ". . . the minority possess their equal rights, which equal laws must protect."[46] His principles and his philosophy justify our conclusion that he was at least as liberal in his view of the equal legal rights to which all were entitled as Americans are today—which no doubt means that he was far more dedicated to the ideal of equality before the law than were most of his contemporaries.

As to the inherent potentialities of Negroes, he said, "No person living wishes more sincerely than I do, to see a complete refutation of the doubts I have myself entertained and expressed on the grade of understanding allotted them by nature, and to find that in this respect they are on a par with ourselves."[47]

However, by far the greater part of his writings provides incontrovertible evidence that he considered the Negro inferior to both the white and the Indian—though, of crucial significance, he clearly did not imagine that inferiority was a justification for slavery. Indeed, he never doubted that slavery was utterly indefensible

---

45. Padover, ed., *Thomas Jefferson on Democracy*, p. 101.
46. Lipscomb and Bergh, 3:318.
47. Padover, ed., *Thomas Jefferson on Democracy*, p. 101.

under any and every circumstance. It was in his willingness to entertain the possibility—and the ardent hope—that the Negro might someday prove himself the equal of the white, and in his lifelong struggle to secure freedom for the Negro by the abolition of slavery, that he was a liberal whose attitudinal orientation was far ahead of that of most men of his time and place.

10

On Social Processes

COMMUNICATION: THE PRESS

From Paris Jefferson wrote a friend in the hyperbole he often used to emphasize a point that "were it left to me to decide whether we should have a government without newspapers, or newspapers without a government, I should not hesitate a moment to prefer the latter," for he believed that a free press was necessary if the people were to restrain the ambitions of their rulers. In this same letter he added:

> I am persuaded that the good sense of the people will always be found to be the best army . . . . The people are the only censors of their governors . . . the only safeguard of the public liberty . . . give them full information of their affairs through the public papers . . . . The basis of our government being the opinion of the people, the very first object should be to keep that right . . . . Every man should receive . . . papers, and be capable of reading them.[1]

As President, however, he seemed on occasion to take a different view. "Nothing can now be believed which is seen in a newspaper," he wrote in the famous Norvell

---

1. Thomas Jefferson, *The Papers of Thomas Jefferson,* ed. Julian P. Boyd (Princeton: Princeton University Press, 1950–   ), 11:49.

letter. "Truth itself becomes suspicious by being put into that polluted vehicle . . . . I really look with commiseration over the great body of my fellow citizens, who, reading newspapers, live and die in the belief that they have known something of what has been passing in the world . . . . The man who never looks into a newspaper is better informed than he who reads them."[2] He had suffered profoundly from the stinging attacks of a partisan press during his active political life; but after his retirement to Monticello, he regained some of his philosophic calm, and in 1823 wrote Lafayette that "the only security of all, is in a free press. The force of public opinion cannot be resisted, when permitted freely to be expressed. The agitation it produces must be submitted to. It is necessary, to keep the waters pure."[3] He thus at last came the full circle, and this statement unquestionably reflects his considered opinion of the press. The apparent inconsistency of his views in this regard may be understood only in the light of the experiences of his life.

Jefferson saw and perhaps stated more clearly than any other political leader the importance of the freedom of the press in a democratic society. Throughout his life he maintained his advocacy of a free press, although he was often deeply disappointed in its performance.

Since he believed in the importance of individuals in a comparatively decentralized society, he was convinced that men should be enlightened and informed. And herein newspapers had a crucial role to play, for the enlightenment of the people was necessary to insure their happiness. The press served as a necessary check upon the government. During the dispute over his relations

2. Thomas Jefferson, *The Writings of Thomas Jefferson,* ed. Andrew A. Lipscomb and Albert E. Bergh, 20 vols. (Washington: Thomas Jefferson Memorial Association, 1903), 11:222–24.
3. *Ibid.,* 15:491.

with Freneau, he wrote President Washington: "No government ought to be without censors; and where the press is free, no one ever will."[4] It was the press which must inform the people of the acts of the government so that they might protect their rights. To a French correspondent, he wrote: "This formidable censor of the public functionaries, by arraigning them at the tribunal of public opinion, produces reform peaceably, which must otherwise be done by revolution."[5]

The role of the free press was therefore a critical one; however, Jefferson had in mind a freedom for it that was less than absolute. His friend George Hay had asserted that no person could be punished for his opinions, however ridiculous "or immoral in their tendency" on any subject, even if the opinions he expressed were malicious untruths. A writer was "safe within the sanctuary of the press" even when he lied outright. Hay drew the line only at libels of private individuals.[6]

Jefferson was largely in agreement with Hay. He would draw the line at deliberate falsehood injurious of private figures, and he insisted upon the right of the states to provide for the control of libel. He included this provision in his 1776 proposals for a Virginia constitution, and also in the Kentucky Resolutions. "While we deny that Congress have a right to control the freedom of the press," he wrote Abigail Adams, "we have ever asserted the right of the States, and their exclusive right, to do so."[7] State laws should hold newspapers responsible for slander and libel but should at the same time protect the rights of the publisher to print truth. Thus, when he declared that "our liberty depends on

---

4. *Ibid.,* 8:406.
5. *Ibid.,* 15:489.
6. Leonard W. Levy, *Freedom of Speech and Press in Early American History: Legacy of Suppression* (New York: Harper & Row, Publishers, 1963), pp. 270–71.
7. Lipscomb and Bergh, 11:51.

the freedom of the press, and that cannot be limited without being lost,"[8] he of course did not have in mind an absolute, limitless freedom which amounted to license, but a press unshackled by arbitrary rules of the government, and unlimited in its right to publish the truth. It was this kind of free press which was essential in a democratic republic and without which liberty was never secure. Perhaps the best single statement of his view is this, penned in 1816: "Where the press is free, and every man able to read, all is safe."[9]

As in other matters, Jefferson and Hamilton disagreed on their views of the press. Hamilton, himself a journalist and founder of the New York *Evening Post,* contended in the Croswell case that truth, when published for good motives, should be permitted as a defense in a prosecution for seditious libel. Croswell had published an account of an alleged deal which Jefferson had made with James T. Callender for the latter to denounce Washington as a traitor, a robber, and a perjurer, and Adams in only slightly less complimentary terms. Croswell was arrested and tried on a common-law indictment for seditious libel; and as a result of the case, the so-called "Hamiltonian Doctrine" was enacted into law in New York.[10] Jefferson's opinion of the case is unknown; however, it is clear that he disagreed with Hamilton's earlier contention that since the federal government had no powers not expressly delegated to it in the Constitution, there was no need for a provision denying it control over the press. Jefferson saw the need for such a provision in order to deter the government from seeking to control the press via the doctrine of implied powers. He was perturbed when he learned of the ab-

8. Thomas Jefferson, *The Writings of Thomas Jefferson,* ed. Paul Leicester Ford, 10 vols. (New York: G. P. Putnam's Sons, 1892-1899), 4:132.

9. Lipscomb and Bergh, 14:384.

10. Levy, pp. 297-99.

sence of a bill of rights in the Constitution, and from Paris he sent Madison his proposed guarantee for freedom of the press: "The people shall not be deprived of their right to speak, to write, or *otherwise* to publish anything but false facts affecting injuriously the life, liberty, or reputation of others, or affecting the peace of the confederacy with other nations."[11] Although his suggestion was not adopted, he was satisfied with Madison's strong and inclusive statement: "Congress shall make no law . . . abridging the freedom of speech or of the press."

When Jefferson as Secretary of State became alarmed at the "monarchical" developments during the Washington administration, he took aim at John Fenno's *Gazette of the United States* as "a paper of pure toryism, disseminating the doctrines of monarchy, aristocracy, and the exclusion of the influence of the people,"[12] for the *Gazette* was by its own declaration a spokesman for government policies. Madison suggested that his former classmate at Princeton, Phillip Freneau, poet, wit, and experienced journalist, might be induced to come to Philadelphia to start a rival newspaper. Jefferson therefore offered Freneau the clerkship for foreign languages in his department; however, Freneau at first declined.

When Jefferson made Freneau a second offer, the young journalist accepted. Soon after he had begun publication of his paper, the *National Gazette,* Jefferson made efforts to secure subscriptions to the paper and wrote his son-in-law that it was "getting into Massachusetts, under the patronage of Hancock" and Samuel Adams.[13] In a short while Freneau had a considerable readership. He began with fairly mild criticisms of the Federalists; before long, however, his attacks became

---

11. Lipscomb and Bergh, 7:450.
12. Ford, *Writings,* 5:336.
13. Lipscomb and Bergh, 8:440.

more personal and vindictive. The Federalists were infuriated, whereupon Fenno published an article questioning the morality of Jefferson's sponsorship of a paper which attacked the administration in which he was a cabinet member. In reply Freneau published a sworn affidavit that Jefferson had no connection whatsoever with the paper, whose editor "was never directed, controlled, or attempted to be influenced in any manner either by the Secretary or any of his friends."[14]

Jefferson wrote Washington a long letter of explanation about his connection with Freneau, absolving himself of any responsibility for Freneau's attacks on the Federalists. Several months later Washington discussed the matter with him, becoming "sore and warm," Jefferson reported. "I took his intention to be, that I should interpose in some way with Freneau, perhaps by withdrawing his appointment as translating clerk in my office. But I will not do it," he declared. "His paper has saved our Constitution, which was galloping fast into monarchy."[15] A few months later, Washington expressed his rage over a lampoon of himself which had appeared in Freneau's paper. Jefferson reported the occasion as follows:

The President was much inflamed; he got into one of those passions when he cannot command himself; ran on much on the personal abuse which had been bestowed on him; defied any man on earth to produce one single act of his since he had been in the government, which was not done on the purest motives; that he had never repented but once having slipped the moment of resigning his office, and that was every moment since; that *by God* he had rather be in his grave than in his present situation; that he had rather be on his farm than be made *Emperor of the World;* and yet that they were charging him with wanting to be a King. That that *rascal Freneau* sent

14. Nathan Schachner, *Thomas Jefferson: A Biography,* 2 vols. (New York: Appleton-Century-Crofts, Inc., 1951), 1:444.
15. *Ibid.,* 1:492.

him three of his papers every day, as if he thought he would become the distributor of his papers; that he could see in this, nothing but an impudent design to insult him: he ended in this high tone.[16]

Jefferson's disavowal of any connection with Freneau's paper was correct, in the terms in which he put it to Washington: "that I never did by myself, or any other, directly or indirectly, write, dictate or procure any one sentence or sentiment to be inserted *in his, or any other gazette,* to which my name was not affixed or that of my office."[17] Jefferson was indeed careful not to write for newspaper publication. "At a very early period in my life I determined never to put a sentence into any newspaper,"[18] he said, and he implored his correspondents to guard his letters lest they "should get into the newspapers, a bear-garden scene into which I have made it a point to enter on no provocation."[19] Yet, it is clear that he was indeed involved with Freneau's paper, at least as a strong supporter; and it is also clear that, for political reasons, he was less than candid with Washington in this matter. Only once did he relax his rule against writing for newspaper publication—at least, under his own name—and that was in his old age, when he replied to accusations of improper conduct while he was President.

Freneau's paper discontinued publication, and a new paper supporting the Republicans appeared in Benjamin Franklin Bache's *Aurora.* Jefferson supported it by calling on his friends to subscribe, for if this paper, and one briefly published by Mathew Carey, failed, he said, "Republicanism will be entirely browbeaten."[20] Bache was

16. Lipscomb and Bergh, 1:382.
17. *Ibid.,* 8:403-4.
18. *Ibid.,* 10:58.
19. *Ibid.,* 10:173.
20. *Ibid.,* 10:32.

indicted for criminal libel just before the enactment of the Sedition Act in 1798, but died before his case came to trial.

The Sedition Act was designed, of course, to silence the opposition press. It provided that any person convicted of writing, printing, or uttering any "false, scandalous and malicious" statement against the government, the Congress, or the President "with intent to defame ... or bring them ... into contempt or disrepute" should be imprisoned for a period of not over two years and fined not more than two thousand dollars.[21]

Jefferson had predicted the enactment of such a bill several months before its passage. "There is now only wanting ... a sedition bill, which we shall certainly soon see proposed," he wrote Madison. "The object of that, is the suppression of the Whig presses."[22] When the Alien and Sedition Acts were passed, he prepared his Kentucky Resolutions to speak out against them, holding that these Acts were "not law, but ... altogether void, and of no force" because they were unconstitutional.[23] One of those indicted under the Act was James T. Callender. Jefferson had known him for some years, and in response to Callender's requests, had sent him money on several occasions after his arrest. When Jefferson became President, Callender requested that he be made postmaster at Richmond; however, Jefferson considered him unfit and refused his petition. The Federalists saw evil implications in Jefferson's contributions of money to Callender, and Callender himself turned violently against Jefferson and circulated numerous vicious stories about him, including the miscegenation charge.[24]

---

21. See Manning J. Dauer, *The Adams Federalists* (Baltimore: The Johns Hopkins Press, 1953), Appendix IV, pp. 343–48.

22. Lipscomb and Bergh, 10:32.

23. *Ibid.,* 17:382.

24. See Dumas Malone, *Jefferson and the Ordeal of Liberty* (Boston: Little, Brown and Company, 1962), pp. 466–72.

Upon his assuming office, Jefferson gave orders for the release of every person imprisoned under the Alien and Sedition laws, writing them each a personal letter apologizing for the government's action. He is justly honored today as the leader of the crusade against this attempt to destroy the freedom of the press.

In his more discouraged moments Jefferson must have wondered whether he had been right in letting the Sedition Act die, for after his election a Federalist free press attacked him with more virulence than perhaps any other American president has suffered. The violence of newspaper attacks during this era was such as to shock even those inured to political invective. And Jefferson was the prime target of the Federalist papers. "Were I to undertake to answer all the calumnies of the newspapers," he said, "it would be more than all my time and that of 20 aids could effect. For while I should answer one, twenty new ones would be invented."[25] He had been accused of almost every conceivable fault and shortcoming during the campaign of 1800, and these attacks continued after his election to the presidency. The abuses heaped upon him led him to say: "I have been for some time used as the property of the newspapers, a fair mark for every man's dirt."[26] But when he was overwhelmingly reelected in 1804, he wrote to a friend:

> The firmness with which the people have withstood the late abuses of the press, the discernment they have manifested between truth and falsehood, show that they may safely be trusted to hear everything true and false, and to form a correct judgment between them.[27]

Events had largely borne out the sentiments Jefferson expressed in his first inaugural address: "If there be any

25. Ford, *Writings*, 7:275.
26. Lipscomb and Bergh, 10:1–2.
27. *Ibid.*, 11:33.

among us who would wish to dissolve the Union or to change its republican form, let them stand undisturbed as monuments of the safety with which error of opinion may be tolerated where reason is left free to combat it."[28]

Jefferson had long been publicly committed to the belief that actions for libel against the press should be limited to private cases, and that public officials should have no such recourse. In 1803 he wrote to a French correspondent that "it is so difficult to draw a clear line between the abuse and the wholesome use of the press, that as yet we have found it better to trust the public judgment, rather than the magistrate, with the discrimination between truth and falsehood."[29]

However, he soon had cause to reconsider. The extreme "licentiousness" and "lying" of the Federalist papers began to appear to him to undermine the credit and reputation of the press in general. He began to feel that perhaps libel against public and political figures should be actionable, and that a few such cases would prove a wholesome corrective "in restoring the integrity of the presses."[30] However, he later reversed his stand and declared near the end of his second term that

as to myself, conscious that there was not a *truth* on earth which I feared should be known, I have lent myself willingly as the subject of a great experiment, which was to prove that an administration, conducting itself with integrity and common understanding, cannot be battered down, even by the falsehoods of a licentious press, and still less by the press, as restrained within legal and wholesome limits of truth. This experiment was wanting for the world to demonstrate the falsehood of the pretext that freedom of the press is incompatible with ordinary government. I have never, therefore, even contradicted the thousands of calumnies so industriously propagated against myself. But the fact being once established, that

28. Ford, *Writings,* 8:3.
29. Lipscomb and Bergh, 10:357.
30. Ford, *Writings,* 8:218.

the press is impotent when it abandons itself to falsehood, I leave to others to restore it to its strength, by recalling it within the pale of truth. Within that it is a noble institution, equally the friend of science and civil liberty.[31]

While Jefferson failed to maintain consistently his announced position that only private libels were actionable, even under the most extreme vituperation he did not discard his dedication to freedom of the press. He did waver under attack, it is true, and he was often deeply disillusioned in the performance of the press, as the Norvell letter makes clear. Even later in life he sometimes expressed his disillusionment. "From forty years' experience of the wretched guesswork of newspapers of what is not done in open daylight, and of their falsehood even as to that, I rarely think them worth reading, and almost never worth notice," he wrote Monroe in 1816.[32] In his old age he gave up newspapers except for Thomas Ritchie's Richmond *Enquirer,* and he said that he read in it "chiefly the advertisements, for they contain the only truths to be relied on in a newspaper."[33] Taken at face value, this would be a surprising statement, for it was Jefferson who suggested to Ritchie that he become a publisher, and Ritchie had remained a loyal supporter of Jefferson and Republicanism. Earlier Jefferson had assisted Samuel H. Smith in establishing the *National Intelligencer* as the spokesman for his administration during his terms as President. He had great respect for both Smith and Ritchie, and despite his protestations to the contrary, he read Ritchie's *Enquirer* to the end.

Jefferson was a sensitive man, and perhaps newspapers always reminded him of the attacks he suffered at their hands during his political career. "Never did a prisoner, released from his chains, feel such relief as I shall on shaking off the shackles of power," he wrote just before

31. Lipscomb and Bergh, 11:155.
32. *Ibid.,* 14:430-31.
33. *Ibid.,* 15:179.

his retirement.[34] And having long since returned to private life, the aged Sage of Monticello declared, "I read but a single paper, and that hastily. I find Horace and Tacitus so much better writers than the champions of the gazettes, that I lay those down to take up these with great reluctance."[35]

From the beginning of his career to its close, however, Jefferson held remarkably steadfast to his conviction that a free press was an essential element of the democratic system—this in spite of his sometimes bitter protests against newspaper attacks and his somewhat injudicious selection of journalists such as Callender to promote his cause. He abhorred censorship— ". . . for God's sake," he wrote, "let us hear both sides"[36] —and he returned at last to that advocacy of freedom of the press for which he is justly honored. Near the end of his life he wrote, "the press . . . is . . . the best instrument for enlightening the mind of man, and improving him as a rational, moral, and social being."[37]

In a democratic republic where an informed electorate is necessary for self-government, Jefferson understood the process of communication to be an essential one. Opinion formation in an atmosphere of freedom and rationality by means of a free press—this to him was both desirable and necessary in a free nation. His confidence in the inevitable victory of truth over falsehood led him to support freedom of expression as the best means to both wholesome protest and eventual consensus in a pluralistic society.

SOCIAL CONFLICT: REVOLUTION AND WAR

Jefferson's statement, "I hold it, that a little rebellion, now and then, is a good thing, and as necessary in the

34. *Ibid.,* 12:259.
35. *Ibid.,* 15:435.
36. *Ibid.,* 14:128.
37. *Ibid.,* 15:489.

political world as storms in the physical,"[38] has been seized upon by some to picture him as an extremist who advocated rebellion or revolution for the simple purpose of keeping the people politically awake to their rights and privileges. But it would be difficult to support this view in light of his frequent references to granting the people their rights in order to avoid the bloody necessity or rebellion.[39] His comment on the necessity of "a little rebellion, now and then" was made in reference to Shays's Rebellion of 1786-1787. Washington and Madison believed that the uprising was designed to secure an abolition of debts, public and private, and to effect a new distribution of property. When Jefferson heard from John Adams that the insurrection was in protest against new and heavy taxation on small farmers, he immediately called for relief from such burdens. After all, it was the group of independent farmers that Jefferson saw as the hope of democracy.

In regard to this same uprising, he wrote Abigail Adams of his hope that the malcontents would be pardoned:

> The spirit of resistance to government is so valuable on certain occasions, that I wish it to be always kept alive. It will often be exercised when wrong, but better so than not to be exercised at all. I like a little rebellion now and then. It is like a storm in the atmosphere.[40]

Jefferson, the superb literary stylist, seems to have been

---

38. Boyd, 11:93.

39. A case in point is his reference to the free press as follows: "This formidable censor of public functionaries, by arraigning them at the tribunal of public opinion, produces reform peaceably, which must otherwise be done by revolution." Lipscomb and Bergh, 15:489. Another example may be quoted from his first Inaugural Address, in which he called for "a jealous care of the right of election by the people—a mild and safe corrective of abuses which are lopped by the sword of revolution where peaceable remedies are unprovided." *Ibid.*, 3:321.

40. Ford, *Writings*, 4:370.

unable to resist the temptation to express himself in epigram or hyperbole, particularly when corresponding with old friends. It appears that many of the statements in his letters can be explained only on this basis—a characteristic of numerous good writers who employ hyperbole and exaggeration for the purpose of gaining attention and emphasizing a point. Jefferson obviously did not *like* rebellion, although he clearly preferred it to oppression. During the period of Shays's Rebellion he was in France, and what he had seen abroad no doubt hardened his opposition to oppression in any form. Furthermore, removed from the American scene as he was, he might well have understood imperfectly what was happening at home.

The statements he made on the desirability of rebellions and revolutions came almost exclusively from references to the Shays's insurrection. In another letter, he said of it: "Can history produce an instance of rebellion so honorably conducted? I say nothing of its motives. They were founded in ignorance, not wickedness . . . . God forbid that we should ever be twenty years without such a rebellion," for if the people remain quiescent under oppressions,

> it is . . . a forerunner of death to the public liberty . . . . And what country can preserve its liberties, if its rulers are not warned from time to time, that this people preserve the spirit of resistance? Let them take arms . . . . What signify a few lives lost in a century or two? The tree of liberty must be refreshed from time to time, with the blood of patriots and tyrants. It is its natural manure.[41]

These words appear extreme indeed, but Jefferson's purpose here was to encourage the officials in question not to punish the insurrectionists too severely. In Europe he had learned of harsh repressions in Holland, and

41. Boyd, 12:356.

he had become strongly aroused by what he took to be the trend away from popular liberties toward despotism in the United States. In a letter to Madison at the same time he clearly reveals his thinking.

> The late rebellion in Massachusetts has given more alarm than I think it should have done. Calculate that one rebellion in thirteen States in the course of eleven years, is but one for each State in a century and a half. No country should be so long without one. Nor will any degree of power in the hands of government, prevent insurrections . . . . And say, finally, whether peace is best preserved by giving energy to the government, or information to the people. This last is the most certain, and the most legitimate engine of government. Educate and inform the mass of the people. Enable them to see that it is their interest to preserve peace and order, and they will preserve them . . . . They are the only sure reliance for the preservation of our liberty.[42]

This position is in keeping with his philosophical justification of revolution in the Declaration of Independence, in which he declared, echoing Locke, that "whenever any form of government becomes destructive of" the rights of the people, it is their privilege "to alter or to abolish it," indeed, "it is their duty, to throw off such governments." Prudence, of course, "will dictate that governments long established, should not be changed for light and transient causes; and accordingly, all experience hath shown, that mankind are more disposed to suffer, while evils are sufferable, than to right themselves" by means of revolution. But, Jefferson clearly thought, rebellion and revolution are preferable to despotism and oppression, even at the cost of human lives. Peace with liberty was, of course, most to be desired—and educating the people the best means of equipping them to maintain their rights by peaceful means. Revolutions and rebellions may indeed have a salutary effect upon governments

---

42. *Ibid.*, 12:442.

—since all are prone to become tyrannical—but violence was to be employed only when peaceful means had failed to secure or protect the rights of the people. This was Jefferson's view.

As minister to France, Jefferson observed the revolution there during its early stages when it was principally philosophical in nature. Later, he said, "I had left France in the first year of its revolution in the fervor of natural rights and zeal for reformation. My conscientious devotion to these rights could not be heightened, but it had been aroused and excited by daily exercise."[43] His attitude toward the French Revolution as it moved through successive stages reflected the ambivalence of his feeling about revolutions.[44] As an experienced statesman who saw the practical danger of pushing too hard and too fast for abstract principles where circumstances were unfavorable, he often advocated caution; furthermore, he believed that the French people were not yet ready for liberty and self-government. And when violence broke out, he reacted with personal distaste, as his letters show. Apparently, the closer he was to bloodshed, the less he liked it.

As the excesses increased, he became apprehensive; yet at home, as Secretary of State, he continued his support of the revolutionary movement. He had been active in outlining its objectives, having consulted with Condorcet and Lafayette and having made suggestions on the latter's draft of the Declaration of Rights. His own Declaration of Independence and *Notes on the State of Virginia* had strongly influenced the revolutionary leaders in France, and shortly before leaving France he was invited to assist in the deliberations of the committee appointed by the National Assembly to draft a constitution, an honor his official position led him to decline.

43. Ford, *Writings,* 1:159.
44. Malone, *Jefferson and the Ordeal of Liberty,* p. 39.

But all along he had cautioned against haste and extremism, and had advocated the acceptance of a constitutional monarchy as the most desirable type of government for the France he knew so well.[45]

He could not turn his back on France; nor could he approve the growing excesses which became a source of great difficulties for him as Secretary of State. The principles for which the Revolution was fought led him to say in a personal letter to William Short:

> In the struggle which was necessary, many guilty persons fell without the forms of trial, and with them some innocent. These I deplore as much as any body, & shall deplore some of them to the day of my death. But I deplore them as I should have done had they fallen in battle . . . . The liberty of the whole earth was depending on the issue of the contest, and was ever such a prize won with so little innocent blood? My own affections have been deeply wounded by some of the martyrs to this cause, but rather than it should have failed, I would have seen half the earth desolated. Were there but an Adam & an Eve left in every country, & left free, it would be better than as it now is.[46]

Here again Jefferson was no doubt speaking in hyperbole—in the most extreme hyperbole of his life, in fact. Such a position could hardly be justified historically, philosophically, or morally, and his own disciplined life shows clearly that in this letter and others of its nature he realized he was speaking in those extremes which sometimes found their way into his private letters but never into his public documents. That his private words have been so widely quoted to a later public would, no doubt, have been a great surprise to him; and had he possessed the foresight, he might well have restricted his flights of rhetorical fancy even in his private letters. Before Lafayette had left the revolutionary movement

45. Ford, *Writings,* 1:141.
46. *Ibid.,* 1:154.

Jefferson had written him, "we are not to expect to be translated from despotism to liberty on a feather-bed."[47] He realized that freedom must be purchased with the blood of martyrs; however, he was not the wild-eyed revolutionary which some of his letters have caused him to appear to be. He understood that the great disruptions accompanying the process of rapid and extreme social change were to be expected; and if they led to liberty for the people, he believed that they were often worth the sacrifices involved.

However, he deplored the bloody excesses of the French Revolution and the oppressions of the Thermidorean Reaction. He regretted the execution of the king,[48] and he felt deep disillusionment in the outcome of this catyclysmic struggle, for he had been convinced that even the continued existence of democracy in America depended upon the success of the French Revolution.[49] His worldwide view of politics led him to believe that republicanism everywhere—even in the United States— would suffer attacks from abroad if the French struggle failed. Jefferson retained his allegiance to France as long as he could, but when war erupted between England and France, he spoke out for neutrality. "We wish not to meddle with the internal affairs of any country, nor with the general affairs of Europe," he wrote.[50] And, of course, as President he went to extreme lengths in his Embargo Act to avoid involvement in the war between France and England. The French Revolution had failed, and it was no doubt a sobered Jefferson who emerged as the political leader soon to assume the helm of government. Never again did he express himself in such extreme terms as those he had used regarding rebellions

47. Boyd, 16:293.
48. Ford, *Writings*, 1:141.
49. Leo Gershoy, *The Era of the French Revolution, 1789–1799* (Princeton, N. J.: D. Van Nostrand Company, Inc., 1957), pp. 77-78.
50. Lipscomb and Bergh, 9:56.

and revolutions at the time of the Shays insurrection and the French Revolution. Again, he was the practical idealist, and if he never lost his dedication to liberty—as, indeed, he did not—his early enthusiasm was tempered by the practicalities of administering a government.

Jefferson's optimism led him in early life to regard warfare as more civilized than it turned out to be.[51] He overemphasized the reasonableness of men. Early in the American Revolution he wrote: "It is the happiness of modern times that the evils of necessary war are softened by the refinement of manners & sentiments and that an enemy is an object of vengeance, in arms, & in the field only."[52] But the actualities of warfare proved somewhat different, as he had occasion to experience as governor of Virginia. Even the English gentleman Cornwallis had laid waste to his fields, crops, and stock; he had also carried off a number of his slaves to die of smallpox.

In the *Notes on Virginia* he declared, "Never was so much false arithmetic employed on any subject, as that which has been employed to persuade nations that it is in their interest to go to war." To avoid the possibility of becoming embroiled in wars he suggested that "it might be better for us to abandon the ocean altogether"[53] —something he tried to effect with his disastrous Embargo Act. "As to myself," he said, "I love peace and I am anxious that we should give the world still another useful lesson by showing to them other modes of punishment than by war, which is as much a punishment to the punisher as to the sufferer." Later he declared: "Peace then has been our principle, peace is our interest, and peace has saved to the world this only plant of free and

51. Dumas Malone, *Jefferson the Virginian* (Boston: Little, Brown and Company, 1948), p. 291.
52. Ford, *Writings,* 1:141, 494.
53. Lipscomb and Bergh, 2:240–41.

rational government now existing in it."[54] During the War of 1812 he decried "the acts of barbarism which do not belong to a civilized age,"[55] and it can certainly be said that he always preferred the ways of peace where he felt peace was possible. It can also be said that his primary dedication was to freedom and natural rights, and that if force became necessary to secure or protect them, he believed the struggle and the sacrifices worth the prize. And even in the time of war he remained still basically an optimist who believed that with the growth of knowledge and science mankind might progress toward the goal of liberty and equality in a world at peace.

SOCIAL CHANGE: INNOVATION AND PROGRESS

Jefferson, on the subject of invention, said:

> He who receives an idea from me, receives instruction himself without lessening mine; as he who lights his taper at mine receives light without darkening me. That ideas should freely spread from one another over the globe, for the moral and mutual instruction of man, and improvement of his condition, seems to have been peculiarly and benevolently designed by nature.[56]

He was a man of ideas as well as of action; he was an innovator who believed that the progress and happiness of mankind depend on both social and mechanical inventions spread freely abroad for the use of all. He emphasized the useful and practical in mechanical and social

---

54. Edward Dumbauld, ed., *The Political Writings of Thomas Jefferson* (Copyright, 1955, by The Liberal Arts Press, Inc.), pp. 181–82. Reprinted by permission of The Liberal Arts Press Division of The Bobbs-Merrill Company, Inc.

55. Lipscomb and Bergh, 14:190.

56. *Ibid.,* 13:334.

inventions—indeed, he made utility the criterion in morality as well as in the technical elements of culture.[57]

Jefferson had a clear idea of the process of innovation. To ask who commenced the Revolution, he said, was like asking who invented the steamboat. "The fact is, that one new idea leads to another, that to a third, and so on through a course of time until some one, with whom no one of these ideas was original, combines all together, and produces what is justly called a new invention."[58] He therefore correctly understood invention and innovation as a recombination of existing culture traits, just as he clearly desired that all beneficial innovations be disseminated widely by the process of cultural diffusion. It is the man who produces a new arrangement of ideas and materials who is the true inventor. He is also the benefactor of mankind.

As a man of the Enlightenment, Jefferson was committed to that view of progress which meant that he looked to the future for the realization of man's hopes. "I like the dreams of the future better than the history of the past," he said. He declared that he was not one "to go backwards instead of forwards to look for improvement; to believe that government, religion, morality, and every other science were in the highest perfection in ages of darkest ignorance, and that nothing can ever be devised more perfect than what was established by our forefathers."[59] He saw the improvement of the condition of man in America as a divinely appointed mission, with implications for the whole of humanity. Here, in a vast and magnificent natural laboratory, the experiment in democratic social interaction might be carried out; and if the people here proved capable of ruling themselves, so might men everywhere grasp the

---

57. *Ibid.*, 14:143.
58. *Ibid.*, 15:163.
59. Ford, *Writings*, 7:328.

opportunity to live in freedom. Thus, he hoped that even the Federal Constitution, by means of amendments, might "keep pace with the advance of the age in science and experience."[60] America offered humanity its first real opportunity to build a society founded upon the doctrine of natural rights, in which Jefferson confidently hoped that the happiness of the species might advance "to an indefinite although not infinite degree."[61] Jefferson was indeed optimistic about the future, although he did not share Condorcet's belief in the inevitability of progress, since to Jefferson man had a "fatal flaw" which would prevent this: his tendency to exploit his fellows. As a friend of Condorcet, he doubtless discussed with him the latter's concept of man's continuous progress from barbarism to ultimate perfection, and parts of the *Equisse d'un tableau historique des progrès de l'esprit humain* reflect ideas that Jefferson had expressed in his *Notes on the State of Virginia.*[62]

Jefferson like Condorcet had tremendous faith in education as a route to human betterment, and this faith, coupled with his zeal to advance the general welfare of mankind by an interchange of useful things,[63] provides a clue to the wide diversity of his activities. He was strongly utilitarian in outlook and once said that the reason for Benjamin Franklin's eminence was that he always tried to direct his efforts toward something useful and beneficial.[64] The same may largely be said of Jefferson. His dedication to science is in part to be explained by his eagerness to see discoveries made which would contribute to the good of mankind. He once spoke of

60. Daniel J. Boorstin, *The Lost World of Thomas Jefferson* (Boston: Beacon Press, 1948), p. 212.

61. Lipscomb and Bergh, 15:400.

62. Marie Kimball, *Jefferson: The Scene of Europe, 1784 to 1789* (New York: Coward-McCann, Inc., 1950), pp. 92–93.

63. Dumas Malone, *Jefferson and the Rights of Man* (Boston: Little, Brown and Company, 1951), p. xv.

64. Lipscomb and Bergh, 15:339.

chemistry as a science "big with future discoveries for the utility and safety of the human race."[65] In America, in particular, the opportunities for scientific progress were outstanding. To the President of Harvard he wrote:

> What a field have we at our doors to signalize ourselves in! The Botany of America is far from being exhausted, its Mineralogy is untouched, and its Natural History or Zoology, totally mistaken and misrepresented . . . . It is for such institutions as that over which you preside so worthily, Sir, to do justice to our country, its productions and its genius. It is the work to which the young men, whom you are forming, should lay their hands. We have spent the prime of our lives in procuring them the precious blessing of liberty. Let them spend theirs in showing that it is the great parent of *science* and virtue; and that a nation will be great in both, always in proportion as it is free.[66]

Liberty, science, national greatness—these were things to which Jefferson was dedicated. Science was a means to progress and to human happiness, and the future was bright with promise for free America. He ardently hoped that all useful science and knowledge might grow in the nation he had helped found. He was convinced that human intelligence could unlock the secrets of the universe and lead mankind toward a richer and better life. This was the faith of the Enlightenment, a faith he shared with Franklin, in particular. His confident hypotheses about universal natural law and natural rights guided his thought and his efforts throughout life. Freedom of inquiry, science, and reason—to him these were both goals and guides, and their natural Enlightenment corollary was progress via innovation and discovery in the advancement of the human species.

It was by means of rational, scientific improvements that Jefferson believed progress and social change would

65. *Ibid.,* 2:76.
66. Boyd, 14:699.

occur. As an innovator, he himself freely combined the ideas of many predecessors in devising plans to effect changes he considered desirable—in education, in government, in religion, in law, in agriculture, in science—and many of his proposals were successfully disseminated and widely adopted. Jefferson believed that man was an imitative creature and that this characteristic of human nature would insure social change and progress. And he was firmly convinced that rational evidence demonstrating the superiority of innovations and new discoveries would lead to their adoption.

Scientific innovation was to him, of course, the principal means of achieving betterment in human life. He encouraged inventions, both social and material, and was himself one of the great innovators of the modern world. Few men are his challengers in the variety and significance of his innovations, and certainly none of his fellow Americans excel him. The breadth and depth of his interests, as well as the variety and importance of his activities, are indeed staggering. It is doubtful that any other man has so shaped the culture of a democratic republic to the extent that he has. None stands out more importantly in the life and values of his nation than Jefferson, the disciple of progress, the wide-ranging and ingenious innovator, the special definer of situations during the crucial years of the nation's birth and troubled youth. And no man's words are more often quoted today to justify or explain its institutions and its ideology, or to point the direction for its future, for he has emerged as the dominant American culture hero.

Part III

Jefferson as Both
Social Scientist and Reformer

11

Apostle of Freedom, Activist, and Student of Society

THE INFLUENCE OF FRENCH THOUGHT

Thomas Jefferson's philosophy was an eclectic one, having radicles in the works and thoughts of many men and many nations. This is not surprising in the light of his effort to understand the whole of the intelligible world, natural and human, an approach common to the men of the Enlightenment. He was critical of the attitude of those who saw "a little of everything and the whole of nothing," just as he objected to the specialist who wrote in a jargon intelligible only to his professional colleagues.[1] He sought during his student days to lay a broad base upon which to build his intellectual life; and, as we have seen, he began with the study of the ancients—of Homer, Demosthenes, Cato, Livy, Tacitus, Cicero—and he continued to read them in the original throughout life.

But Jefferson was a man who looked less to the past than to the future, and the writers who influenced him most were not the ancients. The principal influences on

---

1. It will be recalled that he castigated lawyers for their specialized legal cant.

his thought were English and French writers of a later era. Many of his contemporaries considered him an excessive Francophile, contending that he took his morals, his "irreligion," his political philosophy, and his manners from the French, and as Patrick Henry said, even "abjured his native victuals" in favor of French foods. Jefferson was indeed strongly pro-French, and his five years in Paris left deep impressions on him.

The greatest single French influence on Jefferson during his formative years was Montesquieu, for whose *Esprit des Lois,* one of the earliest works of descriptive social science, he showed an ardent enthusiasm, transcribing voluminous notes from this great work into his *Commonplace Book.* He was profoundly interested in Montesquieu's definitions of popular sovereignty, his theory of federative republics, his examples of the relativity of laws and constitutions and the necessity for their modification in accordance with climate, local conditions, and new circumstances, and particularly Montesquieu's views on civil liberties and the processes by which democracies prosper or become corrupted. In his *Commonplace Book* Jefferson noted that Montesquieu

> considers political virtue or the Amor Patriae, as the energetic principle of a democratic republic; moderation, that of an aristocratic republic; honor, that of a limited monarchy; and fear, that of despotism; and shews that every government should provide that it's energetic principle should be the object of the education of its youth.
> That it's laws also should be relative to the same principle. In a democracy, equality and frugality should be promoted by the laws, as they nurse the amor patriae.[2]

Later in life he turned violently against Montesquieu because of the latter's advocacy of an English type of

---

2. Thomas Jefferson, *The Commonplace Book of Thomas Jefferson,* ed. Gilbert Chinard (Baltimore: The Johns Hopkins Press, 1926), pp. 37–38.

monarchy, and his doctrine that a republic could exist only in a small and restricted territory—two dogmas Jefferson thought he discovered in the Federalist approach. In 1810 he declared vehemently: "I am glad to hear of everything which reduces that author to his just level, as his predilection for monarchy, and English monarchy in particular, has done mischief everywhere, and here also, to a certain degree."[3]

Some have attributed to Rousseau a strong influence on Jefferson; however, such a position is insupportable. There is no evidence that he read Rousseau with any care, although he expressed himself quite clearly on the subject of the "natural" man, stating, "I have long been fatigued with the eternal repetition of the term *'man in the state of nature,'* by which is meant man in his savage and stupid state, with his faculties entirely undeveloped."[4] Jefferson found nothing appealing in such a doctrine.

He spoke occasionally of Voltaire, but Voltaire was certainly no great influence on him. On a number of occasions he referred favorably to Turgot and was obviously familiar with his work, but there is no evidence that Turgot was a formative influence on him, although he displayed a bust of this French savant at Monticello. The same can be said of Helvetius and of Descartes, whose *cogito ergo sum* he quoted from time to time.

As time went on, he often included ideas and quotations in his remarks from the *encyclopedistes, philosophes, idealogues* and physiocrats. He knew Turgot, Diderot, D'Alembert, Cabanis, Destutt de Tracy, Du Pont de Nemours, and Condorcet, and thought highly of them, particularly the latter two; he was a friend of

---

3. Thomas Jefferson, *The Writings of Thomas Jefferson,* ed. Andrew A. Lipscomb and Albert E. Bergh, 20 vols. (Washington: Thomas Jefferson Memorial Association, 1903), 12:404.
4. Nathan Schachner, *Thomas Jefferson: A Biography* (New York: Appleton-Century-Crofts, Inc., 1951), 2:728.

Lafayette, of course, and of Madame de Helvetius and the Comtesse d'Houdetot and Madame de Corny, of whom he seemed particularly fond, and of the Duc de La Rochefoucauld and his Duchesse. There can be no question that Jefferson was influenced by his many French friends, and throughout life he was fond of things French: cuisine, wines, architecture, sculpture, painting, music, and especially the French language.

Of all things French, however, he appears to have been most enthusiastic over the writings of Condorcet, Du Pont de Nemours, and Destutt de Tracy. He was particularly impressed with Comte Antoine Louis Claude Destutt de Tracy's *A Treatise on Political Economy,* and Jefferson himself translated this work from the French for printing in the United States.[5] Destutt de Tracy was a follower of the doctrines of Adam Smith, as was Jefferson. During his presidency, Lafayette sent him a copy of Jean-Baptiste Say's treatise on political economy and Destutt de Tracy's *Idéalogie.* Jefferson's enthusiasm for the latter writer was almost boundless: he considered Destutt de Tracy the greatest political and social philosopher of his age.[6] He was so eager to see Tracy's works published, particularly as an antidote to Montesquieu and Hume, that he went to great lengths to bring them before the public. Tracy was a strong liberal, following the "indisputable" laws of nature, and Jefferson thought it worth "ten-times" the work he had gone through—some four or five hours a day for a period of three months, in translating Tracy's *Political Economy* —to gain publication for the French thinker's work. He confessed, however, that he had never got entirely through the basic volumes on ideology, since "I am not

---

5. Manning J. Dauer, *The Adams Federalists* (Baltimore: The Johns Hopkins Press, 1953), p. 59.
6. Schachner, 2:893.

fond of reading what is merely abstract, and unapplied immediately to some useful science."[7]

Jefferson was also enthusiastic over the work of Cabanis, whose materialism reinforced his own, but he found a particularly warm spot in his heart for Pierre Samuel Du Pont de Nemours, whom he had known well in France; and when Du Pont decided in 1800 to emigrate to America, Jefferson was more than delighted. To Priestley, who had arrived from England in 1794, he wrote of an expected visit from Du Pont and expressed the hope that Priestley might visit at the same time. What a joy it would be, he said, to see "two such illustrious foreigners embracing each other in my own country, as an asylum for whatever is great and good."[8] Du Pont was a physiocrat. His work, *De l'Origine et des progrès d'une science nouvelle,* had expounded the doctrines that economic behavior is subject to natural laws, that everyone pursues his own self-interest, and that the only source of new wealth is agriculture, all other human activities being largely parasitical. He was a supporter of the laissez-faire policy, in the tradition of Quesnay and Turgot, from whom Adam Smith developed many of his ideas. There were of course strong elements of physiocracy in Jefferson's thinking and he was a great admirer of Du Pont, whom he considered "the ablest man in France," as he said to his son-in-law.[9] Du Pont eventually settled in Virginia, where his son established a gunpowder plant. Jefferson sought and received Du Pont's advice on education, as he did Priestley's, and suggested that the former might be appointed the first president of his proposed national university.

7. Lipscomb and Bergh, 15:73. For a more detailed discussion of Jefferson's views of Tracy, Cabanis, and others, see Adrienne Koch, *The Philosophy of Thomas Jefferson* (Chicago: Quadrangle Books, 1964).
8. Lipscomb and Bergh, 10:148.
9. Schachner, 2:634.

He always maintained a warm relationship with Du Pont and consulted with him on various matters.

During Jefferson's stay in France he had been on close terms with Condorcet, who was one of the three liberal noblemen he had entertained at a farewell dinner (the other two being Lafayette and La Rochefoucauld) before his return to America in 1789; and when the troublesome young "Citizen" Genet arrived from France, he brought with him a letter to Jefferson from Condorcet, in which the latter expressed the opinion that "our republic, founded like yours on reason, on the rights of nature, on equality, ought to be your true ally; we ought in some sort to form one people."[10] Such words could hardly fail to elicit a warm response from Jefferson, whose admiration for Condorcet was profound and sincere. Condorcet was one of the writers he suggested that law students read, and he was obviously impressed by Condorcet's concept of the inevitability of progress.

These men clearly exerted considerable influence on Jefferson—perhaps because they reinforced many of his own views.[11] It is certainly true that Jefferson adopted and promulgated the ideas of these French thinkers. Indeed, he regarded himself as being in some respects the American representative of the *idéalogues,* and he felt that their work would be of inestimable value to Americans and should therefore be emphasized in the curriculum of the university which he had founded.[12]

The ideas of progress put forward by Condorcet, Tracy, and Turgot, in particular, were strongly reflected in Jefferson's thought. And the words of Condorcet—

10. Dumas Malone, *Jefferson and the Ordeal of Liberty* (Boston: Little, Brown and Company, 1962), p. 96.

11. Dumas Malone, *Jefferson and the Rights of Man* (Boston: Little, Brown and Company, 1951), p. 154.

12. Lipscomb and Bergh, 19:263; see also Gilbert Chinard, *Jefferson et les idéalogues* (Baltimore: The Johns Hopkins Press, 1925), pp. 215–16.

awaiting death under sentence of the revolutionary tribunal—that the sun would one day shine "on an earth of none but free man, with no master save reason; for tyrants and slaves, priests and their stupid or hypocritical tools, will have disappeared,"[13] could not have failed to inspire Jefferson. His own optimistic faith in progress, if a lesser one than Condorcet's, had its impact upon American thought and values. As a culture hero, Jefferson personified the diffuse constellation of beliefs and attitudes which Robin Williams calls "the cult of progress," a major American value-orientation.[14] To fail to attribute in part the origin of this American belief in progress to these French thinkers, especially through Jefferson, would be less than honest.

A letter which Jefferson wrote Priestley in 1800 sums up his own ideas of progress, in words that might almost have come from the pen of Condorcet, Turgot, or another of the French writers:

> The Gothic idea that we are to look backwards instead of forwards for the improvement of the human mind, and to recur to the annals of our ancestors for what is most perfect in government, in religion, and in learning, is worthy of . . . bigots . . . . But it is not an idea which this country will endure; and the moment of their showing is fast ripening.[15]

THE INFLUENCE OF ENGLISH THOUGHT

Jefferson once described his philosophy of life as Epicurean, though he hastened to add that this term was widely misunderstood. He came to see the achievement

---

13. Page Smith, *The Historian and History* (New York: Alfred A. Knopf, 1964), p. 33.

14. Robin M. Williams, Jr., *American Society: A Sociological Interpretation* (New York: Alfred A. Knopf, 1965), p. 431. See also Kurt Riezler, "Political Science," in Edward N. Saveth, ed., *American History and the Social Sciences* (New York: The Free Press of Glencoe, 1964), pp. 81–82.

15. Lipscomb and Bergh, 10:148.

of happiness as the purpose of life, and to believe that happiness was to be gained by self-discipline within the framework of personal and political freedom.[16] His emphasis was obviously not on mere pleasure for its own sake. Happiness to him meant the possession of natural rights: life, liberty, knowledge, human fulfillment in a world designed by a benevolent Creator for man's use and enjoyment.

The chief source of Jefferson's doctrine of natural rights is generally agreed to have been John Locke. Among the English writers whom Jefferson carefully studied, as we have seen, was Lord Kames, the Scottish jurist and philosopher whose ideas were derived from Locke; and it was Kames who was the major source of Jefferson's Lockian concepts. He also read Sir Edward Coke and Lord Bolingbroke, as well as David Hume and Thomas Hobbes—and later in life the practical philosophy of the Scotsman Dugald Stewart. But it was Locke whose ideas were the most decisive and formative for Jefferson.

He copied relatively little from Locke in his student notebooks because, as a disciple of the Enlightenment, he was already familiar with the basic postulates of this writer. He accepted Locke's doctrine of the social contract without specifically terming it that. Like many of his enlightened contemporaries, he confidently accepted virtually all the major Lockian ideas that were such an important element in the thought of England, France, and America during his formative years.

Locke's influential restatement of the classical political doctrines of natural rights gained wide currency from his *Two Treatises of Government*. He had quoted the memorable dictum of the Roman jurist Ulpian that men

---

16. Thomas Jefferson, *The Writings of Thomas Jefferson,* ed. Paul Leicester Ford, 10 vols. (New York: G. P. Putnam's Sons, 1892–1899), 10:143.

are by nature created free and equal. Locke emphasized that government rested on a social contract of free men who gave up their primitive "state of nature" to preserve their inalienable "natural rights" of life, liberty, and property in a civil state. "Men being . . . by nature all free, equal, and independent, no one can be put out of this estate, and subjected to the political power of another without his consent,"[17] Locke declared. And, thinking in terms of the Glorious Revolution of 1688, Locke further asserted that whenever the social contract was violated by arbitrary rulers, the people were justified in revolting—a statement rephrased in the Declaration of Independence along with Locke's "life, liberty, and property." The influence of this doctrine on Jefferson is obvious.

Locke also, in his *Essay on Human Understanding,* offered a doctrine of materialism which gained wide acceptance and which may be detected in Jefferson's basic concepts. Rejecting Plato's mystical postulate of "innate ideas," Locke declared that "there is nothing in the mind except what was first in the senses"—that the mind was at birth a "tabula rasa," and that experience was the sole source of knowledge.[18] This empiricist doctrine owed much to the philosophy of the ancient Epicureans and Stoics. Locke's theory suggested that man was not an innately depraved creature, marred by original sin, but that he was capable of vast improvement, perhaps even perfection, in an invironment devoid of destructive elements. It also suggested by implication that the sanctity of property led men to seek their own self-interest and that therefore checks and balances were necessary in governmental administration in order to contain this predatory inclination of man—the fatal flaw in human

17. Harvey Wish, *Society and Thought in Early America* (New York: Longmans, Green and Company, 1950), p. 145.
18. *Ibid.,* p. 144.

nature to which Jefferson referred. Jefferson, however, placed less emphasis upon the sanctity of property than did many of Locke's followers, preferring instead to emphasize the Epicurean and utilitarian pursuit of happiness.

That Jefferson recognized his obligation to the Lockian doctrine is clear from the fact that he referred to Locke, Newton, and Bacon as his "trinity of immortals."[19] He considered these the real founders of the Enlightenment, much of the spirit of which he absorbed at Williamsburg from Small, Wythe, and Fauquier; and he himself became the almost perfect embodiment of the Enlightenment and in many ways its most conspicuous apostle on his side of the Atlantic,[20] although in many respects he moved far beyond Locke. His references to Locke were not numerous, but in a letter to his son-in-law he said that "Locke's little book on Government, is perfect as far as it goes."[21] Because his own thought embodied so much that was Lockian, perhaps he did not need to say more. Although much of it came to him through Kames, he recognized its ancestry.

He was familiar, of course, with the works of Hobbes; however, this writer's view that the social contract was irrevocable and therefore gave to the Leviathan state absolute power over the ruled was anathema to Jefferson. He may have agreed with Hobbes that life in a state of nature would be "solitary, poore, nasty, brutish and short"—he certainly had no sympathy for the "noble

---

19. Dumas Malone, *Jefferson the Virginian* (Boston: Little, Brown and Company, 1948), p. 101.

20. *Ibid.*, pp. 101–2.

21. Thomas Jefferson, *The Papers of Thomas Jefferson,* ed. Julian P. Boyd (Princeton: Princeton University Press, 1950–   ), 16:449. Locke was, of course, a constitutional monarchist who did not completely trust democracy. It was in this respect that Jefferson considered he did not go far enough. Vernon L. Parrington, "The Great Debate," in Earl Latham, ed., *The Declaration of Independence and the Constitution* (Boston: D. C. Heath and Company, 1956), p. 62.

savage" view of Rousseau, as we have seen—and he found no argument with Hobbes's materialism and empiricism; but no two views of government could be further apart than the Jeffersonian and the Hobbesian.

He had only a little less antipathy for Hume, whom, together with Montesquieu and Blackstone, he railed against for supporting the English monarchy. "In truth," he wrote, "Blackstone and Hume have made tories of all England, and are making tories of those young Americans whose native feelings of independence do not place them above the wily sophistries of a Hume or a Blackstone."[22] To these two favorite enemies he ascribed a greater "suppression of the liberties of man, than all the millions of men in arms of Bonaparte and the millions of human lives with the sacrifice of which he will stand loaded before the judgment seat of his Maker."[23] So great was his abhorrence of Hume, whom he admitted to be an excellent historian aside from his biases and distortions, that Jefferson advocated the use of Baxter's *History of England* for students because Baxter, in quoting Hume, "then alters the text silently"—in other words, so skillfully that the reader is unaware of the changes made in Hume's text. This seems to be about as close as Jefferson ever came to approving censorship, and it is indicative of how pernicious he believed the influence of Hume to be.

Jefferson was also impressed with James Harrington's *The Commonwealth of Oceana,* which was intended to be a constructive answer to Hobbes's Leviathan. In Harrington's utopia the head of the state was elected by the people; there was freedom with equality, property was limited, and war was disapproved. Harrington was an advocate of natural rights and therefore appealed to Jefferson.

---

22. Lipscomb and Bergh, 14:118–20.
23. *Ibid.*

He of course read Bacon, Gibbon, Shakespeare, Milton, Pope, Dryden, and other English writers, but it was the social contract theorists who influenced him most strongly; and, of course, it was Locke whose ideas he most consistently reflected and whose doctrines were such a crucial influence on Jefferson's basic approach to life, in politics and otherwise.

JEFFERSON AS REVOLUTIONIST

A major writer on Jefferson, Daniel Boorstin, contends that Jefferson and his Virginia colleagues owed no debt to the French and English thinkers who preceded them. Instead, Boorstin sees the thinking of the Virginia Revolutionary leaders as a natural outgrowth of the aristocratic republicanism which developed in that colony at the hands of a gentry of land and birth sincerely dedicated to public service, which Charles Sydnor has so well depicted. When we understand this background, Boorstin says, "the philosophers of the European Enlightenment who have been hauled into the court of historians as putative fathers of the Revolution may then seem . . . irrelevant."[24] He points out that this Virginia aristocracy consciously patterned itself after the English gentry and was therefore basically conservative; it was, however, an aristocracy of men seeking to enhance their wealth and position as well as to preserve them. Its proudly independent spirit was rooted in the plantation system with its many responsibilities; the value it placed on individual liberty was shaped by the ever-present contrast with slavery; its "habit of command" was based on the belief that the aristocrats could make better decisions for the community than could the people them-

---

24. Daniel J., *The Americans: The Colonial Experience* (New York: Random House, 1958), p. 110.

selves. These characteristics, Boorstin suggests, produced the Virginia revolutionaries.[25]

Boorstin is, of course, in a sense right; however, the local circumstances which brought forth the Virginia Revolutionary leadership did not exist in a vacuum. The aristocracy of Virginia, generally speaking, was an educated one; and to deny influence to the knowledge and information these men had absorbed from their studies would be unrealistic. When Jefferson spoke of one idea leading to others through a course of time until someone, with whom none of the ideas was perhaps original, combines them into a new invention,[26] he displayed a clearer understanding of both the general process of change and the emergence of a specific new social movement than has Boorstin. Even if the origins of the American Revolution were principally local in character, the philosophical justification of this movement had clear roots in Locke and the thinkers of the European Enlightenment, as the Declaration of Independence makes obvious.

The sense in which Boorstin is largely right is his emphasis upon the essentially conservative outlook of the Virginia Revolutionaries. These Revolutionary leaders thought of themselves as Englishmen being denied their fundamental rights by a misguided Parliament; and, furthermore, the colonies had in fact been subject to really serious exploitation only since 1763. Their primary objective was to preserve the English rights guaranteed to them in their charters, and what perturbed them most, as Marcus Cunliffe says, was the assumption of the mother country that they were not parts of Britain but possessions of Britain.[27] It is certainly true that the Amer-

---

25. *Ibid.,* p. 140.
26. Lipscomb and Bergh, 15:163.
27. *George Washington, Man and Monument* (New York: Mentor Books, 1960), p. 63.

ican colonies had developed somewhat divergent interests from those of the mother country—economic, social, and political—but it was largely the ineptness of the British leadership which forced the Americans to take up arms and seek independence.[28] The social and economic consequences of the Revolution were largely by-products of the struggle for political independence. The insistence that all government is limited, and that even rulers are subject to law, bound the Revolutionary patriots together.

It was of such men as these that Jefferson was a leader. In his private letters he often spoke in hyperbole, as we have seen, but in his public documents he was careful to justify his proposals on the basis of history, morality, law, and philosophy. In the *Summary View* and the Declaration of Independence he articulated the feelings of most of his fellow revolutionaries that what the Americans had desired was not separation from England but the enjoyment of their natural rights as Englishmen. It was only when any hope of receiving such rights had faded that he and his colleagues sought independence. In this sense, he too was conservative.

If we take the term revolutionary to mean a believer in sudden and sweeping change, it would be difficult to think of Washington as revolutionary—indeed, as an intemperate radical of any sort.[29] The same might be said of Pendleton, Madison, Edmund Randolph, and most of the Virginia Revolutionary leadership. And, in a sense, the same may be said of Jefferson, the disciple of reason, science, and the Enlightenment. That he was more radical than most of his contemporaries among the

---

28. John C. Miller, *The Federalist Era, 1789–1801* (New York: Harper and Row, Publishers, 1963), pp. 1–10. See also Lawrence Harvey Gipson, *The Coming of the Revolution, 1763–1775* (New York: Harper and Row, Publishers, 1962), pp. 1–27, and John C. Walhke, ed., *The Causes of the American Revolution* (Boston: D. C. Heath and Company, 1962).

29. See Cunliffe, pp. 62–82.

elite is clear, for he, perhaps more than any of them, wished the Revolution to be a social as well as a political movement: he wished to free the people from "every form of tyranny over . . . man," religious, intellectual, and political. He insisted first and fundamentally upon the primacy of human rights in every area of life, and as time passed he became increasingly democratic. Yet as a reformer, he was essentially a gradualist in temperament, who looked forward with longing to the establishment of the rule of reason. His preference for gradualism was clearly demonstrated during the French Revolution, when he said, "It is to be feared that an impatience to rectify every thing at once, which prevails in some minds, may . . . lead . . . to force."[30]

This may not sound like the Jefferson of the American Revolution, who is often pictured as a fierce rebel and firebrand; and it appears to be true that he mellowed on the subject of rebellion and revolution as time passed. It must be remembered, however, that Jefferson no more had in mind an utterly complete restructuring of American life following the Revolution than did many of his fellow leaders. He did not wish to discard the system of law, property rights, and representative legislatures: he wished only to improve and correct them. He was certainly not a man who feared change or despaired of the future; rather, he was one whose optimism and belief in progress led him to look forward confidently to greater happiness for all by means of rectifying the ideology as well as the institutions within which corporate interaction takes place—all in consonance with his natural rights doctrine.

Jefferson has often been called "the Pen of the Revolution," and the phrase is an apt one. He fought no battles and harangued no crowds. It was his facility for written

---

30. Boyd, 14:213.

expression that more than anything else projected him into the forefront of the Revolutionary struggle, and he stated its origins and goals with greater clarity and eloquence than did any others. There is no doubt that his words inspired many of his contemporaries and elevated the objectives of this struggle to a higher plane than the purposes of many who entered it for less noble reasons than his. He was the propagandizer, and such he continued to be throughout life. In this sense he was a true revolutionary whose leadership was more decisive in the long run than that of the military commanders and the administrative functionaries. It is also true that his words helped to stabilize the determination of the people and to develop the degree of consensus necessary if the struggle were not to fail.

Thus, Jefferson the intellectual helped give legitimacy to the revolutionary struggle and awakened the masses to a consciousness of injustice, linking the leaders of the movement with the people in the struggle for the rights he insisted were theirs, just as he had earlier helped establish ideological consensus among the leaders of the interest groups supporting the movement.

It may be true that revolutions change men's minds more than they change men's habits,[31] and it was men's minds that Jefferson sought to change, confident that a change in their behavior would follow. Not only was he a leader in the political revolution by means of which the colonies attained their independence; he was even more of a revolutionist in the fields of education, law, and church-state relations. The changes which he advocated and actively promoted were designed to alter the whole spectrum of American life—again, not abruptly but gradually, preserving from the old that which he felt to be desirable and changing that which he felt to be objectionable.

---

31. Crane Brinton, *The Anatomy of Revolution* (New York: Vintage Books, 1959), p. 261.

He was not, of course, the same type of revolutionary as those who sought to overturn complete social systems, any more than were the other leaders of the American Revolution. Social, economic, and political changes resulted from this struggle, and many of them were of far-reaching consequence. Furthermore, the Revolution resulted in the establishment of a republican form of government in a large nation, the first in modern history. But it must not be forgotten that the justification of the Revolution was the claim of Americans to their natural rights of self-government and freedom from arbitrary and authoritarian power—a very English justification originally proposed by an Englishman to vindicate an English revolution which had taken place almost a hundred years earlier. Still, it must be remembered that these "English" rights were those not yet actually enjoyed by the people of Great Britain, and that Jefferson as a revolutionist perceived and expressed these rights better than his contemporaries—and, indeed, went far beyond them, particularly in his dedication to the rights of the people. Politically, it was in the area of democracy that Jefferson was most decidedly the revolutionary.

Although Daniel Boorstin, Clinton Rossiter, and a number of other historians have in recent years advanced the view that there was little about the American Revolution which was democratic, others have correctly taken the position that in spite of the paradoxes involved, the Revolution was still essentially, if relatively, a democratic movement, and that its significance lay in the fact that it tended to increase the political power of the majority of the people. It was here that Jefferson was the spokesman supreme for the kind of rights which were not yet English. "The first principle of republicanism," he said, "is, that the *lex majoris partis* [majority rule] is the fundamental law of every society of individuals of equal parts; to consider the will of society enounced by the majority . . . as sacred . . . is the first of all lessons of importance"—though in most of the world he saw the democratic rights of the people as frustrated by "the blinds of bigotry, the shackles of the priesthood, and the fascinating glare of rank and wealth."[32] In his First Inaugural Address he asserted that "though the will of the majority is in all cases to prevail, that will, to be rightful, must be reasonable . . . the minority possess their equal rights, which equal laws must protect, and to violate which would be oppression."[33]

Few of his contemporaries conceptualized so well, or phrased so effectively, or fought for so tirelessly, the democratic rights of the people as did Jefferson. Washington, Adams, Hamilton, and others so important during the Revolutionary and post-Revolutionary periods had far too little confidence in the people to be called democrats in the sense that Jefferson was—and even he recognized clearly the necessity for the people to be educated if they were to be capable of governing themselves.

Jefferson, though far more the revolutionist—that is, the believer in rather sudden and sweeping change—than his contemporaries, was not, however, an erratic democratic firebrand. In spite of the rashness to be found in some of his private letters, he had few illusions about what the Revolutionary struggle would accomplish. Before it had ended, he said:

> From the conclusion of this war we shall be going down hill. It will not then be necessary to resort every moment to the people for support. They will be forgotten, therefore, and their rights disregarded. They will forget themselves . . . . The shackles, therefore, which shall not be knocked off at the conclusion of this war, will remain on us long.[34]

What better justification could be found for needed sud-

32. Lipscomb and Bergh, 15:127.
33. *Ibid.*, 3:318.
34. *Ibid.*, 2:225.

den and sweeping changes while the opportunity was at hand? He may therefore properly be called a radical by comparison with most of his contemporaries; for, among other things, the democratic changes he advocated would indeed eventually sweep away the aristocratic structure which had enabled him to gain entrance into the power elite, an end he consciously sought but one which few among the Virginia Revolutionary leadership desired.

Always, in the final consideration a practical idealist, he might well be called a rational revolutionist.

JEFFERSON AS POLITICIAN

If politics may be characterized as the art of the possible, then the successful politician must be an exceedingly practical man. That Jefferson was an idealist few will deny; that he was an eminently successful politician none can doubt. The emergence of the philosopher of the Revolution, often speaking in highly eloquent if highly generalized terms, as the leader of a broadly-based popular political party involves one of the most striking and fascinating aspects of Jeffersonian study. Originally unconvinced of the desirability of political parties, he came at last to view them as the hope of democracy, and as President his administration achieved an almost ideal "model of responsible democratic party government in office."[35]

The practical fulfillment of the democratic promise contained in the Declaration of Independence depended no less upon the establishment of a government than upon the establishment of a viable system of political parties. Indeed, if democracy were to work, the legitimacy and authority of government had to be undergirded by a party system in which the conflict of interests and

---

35. William Nisbet Chambers, *Political Parties in a New Nation* (New York: Oxford University Press, 1963), pp. 10-11.

opinions might be resolved peaceably within the framework of national unity. It is one of the impressive facts
of our history that the man who wrote the Declaration
of Independence was also the founder and leader of
the first opposition party, an accomplishment which in
the long run gave legitimacy to a system of free choice
via which the people might express the will of the majority in a plural society.

It was, of course, the differing views of which Hamilton and Jefferson were the spokesmen which led to the
appearance of contesting parties, and Hamilton was no
less the founder of a political party than was Jefferson.
Washington himself, although disapproving of parties,
came eventually to be identified with partisan politics,
and by 1793, when Jefferson resigned as Secretary of
State, sought advice almost entirely from a coterie of
Federalist-minded leaders. "Active leadership" and a
"freely recruited following," as Max Weber observed,
"are the necessary elements in the life of any party,"[36]
and Hamilton provided this leadership for those whom
he recruited as supporters of the Federalist party, while
at the same time, by his attacks on Jefferson, he established the latter as the symbol of opposition to Hamiltonian principles and policies.

In 1792 Jefferson announced what he called his "Catholic principle of republicanism" as follows:

> We certainly cannot deny to other nations that principle
> whereon our government is founded, that every nation has a
> right to govern itself internally under whatever forms it
> pleases, and to change these forms at its own will . . . . The
> only thing essential is the will of the nation.[37]

His statement "the will of the nation" implied, of
course, the will of the people, and he may have had in

36. *Ibid.,* p. 45.
37. Lipscomb and Bergh, 9:7–8.

mind this statement as the foundation upon which an opposition political party would be erected. After leaving the Washington cabinet, he made no secret of his feeling that "where the principle of difference is as substantial and as strongly pronounced as between the republicans and the Monocrats of our country, I hold it honorable to take a firm and decided part, and as immoral to pursue a middle line, as between parties of honest men and rogues."[38] From this time on, he wrote numerous letters to those who sympathized with his views, crystallizing the anti-Federalist sentiment around himself as opposition leader. Finally, in 1797, he fully accepted the leadership of the now important opposition party—an action he justified on patriotic and philosophical grounds—and from that date forward partisanship colored his actions and judgments to a far greater degree than in his earlier career.[39] Although as Vice-President he could not act openly, he continued to structure the party for the fateful election of 1800, and by means of the Kentucky Resolutions, in particular, he drew dramatic attention to what he saw as the evils of Federalist policies and principles without overtly attacking the administration of which he was a part. By campaign time, he had organized a well-disciplined and effective political party which provided the means to gain the presidency.

It appears clear that Jefferson's primary motivation was to save the nation he had helped found. Ever since his return from France in 1789, he had become increasingly agitated over the undemocratic tendencies of the leadership in power, and he was doubtless honest both in his desire not to enter the political arena and in his determination to unseat the Federalists and redirect the nation on the democratic course he had been such a formative influence in designing for it. The party he

38. Ford, *Writings,* 7:43.
39. Malone, *Jefferson and the Ordeal of Liberty,* p. 334.

helped organize and of which he was the most important
leader was a broadly based one of wide appeal to the
people, who to him were the rightful holders of power
in a democratic republic.

Through the efforts of Jefferson and his followers,
the New York-Virginia alliance became the axis of Republican electoral strength, with local cadremen and
activists setting up a grass-roots political organization
which soon extended into other states. Rallies were held
in numerous localities and the lines of political battle
were drawn. Support crystallized around Jefferson, in
whose personality there was little of drama and urgency
but who possessed something of a charismatic appeal that
drew men to him.

The contrast between the parties, however, was dramatic. The Federalist tendency was basically aristocratic;
it was also Anglican, legalistic, and hierarchical. On the
other hand, the Republican ideology—reflecting both the
Enlightenment and Puritanism—was democratic, noncon-
formist, deistic, individualistic, romantic, and anti-his-
torical.[40] Jefferson was the embodiment of Republicanism
just as Locke was in a very real sense its ideological
father.

Careful planning for the election of 1800 characterized Republican efforts in the months before the campaign. Jefferson insisted that for success "the engine is
the press" and advocated that "every man lay his purse
and pen under contribution,"[41] although, as we have seen,
the Federalist newspapers attacked him viciously. But
appeal to the people through the press was not enough,
and the careful organization and planning of the Republicans brought the issues to the fore through rallies,
propaganda, conventions, caucuses, committees, and
"celebrations." The overwhelming Republican victory

---

40. Chambers, p. 92.
41. Lipscomb and Bergh, 10:334.

was a vindication of majority rule, and the peaceful transfer of power from the Federalists to the Republicans
represented a major step toward full acceptance of rational legitimacy.[42]

Jefferson spoke of his election as "the revolution of
1800" and set about, as a strong executive, to fulfill
the mandate of the people, maintaining a close and successful relationship with Congress, seeking cohesion by
means of the caucus, the speakership, the committees,
and floor leaders, as well as informal connections with
the legislators, with whom he conferred regularly. His
leadership was efficient and effective, particularly during
his first term.

He was a man who understood politics eminently well.
Striving for national consensus, he attempted to reassure
the moderates and to allay the passions which the bitter
campaign had excited. "We are all Republicans, we are
all Federalists,"[43] he declared in his First Inaugural Address.

In office he sought the support of all elements of the
population, even the mercantile interests; he acted cau-
tiously to undo the Federalist innovations, moving quickly
in the case of the Alien and Sedition Acts but never
destroying the Hamiltonian bank. He sought to make
real the guarantees of the Constitution as he understood
them and above all to insure the rights of the people,
generally demonstrating an exceedingly high sense of
political responsibility. The remarkable consensus he
achieved among the people was reflected in the election
of 1804, when the Republicans won 162 of the electoral
votes and the Federalists only 14. If his second administration was less successful than his first, as indeed it
was, international tensions and the threat of war were
to blame, along with the fateful embargo he sought to

---

42. Chambers, p. 168.
43. Lipscomb and Bergh, 3:319.

employ as a means to avoid embroiling the nation in the struggle between European powers. Even so, the continued success of the Jeffersonian principles as embodied in the administrations of Madison and Monroe give adequate testimony to the broad appeal of the popular party he had helped found and which he so effectively led.

As one of the most successful politicians in the nation's history, Jefferson would no longer be known only as the idealist and the disciple of rationalism and science. He had proven himself, magnificently, as the activist and practical man of affairs.

JEFFERSON AS SOCIAL THINKER AND PLANNER

The confident hypotheses which underlay Jefferson's thinking were based on the doctrine of natural rights and natural law. The species "man" was to be understood in the context of nature, not in the context of social institutions, which were but imperfect human inventions. The objective of Jeffersonian social science was therefore not to work out a blueprint for society but to discover the plan implicit in nature, which he, like the *philosophes,* had imbued with divinity. The realization of man's highest possibilities was to occur in fulfilling the *natural* potentialities of the species. It was thus the natural laws of society which men must discover and under which they must live if their pursuit of happiness was to prove successful—following "those moral rules which the Author of our nature has implanted in man as the law of his nature, to govern him in his associated, as well as individual character."[44]

"Man was destined for society," Jefferson declared.

---

44. Adrienne Koch and William Peden, eds. *The Life and Selected Writings of Thomas Jefferson* (New York: Random House, Inc., 1944), p. 345.

He was endowed with a sense of right and wrong, merely relative to this. This sense is as much a part of his nature, as the sense of hearing, seeing, feeling; it is the true foundation of morality.[45]

Jefferson's approach was of course materialistic. A moral sense, made necessary by the demands of social living, was implanted in man by an all-wise Creator. This was not theological or metaphysical reasoning, as Jefferson saw it, but was consonant with his materialism, for the

moral sense, or conscience, is as much a part of man as his arm or leg. It is given to all human beings in a stronger or weaker degree, as force of members is given them in a greater or lesser degree. It may be strengthened by exercise, as may any particular limb of the body. This sense is submitted, indeed, in some degree, to the guidance of reason; but it is a small stock which is required for this.[46]

On another occasion he stated this concept somewhat differently, saying "Nature hath implanted in our breasts a love of others, a sense of duty to them, a moral instinct, in short."[47] These were social virtues without which corporate life was impossible. "The Creator would have been a bungling artist," he continued, "had he intended man for a social animal, without planting in him social dispositions." However, it is unfortunately "true they are not planted in every man, because there is no rule without exceptions." For example, "some men are born without organs of sight, or of hearing, or without hands. Yet it would be wrong to say that man is born without these faculties."[48]

When the moral sense is lacking in individuals,

---

45. Boyd, 12:15.
46. *Ibid.*
47. Lipscomb and Bergh, 14:141.
48. *Ibid.*, 14:142.

we endeavor to supply the defect by education, by appeals to reason and calculation, by presenting to the individual so un-happily conformed, other motives to do good and to eschew evil, such as the love, or the hatred, or rejection of those among whom he lives, and whose society is necessary to his happiness and even existence.[49]

Here Jefferson suggests the role institutions are to play in order to effect the social control necessary in human society. He states that the individual devoid of the moral sense must be presented

demonstrations by sound calculation that honesty promotes in-terest in the long run; the rewards and penalties established by the laws; and ultimately the prospects of a future state of retribution for the evil as well as the good done while here. These are the correctives which are supplied by education, and which exercise the functions of the moralist, the preacher, and legislator; and they lead into a course of correct action all those whose disparity is not too profound to be eradicated.[50]

Jefferson's great concern for social control derived from his conviction that moral norms were necessary for social life. But if this moral sense is a natural instinct, how is it that the definition of morality differs from cul-ture to culture? How can it be that moral norms vary from one society to another? Recognizing that "the same actions are deemed virtuous in one country and vicious in another," he contends

that nature has constituted *utility* to man, the standard and test of virtue. Men living in different countries, under different circumstances, different habits and regimens, may have different utilities; the same act, therefore, may be useful, and conse-quently virtuous in one country which is injurious and vicious in another differently circumstanced.[51]

49. *Ibid.*
50. *Ibid.,* 14:142–43.
51. *Ibid.,* 14:143. It is interesting that Jefferson here anticipated the conclusions of contemporary anthropologists and sociologists, as well as of those modern moralists who concern themselves with "situation ethics."

If Jefferson's belief in a moral instinct was erroneous according to the understandings of modern psychology and sociology, his recognition of the variability of culture was not; furthermore, his standard of utility in the sense of fulfilling human needs is entirely consonant with the postulates of contemporary sociological functionalists, just as his concept of a moral instinct was with the views of earlier social psychologists. His social thought and social planning were based on his belief in this inborn moral sense, which he considered "the brightest gem with which the human character is studded."[52]

However, he believed that the moral conceptions which men developed regarding their social obligations varied. Politically, "men by their constitutions are naturally divided into two parties," he said:

> 1. Those who fear and distrust the people and wish to draw all powers from them into the hands of the higher classes. 2. Those who identify themselves with the people, have confidence in them, cherish and consider them as the most honest and safe, although not the most wise depository of the public interests.[53]

It was, of course, the "natural aristocracy of virtue and talents," educated and trained for public service, which was to provide the wisdom for leadership. Education was therefore essential, even for those possessing a healthy moral instinct. And even among them there existed the natural division into two orientations regarding the people, for the moral instinct only inspired "a love of others, a sense of duty toward them"; it did not include a blueprint for fulfilling this moral and social duty. Utility to society was the criterion of morality, and this was determined by the culture and its values. The two political orientations were universal:

---

52. *Ibid.*
53. *Ibid.*, 14:73-74.

> In every country these two parties exist . . . . Call them
> . . . Liberals and Serviles, Jacobins and Ultras, Whigs and
> Tories, Republicans and Federalists, Aristocrats and Demo-
> crats, or by whatever name you please, they are the same
> parties still, and pursue the same object. The last appellation
> of Aristocrats and Democrats is the true one expressing the
> essence of them all.[54]

There can be no question regarding which of these
orientations Jefferson felt to be consistent with the design
of nature. But since political institutions were of human
origin, no specific political party could be considered
either perfect or permanent. "I had always expected that
when the republicans should have put down all things
under their feet, they would schismatize among themselves,"[55] he wrote. Human institutions were but imperfect instruments; the objective of man was to discover
and adapt to the plan inherent in nature, for the human
species was a part of nature and therefore subject to
the laws of nature. Jefferson's science of society was
based on natural laws and not on human institutions.

Man, because of his exploitative character, was of
course not perfect; in all the animal kingdom there is
no "single species but man which is eternally and sys-
tematically engaged in the destruction of its own species
. . . the lions and tigers are mere lambs compared with
man as a destroyer."[56] Jefferson never explained in any
detail the functional reason for this fatal flaw which
existed in humanity in spite of the moral instinct, but he
appeared to believe that it served the purpose of maintaining a demographic balance and preventing overpopulation. "This pugnacious humor," he observed, "seems
to be the law of his nature, one of the obstacles to too
great multiplication provided in the mechanism of the

---

54. *Ibid.*, 14:74.
55. *Ibid.*, 11:265.
56. *Ibid.*, 9:359.

universe."⁵⁷ It is also clear that as a humanitarian Jefferson recoiled from the evidence of man's destructive nature. In writing of the excesses committed by the people during the French Revolution in the name of liberty, he said, "Yet these were men, and we and our descendants will be no more."⁵⁸

Whatever his view of the origin of mankind's exploitative propensities, he was optimistic about the future of man, particularly in America, where he confidently hoped that human happiness might advance "to an indefinite, although not an infinite degree."⁵⁹ His view of man was not unrealistically idealistic; he was aware of the defects of the species—defects which he no doubt saw as a part of the plan of nature. This did not lead him to any such conclusion as that implied in the "natural selection" or "survival of the fittest" doctrine of social Darwinism. He was profoundly and unchangingly humanitarian, and most of the efforts of his life were directed toward the attainment of man's happiness and well-being.

Because institutions were of human invention and development, they were not sacred. Man's goal was to fit the perfect plan of nature: this concept, also held by the Physiocrats, was the foundation of his social thought. However, human institutions were the means whereby man sought to discover the plan of nature and adapt to it. They were therefore important elements in his social science, and he spent the major portion of his life actively promoting those forms of institutional behavior which he felt would guide man toward the attainment of the happiness which the Creator had intended. He firmly

---

57. *Ibid.*, 15:372. He appeared to agree with Malthus that war was among the checks on overpopulation and a part of "the economy of nature." He praised the "masterly work" of Malthus but felt the latter's doctrines required considerable modification before being applied to America. *Ibid.*, 10:477 and 11:1.
58. *Ibid.*, 15:360.
59. *Ibid.*, 15:400.

believed that great progress was possible, but he was no utopian, for he saw the nature of man as unchangeable, although he believed that man's capacity for adjustment was susceptible of much improvement. What he sought was a state of equilibrium in society analogous to that in the natural world. Integration he saw as not only desirable but necessary; however, he understood that stresses and strains were a natural and inevitable aspect of human interaction. The life of individual and collective man was to him a process of dynamic searching, attempting, adjusting, adapting—all within the framework of the institutions available for man's use.

Perhaps the best single clue to Jefferson is to be found in his conviction that men should be free so that they might progress toward happiness and fulfillment by the use of ever-expanding knowledge.[60] He was both a thinker and an activist, and his plans for the improvement of the society in which he lived were oriented toward the institutions of that society: education, politics, law, and all other institutional structures. The most crucial of these was education. Political and governmental structures and functions were important indeed; but in the larger sense, it was knowledge, reason, and science which held out the best hope for the betterment of humanity. His conclusion that the people were governed best who were governed least emphasized his view that governments existed only to protect the natural, inalienable rights. It was education which was to save the people from that tyranny of which he was always the ardent and watchful enemy—tyranny over the mind, the conscience, the person. Freedom was essential for happiness, for the realization of man's natural potentials according to the plans of nature. And it was education which was to equip the people to defend themselves from the am-

---

60. Malone, *Jefferson and the Rights of Man,* p. xvi.

bitions that political structures provided potential tyrants the best means of attaining. Jefferson may be said to have believed in salvation by knowledge and in human fulfillment by science and reason in the liberating atmosphere of freedom from "every form of tyranny over the mind of man."[61]

This was the high purpose which motivated his thought and efforts, and in the accomplishment of this purpose, human institutions were to be utilized, always modifying, shaping, and adapting them as implements in the struggle for the eternal goal of man's freedom from tyranny, which was his primary natural right. Jefferson the social planner and activist sought to improve the efficiency and effectiveness of the institutions of his society by wide-ranging reforms. Recognizing the desirability of seeking the facts as they exist—for only "truth and reason are eternal"[62]—his social science was nevertheless chiefly a utilitarian, meliorative one. It was the use which could be made of knowledge and science that was of primary importance to him; and here he was not so far removed from those modern social scientists who feel that "science must eventually pay her debts" to society by providing solutions to practical problems.[63]

Jefferson the idealist-reformer may have seen little need for scientific detachment and objectivity in the study of man, for his approach was one whose broad theory had already been established and whose hypotheses he accepted without question: the Lockian delineation of natural rights and natural law. Jefferson the scientist—in

61. Lipscomb and Bergh, 10:175.
62. *Ibid.*, 12:360.
63. W. I. Thomas and Florian Znaniecki, *The Polish Peasant in Europe and America*, 2 vols. (New York: Dover Publications, Inc., 1958), p. 19. See also Robert S. Lynd, *Knowledge for What?* (Princeton: Princeton University Press, 1939); George A. Lundberg, *Can Science Save Us?* (New York: David McKay Company, Inc., 1961); Thomas Ford Hoult, ". . . Who Shall Prepare Himself to the Battle?", *The American Sociologist* 3 (February, 1968) :3-7.

spite of his generally scientific frame of mind and approach—was in his consideration of social matters always the reformer seeking to attain the ideals of the Enlightenment in the real world of men. His scientific bent displayed itself clearly in his empirical approach to the considerations of natural science, as well as in his open-minded willingness to experiment with social institutions. But in the final sense, it was his unquestioning acceptance of the postulates of natural law and natural rights which underlay his view of social phenomena. The Lockian approach was an empiricial and positive one; however, it was an approach whose hypotheses, like those of the so-called "grand theory" in sociology, were untestable.

Jefferson understood human behavior as an appropriate subject for empirical investigation; he believed that there were laws of human behavior, understandable and predictable regularities which science could at least in part comprehend. He may therefore correctly be considered a proto-social scientist. But his social science was purposive and teleological, as many sociologists have contended social science should be; its objective was prediction and control. So perhaps the goal of all science at last is, just as it may finally be, melioristic. Jefferson's social science was not a "pure" science but a practical applied one. In this respect he was at one with the company of those who founded the discipline of sociology as well as of many who guided it through its often uncertain and troubled youth. Indeed, since its origin sociology has in the work of many of its leading figures always involved not only the theoretical and empirical enquiry into social structures and functions which is social science, but also the concern for social practices and social change which characterize social policy and social criticism. With such men as Comte, Ward, and Ross, in particular, he had much in common, for the desire to reorganize or improve society inspired and motivated their thoughts and efforts as it did his. But, in contrast to them, Jefferson made no effort to construct a system nor to develop a theory of logically interrelated postulates within the specific framework of a science of society. Among other reasons, the broadness of his mind and interests precluded his doing so.

12

Conclusion

The image of Thomas Jefferson which emerges from a careful study of his writings and works is that of an astonishingly broad and versatile genius who, like one of his heroes, Sir Francis Bacon, had taken all knowledge to be his province. It is difficult to disagree with the assertion of one of his biographers that "no man in this or any other country in the Western world—excepting only Leonardo da Vinci—ever matched Jefferson in the range of his activities, in the fertility of his thinking, and in the multiplicity of his interests."[1] He was a scientist, legislator, mathematician, architect, philologist, lawyer, farmer, politician, inventor, diplomat, musician, writer, statesman. Philosophers may arbitrarily deny him membership in their fraternity, yet he is widely known as the philosopher of democracy, for his thought was strongly philosophical. He developed an educational system and built a university; he founded a great political party, helped design the national capital, and was instrumental in establishing America's coinage; he collected scientific materials in the fields of anthropology, geology, and zoology; he was a paleontologist; he wrote an essay on poetry, codified the laws of his state, and designed a plow of least resistance which, with modifica-

1. Saul K. Padover, *Jefferson* (New York: Mentor Books, 1963), p. 7.

tions, is still used. He was an almost uniquely brilliant and creative human being, as he was a subtle and elusive one, consistent in the ends he sought, but often inconsistent in the means he utilized. Although an aristocrat by birth, the overriding passion of his life was the freedom, rights, and dignity of all men. He was also, in the broad sense of the term, a serious student of society and a proto-sociologist.

As his most competent biographer, Dumas Malone, points out, "he exemplified more conspicuously than any of his fellows the liberal and humane spirit, the incessant scientific curiosity and zeal for universal knowledge, and the fundamental belief in the powers of human intelligence which characterized what historians call the Enlightenment."[2] The humanitarianism, empiricism, skepticism, toleration, liberalism, rationalism, and utilitarianism characteristic of the Enlightenment permeated his thought and action, as did the Enlightenment faith that what science had achieved in the material world it could also achieve in the social sphere: the discovery of laws of social behavior analogous to the laws of the material world which Newton had demonstrated. Thus men of the Enlightenment—of whom Jefferson was the American exemplar—confidently believed that they could develop "a science of rational sociology" which would make the search for human justice, virtue and happiness "no longer utopian."[3] Jefferson shared the Enlightenment theory of society as well as the ideas of the social contract, natural law, and natural rights; in him, Alfred Cobban says, "the pure milk of Lockian doctrine was . . . undefiled."[4]

2. Dumas Malone, *Jefferson the Virginian* (Boston: Little, Brown and Company, 1948), p. xv.
3. Sir Isaiah Berlin, ed. *The Age of the Enlightenment* (New York: Mentor Books, 1963), pp. 27-28.
4. *In Search of Humanity: The Role of the Enlightenment in Modern History* (New York: George Braziller, 1960), p. 172.

It is true that as a student of society Jefferson proceeded on the basis of Locke's postulates. He concerned himself with those areas of interest which have formed the major subject matter of sociology since its beginning: groups, society, culture, norms, institutions, social control, status and role, socialization, stratification, and the social processes. His insights were often profound, and his approach was usually scientific and empirical.

He asserted that "I have never submitted the whole system of my opinions to the creed of any party of men whatever, in religion, in philosophy, in politics, or in anything else";[5] however, his writings and works show that he clearly accepted the major hypotheses and general approach of the Enlightenment. Yet it is a fatal mistake to freeze him in the static image of Enlightenment spokesman, for his thought was often profoundly original and strikingly innovative, and his specific proposals were largely his own. He was strongly empiricist and positivistic, and he was utilitarian and reformist in his outlook. He himself constructed no systematic general theories; and, indeed, was impatient of those theories he came across. "The moment a person forms a theory his imagination sees in every object only the traits which favor that theory,"[6] he said. It is well to recall that, in spite of his enthusiasm for Destutt de Tracy, he confessed he had never completed reading the volumes on ideology, since "I am not fond of reading what is merely abstract, and unapplied immediately to some useful science."[7] Jefferson's social science was designed to chart

5. Thomas Jefferson, *The Papers of Thomas Jefferson*, ed. Julian P. Boyd (Princeton: Princeton University Press, 1950–   ), 14:650.

6. Thomas Jefferson, *The Writings of Thomas Jefferson*, ed. Paul Leicester Ford, 10 vols. (New York: G. P. Putnam's Sons, 1892–1899), 4:447.

7. Thomas Jefferson, *The Writings of Thomas Jefferson*, ed. Andrew A. Lipscomb and Albert E. Bergh, 20 vols. (Washington: Thomas Jefferson Memorial Association, 1903), 15:73.

the course by which man's progress toward fulfillment
might be achieved. To him, it was the goal of human
happiness to which social science should lead the way.
It was the practical and therefore the purposive which
in the final consideration really counted.

But Jefferson was far more than the spokesman and
exemplar of the Enlightenment, great as these roles were.
He adapted the liberal and progressive ideas of that
movement to the needs and circumstances of America,
and in doing so altered many of the accepted Enlightenment views in order to fit the realities of the American
experience. He was an eclectic who was no mere echo
of any single philosophy or creed. One of his most significant innovations may be found in his efforts to apply
his social science to the practical realization of the goals
he believed most highly desirable for America and Americans.

While he developed no systematic theory, as we understand the term today, he was consistently motivated
by principles that were essentially scientific in nature,
which a careful study of his writings reveals but which
a cursory examination often only obfuscates. In words
of deathless eloquence, he wrote *something* about almost
the entire range of human knowledge and interests.

His words have been used to justify opposition to,
and defense of, an almost endless variety of social views
and ideologies; in a sense, he has been all things to all
men. He has been properly claimed as a predecessor or
practitioner of almost every discipline, from architecture
to zoology. It is surprising that he has not also been
claimed as a founder of modern social science—as indeed
he was, for few other men before Auguste Comte gave
more careful and extensive consideration to the facts of
society as seen within the framework of the scientific and
empirical approach. In fact, Jefferson proposed that a
"new science" should be developed, "the science of

man,"[8] and he contributed significantly to such a science, as his writings and activities make clear he intended.

It is important to recall that modern sociology began as an effort to apply scientific methods to the study of human behavior for the express purpose of reconstructing society to incorporate that design and those features which its founders considered desirable. Sociology was to be "positive" or scientific to the extent of discovering the nature of man and the laws of his behavior. But it was also to be teleological and reformist, with the scientific laws discovered to be utilized in designing, instituting, and controlling the social system. Certainly Jefferson was not alone among the men of his age in pursuing such a goal—Turgot, Saint-Simon, and Condorcet in particular were others, and of course in Auguste Comte this approach reached its zenith. It is certainly true that the social system which Comte designed was a basically authoritarian one, the antithesis of that sought for by Jefferson.

The similarity between the two men exists not in their values and ideals but in their conviction that human social systems were amenable to the application of rational, positive, scientific approaches.

It is therefore no mere coincidence that in July, 1824, two years before Jefferson's death, the young Comte sent him a "petit cahier"[9] in which he proposed that the

---

8. Gilbert Chinard, "Jefferson Among the Philosophers," *Ethics* 53 (July, 1943) :266. Chinard shows that Jefferson was pleased with the works of Cabanis and Destutt de Tracy in this regard. He referred to the new "science of man" as "anthropology, to use a term coined in Germany."

9. This was the *Plan of the Scientific Operations Necessary for the Reorganization of Society,* which Comte later called "the great discovery of the year 1822" and in which he outlined his positive system. This outline was first published in the *Catéchisme des industriels de Saint-Simon* in 1824, of which Comte received a hundred copies, one of which he forwarded to Jefferson. He also sent copies to other prominent leaders. See Gilbert Chinard, *Jefferson et les Idéalogues* (Baltimore: The Johns Hopkins Press, 1925), p. 285; McQuilkin DeGrange, "Comte's Sociologies," *American Sociological Review* 4 (February, 1939) :17; and Nicho-

methods of the physical sciences be applied to the study of social phenomena. Jefferson's positivistic epistemology showed clearly in his consideration of social facts, as he demonstrated in the *Notes on the State of Virginia,* which along with his other writings had been fairly widely distributed among French intellectuals. They evidently came into the hands of young Comte and provided him with inspiration. Apparently recognizing Jefferson's contributions to a science of society, the founder of modern sociology wrote him a rather lengthy letter to accompany the copy of the outline of his positive system, a letter in which he sought Jefferson's intellectual patronage.[10]

---

las S. Timasheff, *Sociological Theory: Its Nature and Growth* (New York: Random House, 1964), p. 17.

10. Chinard, *Jefferson et les Idéalogues,* pp. 285-86.

"I request Mr. Jefferson to be so kind as to excuse the liberty I am taking, without having had the honor of being personally acquainted with him, in paying him respectful homage through the work I am herewith presenting to him. I am eager to submit this work to him as the most competent judge of the ideas offered therein.

"This document is only the beginning of a more extensive work the purpose of which is to superimpose upon politics the character of physical science, and consequently to subject the study of social phenomena to the method so successfully employed at present for all other classes of phenomena. A thorough examination of the present state of affairs and a discussion of the fruitless attempts carried on up to now to change its character seem to me to point out this method as the only one capable of terminating decisively the intellectual strife which torments our old Europe, and which prevents her civilization from taking the forward flight which the natural progress of mankind demands of it so strongly today. On the other hand, a close observation of the historical development of human knowledge seems clearly to manifest a constant and progressive tendency of the human mind to consider, in an entirely positive manner, freed of every theological or metaphysical notion, all classes of phenomena. This intellectual revolution appears due to come to a head in our day, and to point out henceforth a completely new era for human intelligence, since social phenomena are now the only ones which are not embraced within the domain of the physical. To submit their study to the same transformation, such is the task I point out to thinkers and to which throughout my life I shall dedicate the employment of my humble talents. But in order to know with certainty whether these endeavors are worthy of being pursued, I must submit this first outline to those thinkers who have meditated the most on this subject and those statesmen who have displayed the greatest capacity to grasp the true character of the present epoch. It is for these dual reasons that I am determined to seek earnestly the opinion of Mr. Jefferson. If my

Comte, in addressing Jefferson as "the most competent judge" of the ideas presented in his work, correctly understood that this great American was a serious student of society. Comte chose to address Jefferson as the most qualified leader to pass on the value of this new scientific method which would substitute a positive approach for those earlier nonscientific approaches which had so long delayed the development of a science of society. Comte viewed Jefferson not as the disciple and spokesman of eighteenth-century Enlightenment thought but as the prophet of a new social philosophy and a new social science.

It is unfortunate that Comte's letter arrived after the time that Jefferson, already an aged man of 81, had largely given up correspondence. However, he may not in any event have replied to Comte, or his reply may well have been acidly unfavorable, for he probably detected in Comte's plan for the reorganization of society that authoritarianism of the French positivist which could only have repelled the hero of democracy to the depths of his being. Even so, at the same time he could not have failed to recognize in Comte's plan the rational, scientific approach which he himself had so long advocated and which unquestionably influenced Comte. Certainly Jefferson was a far broader man than Comte, and a man deeply committed to an antithetically different basic philosophy.

---

ideas appear to him worthy of some consideration, such a triumph, granted by the illustrious man who either as a thinker or as a statesman is placed so high in the history of his own country and in that of humankind, would be the greatest reward and the noblest encouragement which my works might ever obtain. But if I were unfortunate enough not to have merited his approbation, I beg of him at least to accept this token of respect as a feeble but very sincere testimony of the deeply-felt esteem which he inspires in all enlightened men and in all friends of humanity, and particularly of the respectful admiration of his devoted servant.

A^{te}. Comte"

Yet it is not difficult to understand Comte's high regard for the great American. For had not Jefferson himself been concerned throughout his long and active life with the vital questions of society? Had his approach not been empirical and positive rather than essentially theological or metaphysical? Had he not worked to apply his social science in the improvement of American society and ardently wished for the reorganization of European society? And, finally, had he himself not proposed "a science of man"? For Thomas Jefferson, scientist, rationalist, and reformer, was also a precursor of modern social science. He was indeed the exemplar of the American Enlightenment, as well as the herald of positivism, but also—as Comte certainly was not—the champion of self-disciplined individualism and the prophet of a new voluntaristic humanism: a man of broad vision who sought a science of society that would chart the way for humanity to achieve the natural rights of life, liberty, and the pursuit of happiness.

If Jefferson's social ideas were not incorporated into Comte's sociology, they did indeed help shape the goals and ideals of American social science with its voluntaristic emphasis, just as they formed the ideological basis of the American creed and of American thought generally. And through the long years since his death the value-orientations expressed by the majority of American thinkers, in all their ever-changing variety, have continued to be—or to be considered—basically Jeffersonian. Indeed, freedom and equality have increasingly, if not yet universally, become the watchwords of the nations of the twentieth century—words with meanings no less varied than the multitude of interpretations Americans have continued to give to Jefferson's ideas. Few in any age have so profoundly influenced the life and ideals of their fellowmen as has Jefferson, a man whose thought will continue to remain significant so long as men desire or cherish the values of democracy and progress, whatever these words may mean to those who use them.

Perhaps in no other age since that in which Jefferson lived could one man have attained superiority in practically all the areas of human knowledge and accomplishment as he did. Even so, it should always be remembered that Jefferson was one of the few who attained that which in his times was possible. It is not only that he did such an astounding variety of things but also that he did them so incredibly well; and that his ideals—so superbly expressed as to have insured their survival—have become the ideals of those everywhere who value freedom, equality, knowledge, and happiness.

Bibliography

BOOKS

Barnett, H. G. *Innovation: The Basis of Cultural Change.* New York: McGraw-Hill Book Company, Inc., 1953.

Beard, Charles A. *An Economic Interpretation of the Constitution of the United States.* New York: The Macmillan Company, 1913.

———. *Economic Origins of Jeffersonian Democracy.* New York: The Macmillan Company, 1915.

Becker, Carl. *The Declaration of Independence: A Study in the History of Political Ideas.* New York: Alfred A. Knopf, 1956.

Benson, Lee. *Turner and Beard: American Historical Writings Reconsidered.* New York: The Free Press, 1960.

Berger, Peter L. *Invitation to Sociology: A Humanistic Perspective.* New York: Doubleday, Anchor Books, 1963.

Berlin, Sir Isaiah, ed. *The Age of the Enlightenment.* New York: Mentor Books, 1963.

Betts, Edwin M., ed. *Thomas Jefferson's Garden Book.* Philadelphia: American Philosophical Society, 1944.

Boorstin, Daniel J. *The Americans: The Colonial Experience.* New York: Random House, 1958.

———. *The Americans: The National Experience.* New York: Random House, 1965.

———. *The Lost World of Thomas Jefferson.* Boston: Beacon Press, 1948.

Bowers, Claude G. *Jefferson and Hamilton: The Struggle for Democracy in America.* New York: Houghton Mifflin Company, 1937.

313

————. *Jefferson in Power: The Death Struggle of the Federalists.* Boston: Houghton Mifflin Company, 1936.

————. *The Young Jefferson, 1743–1789.* Boston: Houghton Mifflin Company, 1945.

Bridenbaugh, Carl. *Myths and Realities: Societies of the Colonial South.* New York: Atheneum, 1965.

Brinton, Crane. *The Anatomy of Revolution.* New York: Vintage Books, 1959.

Brown, Robert E. *Middle Class Democracy and the Revolution.* Princeton: Princeton University Press, 1956.

Brown, Stuart Gerry. *The First Republicans.* Syracuse: Syracuse University Press, 1954.

————. *Thomas Jefferson.* New York: Washington Square Press, 1963.

Bruckberger, Raymond Leopold. *Image of America.* New York: Viking Press, 1959.

Bullock, Helen Duprey. *My Head and My Heart: A Little Chronicle of Thomas Jefferson and Maria Cosway.* New York: G. P. Putnam's Sons, 1945.

Byrd, William. *The Secret Diary of William Byrd of Westover, 1709–1712.* Edited by Louis B. Wright and Marion Tinling. Richmond: Dietz Press, Inc., 1941.

Cappon, Lester J., ed. *Adams-Jefferson Letters.* Chapel Hill: University of North Carolina Press, 1959.

Chambers, William Nisbet. *Political Parties in a New Nation.* New York: Oxford University Press, 1963.

Channing, Edward. *The Jeffersonian System.* New York: Harper and Brothers, 1906.

Charles, Joseph. *The Origins of the American Party System: Three Essays.* Williamsburg: Institute of Early American History and Culture, 1956.

Chinard, Gilbert. *Jefferson et les Idéalogues.* Baltimore: The Johns Hopkins Press, 1925.

————. *Thomas Jefferson, The Apostle of Americanism.* Boston: Little, Brown and Company, 1929.

Cobban, Alfred. *In Search of Humanity: The Role of the Enlightenment in Modern History.* New York: George Braziller, 1960.

Conant, James B. *Thomas Jefferson and the Development of*

American Public Education. Berkeley: University of California Press, 1963.

Crèvecoeur, J. Hector St. John. *Letters from an American Farmer.* New York: Dolphin Books, n. d.

Cunliffe, Marcus. *George Washington, Man and Monument.* New York: Mentor Books, 1960.

Cunningham, Noble E., Jr. *The Jeffersonian Republicans: The Formation of Party Organization, 1789–1801.* Chapel Hill: University of North Carolina Press, 1957.

Curti, Merle. *The Growth of American Thought.* New York: Harper and Brothers, Publishers, 1943.

Dauer, Manning J. *The Adams Federalists.* Baltimore: The Johns Hopkins Press, 1953.

Dorfman, Joseph. *The Economic Mind in American Civilization.* vol. 1. New York: The Viking Press, 1946.

Dumbauld, Edward. *Thomas Jefferson, American Tourist.* Norman: University of Oklahoma Press, 1946.

————, ed. *The Political Writings of Thomas Jefferson.* Indianapolis: The Bobbs-Merrill Company, Inc., 1955.

Eckenrode, H. J. *Separation of Church and State in Virginia.* Richmond: Virginia State Library, 1916.

Fäy, Bernard. *The Revolutionary Spirit in France and America.* New York: Harcourt, Brace, 1927.

Foner, Philip S., ed. *Basic Writings of Thomas Jefferson.* New York: Willey Book Company, 1944.

Foote, Henry Wilder. *The Religion of Thomas Jefferson.* Boston: Beacon Press, 1960.

Gershoy, Leo. *The Era of the French Revolution, 1789–1799.* Princeton: D. Van Nostrand Company, Inc., 1957.

Gipson, Lawrence Henry. *The Coming of the Revolution, 1763–1775.* New York: Harper and Row, Publishers, 1962.

Goode, William J., and Hatt, Paul K. *Methods in Social Research.* New York: McGraw-Hill Book Company, Inc., 1952.

Goodwin, Edward Lewis. *The Colonial Church in Virginia.* Milwaukee and London: Morehouse Publishing Company and A. R. Mowbray and Company, 1927.

Greene, Evarts B. *Religion and the State.* Ithaca: Great Seal Books, 1959.

————. *The Revolutionary Generation.* New York: The Macmillan Company, 1943.

Griswold, Alfred Whitney. *Farming and Democracy.* New Haven: Yale University Press, 1948.

Handlin, Oscar. *The Americans.* Boston: Little, Brown and Company, 1963.

Hartz, Louis. *The Founding of New Societies.* New York: Harcourt, Brace and World, Inc., 1964.

————. *The Liberal Tradition in America.* New York: Harcourt, Brace and World, Inc., 1955.

Hofstadter, Richard. *The American Political Tradition.* New York: Vintage Books, 1948.

Honeywell, Roy J. *The Educational Work of Thomas Jefferson.* Cambridge: Harvard University Press, 1931.

Jameson, J. Franklin. *The American Revolution Considered as a Social Movement.* Princeton: Princeton University Press, 1940.

Jefferson, Thomas. *The Commonplace Book of Thomas Jefferson.* Edited by Gilbert Chinard. Baltimore: The Johns Hopkins Press, 1926.

————. *Notes on the State of Virginia.* Edited by Thomas Perkins Abernethy. New York: Harper and Row, Publishers, 1964.

————. *Notes on the State of Virginia.* Edited by William Peden. Chapel Hill: University of North Carolina Press, 1955.

————. *The Papers of Thomas Jefferson.* Edited by Julian P. Boyd. Princeton: Princeton University Press, 1950–   .

————. *The Works of Thomas Jefferson.* Edited by Paul Leicester Ford. 12 vols. New York: G. P. Putnam's Sons, 1904.

————. *The Writings of Thomas Jefferson.* Edited by Paul Leicester Ford. 10 vols. New York: G. P. Putnam's Sons, 1892–1899.

————. *The Writings of Thomas Jefferson.* Edited by Andrew A. Lipscomb and Albert E. Bergh. 20 vols. Washington: Thomas Jefferson Memorial Association, 1903.

Jensen, Merrill. *The New Nation.* New York: Alfred A. Knopf, 1950.

Johnson, Allen. *The Age of Jefferson and Marshall.* New Haven: Yale University Press, 1926.

Jones, Howard Mumford. *The Pursuit of Happiness.* Ithaca: Cornell University Press, 1966.

Kimball, Fiske. *Thomas Jefferson, Architect.* Boston: n. p., 1916.

Kimball, Marie. *Jefferson: The Scene of Europe, 1784–1789.* New York: Coward-McCann, Inc., 1950.

Klapp, Orrin E. *Symbolic Leaders.* Chicago: Aldine Publishing Company, 1964.

Koch, Adrienne. *Jefferson and Madison: The Great Collaboration.* New York: Alfred A. Knopf, 1950.

———. *The Philosophy of Thomas Jefferson.* Chicago: Quadrangle Books, 1964.

———. *Power, Morals, and the Founding Fathers.* Ithaca: Cornell University Press, 1966.

Koch, Adrienne, and Peden, William, eds. *The Life and Selected Writings of Thomas Jefferson.* New York: Random House, Inc., 1944.

Korn, Richard R., and McCorkle, Lloyd W. *Criminology and Penology.* New York: Holt, Rinehart and Winston, Inc., 1961.

LaPiere, Richard L. *A Theory of Social Control.* New York: McGraw-Hill Book Company, Inc., 1954.

Lastrucci, Carlo L. *The Scientific Approach: Basic Principles of the Scientific Method.* Cambridge, Mass.: Schenkman Publishing Company, Inc., 1963.

Latham, Earl, ed. *The Declaration of Independence and the Constitution.* Boston: D. C. Heath and Company, 1956.

Lehmann, Karl. *Thomas Jefferson: American Humanist.* New York: The Macmillan Company, 1947.

Levy, Leonard W. *Freedom of Speech and Press in Early American History: Legacy of Suppression.* New York: Harper and Row, Publishers, 1963.

———, ed. *Freedom of the Press from Zenger to Jefferson.* Indianapolis: The Bobbs-Merrill Company, Inc., 1966.

Lipset, Seymour Martin. *The United States—The First New Nation.* Berkeley: Institute of International Studies, 1964.

Lipset, Seymour Martin, and Bendix, Reinhard. *Social Mobility in Industrial Society.* Berkeley: University of California Press, 1959.

Lundberg, George A. *Can Science Save Us?* New York: David McKay Company, Inc., 1961.

Lynd, Robert S. *Knowledge for What?* Princeton: Princeton University Press, 1939.

MacIver, R. M. *Social Causation.* New York: Harper and Row, Publishers, 1964.

Macridis, Roy C. *The Study of Comparative Government.* New York: Random House, Inc., 1962.

Main, Jackson Turner. *The Social Structure of Revolutionary America.* Princeton: Princeton University Press, 1965.

Malone, Dumas. *Jefferson and His Time.* Vol. I: *Jefferson the Virginian.* Vol. II: *Jefferson and the Rights of Man.* Vol. III: *Jefferson and the Ordeal of Liberty.* Boston: Little, Brown and Company, 1948–   .

Martin, Edwin T. *Thomas Jefferson: Scientist.* New York: Henry Schuman, Inc., 1952.

Martindale, Don. *The Nature and Types of Sociological Theory.* Boston: Houghton Mifflin Company, 1960.

Mayo, Bernard. *Myths and Men.* New York: Harper and Row, Publishers, 1963.

Merton, Robert K. *Social Theory and Social Structure.* Glencoe: The Free Press, 1957.

Miller, John C. *The Federalist Era, 1789–1801.* New York: Harper and Row, Publishers, 1963.

Mills, C. Wright. *The Sociological Imagination.* New York: Oxford University Press, 1959.

Morgan, Edmund S. *The Birth of the Republic.* Chicago: University of Chicago Press, 1956.

Morrison, Samuel Eliot, and Commager, Henry Steele. *The Growth of the American Republic.* 2 vols. New York: Oxford University Press, 1962.

Mott, Frank L. *Jefferson and the Press.* Baton Rouge: Louisiana State University Press, 1943.

Nock, Albert Jay. *Jefferson.* New York: Hill and Wang, 1963.

Nye, Russel Blaine. *The Cultural Life of the New Nation.* New York: Harper and Row, Publishers, 1963.

Ostrander, Gilman. *The Rights of Man in America.* Columbia: University of Missouri Press, 1960.

Padover, Saul K., ed. *The Complete Jefferson.* New York: Duell, Sloan and Pearce, 1943.

————, *Jefferson.* New York: Mentor Books, 1963.

———, ed. *Thomas Jefferson on Democracy*. New York: Mentor Books, 1954.

Parrington, Vernon L. *Main Currents in American Thought*. New York: Harcourt, Brace and Company, Inc., 1930.

Perry, Ralph Barton. *Puritanism and Democracy*. New York: Vanguard Press, 1944.

Peterson, Merrill D. *The Jefferson Image in the American Mind*. New York: Oxford University Press, 1962.

Randall, Henry S. *The Life of Thomas Jefferson*. 3 vols. New York: Derby and Jackson, 1858.

Randolph, Sarah N. *The Domestic Life of Thomas Jefferson*. New York: Frederick Ungar Publishing Company, 1958.

Rheinstein, Max, ed. *Max Weber on Law in Economy and Society*. Cambridge: Harvard University Press, 1954.

Robinson, William A. *Jeffersonian Democracy in New England*. New Haven: Yale University Press, 1916.

Saveth, Edward N., ed. *American History and the Social Sciences*. New York: The Free Press of Glencoe, 1964.

Sawer, Geoffrey, ed. *Studies in the Sociology of Law*. Canberra: The Australian National University, 1961.

Schachner, Nathan. *Thomas Jefferson: A Biography*. 2 vols. New York: Appleton-Century-Crofts, Inc., 1951.

Schlesinger, Arthur M. *The Colonial Merchant and the American Revolution*. New York: Frederick Ungar Publishing Company, 1957.

Selltiz, Claire, et al. *Research Methods in Social Relations*. New York: Holt, Rinehart and Winston, 1963.

Smith, James Morton. *Freedom's Fetters: The Alien and Sedition Laws and American Civil Liberties*. Ithaca: Cornell University Press, 1956.

Smith, Page. *The Historian and History*. New York: Alfred A. Knopf, 1964.

Smith, Preserved. *History of Modern Culture*. New York: Henry Holt and Company, 1934.

Sowerby, E. Millicent. *Catalogue of the Library of Thomas Jefferson*. 5 vols. Washington: Library of Congress, 1952–1959.

Sutherland, Edwin H., and Cressey, Donald R. *Principles of Criminology*. Philadelphia: J. B. Lippincott Company, 1960.

Sydnor, Charles S. *American Revolutionaries in the Making.* New York: The Free Press, 1965.

Thomas, W. I. *Primitive Behavior.* New York: McGraw-Hill Book Company, 1937.

Thomas, W. I., and Znaniecki, Florian. *The Polish Peasant in Europe and America.* 2 vols. New York: Dover Publications, Inc., 1958.

Timasheff, Nicholas S. *Sociological Theory: Its Nature and Growth.* New York: Random House, Inc., 1964.

Turner, Frederick Jackson. *The Frontier in American History.* New York: Henry Holt and Company, 1958.

Vander Zanden, James W. *American Minority Relations.* New York: The Ronald Press Company, 1963.

Von Bar, Carl Ludwig. *A History of Continental Criminal Law.* London: John Murray, 1916.

Walhke, John C., ed. *The Causes of the American Revolution.* Boston: D. C. Heath and Company, 1962.

Wertenbaker, Thomas J. *The Golden Age of American Culture.* New York: New York University Press, 1949.

———. *The Old South.* New York: Charles Scribner's Sons, 1942.

Williams, Robin M., Jr. *American Society: A Sociological Interpretation.* New York: Alfred A. Knopf, 1965.

Wilstach, Paul. *Jefferson and Monticello.* Garden City: Doubleday, Doran and Company, Inc., 1931.

Wish, Harvey. *Society and Thought in Early America.* New York: Longmans, Green and Company, 1950.

Wright, Louis B. *The Cultural Life of the American Colonies.* New York: Harper and Row, Publishers, 1962.

———. *The First Gentlemen of Virginia.* Charlottesville: Dominion Books, 1964.

Zetterberg, Hans L. *On Theory and Verification in Sociology.* Totowa: The Bedminster Press, 1965.

Zollschan, George K., and Hirsch, Walter, eds. *Explorations in Social Change.* Boston: Houghton Mifflin Company, 1964.

ARTICLES AND PERIODICALS

Ammon, Harry. "The Formation of the Republican Party in

Virginia, 1789–1796," *Journal of Southern History* 19 (August, 1953) : 283–310.

Anderson, Dice R. "Jefferson and the Virginia Constitution," *American Historical Review* 31 (July, 1916) : 750–54.

Beard, Charles A. "Thomas Jefferson: A Civilized Man," *The Mississippi Valley Historical Review* 30 (September, 1943) : 159–70.

Bowman, Albert H. "Jefferson, Hamilton, and American Foreign Policy," *Political Science Quarterly* 71 (March, 1956) : 18–41.

Brown, Roland W. "Jefferson's Contributions to Paleontology," *Journal of the Washington Academy of Science* 33 (September 15, 1943) : 257–59.

Browne, Charles A. "Thomas Jefferson and the Scientific Trends of His Time," *Chronica Botanica* 8 (Summer, 1944) : 363–423.

Chamberlain, Alexander F. "Thomas Jefferson's Ethnological Opinions and Activities," *American Anthropologist,* New Series 9 (July, 1907) : 499–509.

Chinard, Gilbert. "Jefferson among the Philosophers," *Ethics* 53 (July, 1943) : 255–68.

———. "Jefferson's Influence Abroad," *The Mississippi Valley Historical Review* 30 (September, 1943) : 171–86.

———. "Thomas Jefferson as a Classical Scholar," *The American Scholar* 1 (March, 1932) : 133–43.

Davis, Richard Beale. "Forgotten Scientists in Old Virginia," *The Virginia Magazine of History and Biography* 46 (April, 1938) : 97–111.

DeGrange, McQuilkin. "Comte's Sociologies," *American Sociological Review* 4 (February, 1939) : 17–26.

Hartz, Louis. "American Political Thought and the American Revolution," *American Political Science Review* 44 (1952) : 321–42.

Grampp, William D. "Everyman His Own Jeffersonian," *Swanee Review* 52 (January, 1944) : 118–26.

———. "Re-examination of Jeffersonian Economics," *Social Economics Journal* 12 (January, 1946) : 263–82.

Griswold, Alfred Whitney. "The Agrarian Democracy of Thomas Jefferson," *American Political Science Review* 40 (August, 1946) : 657–81.

Hoult, Thomas Ford. ". . . Who Shall Prepare Himself to the Battle?", *The American Sociologist* 3 (February, 1968): 3–7.

Knoles, George Harmon. "The Religious Ideas of Thomas Jefferson," *The Mississippi Valley Historical Review* 30 (September, 1943): 187–204.

Lehmann-Hartleben, Karl. "Thomas Jefferson, Archaeologist," *American Journal of Archaeology* 47 (April-June, 1943): 161–63.

"The Letters of Thomas Jefferson to William Short," *William and Mary Quarterly* 11. 2nd Series (October, 1931): 336–420.

Lucas, Frederic A. "Thomas Jefferson—Paleontologist," *Natural History* 26 (May, 1926): 328–30.

Main, Jackson Turner. "The One Hundred," *William and Mary Quarterly* 14. 3rd Series (1954): 354–84.

Malone, Dumas. "Jefferson Goes to School in Williamsburg," *Virginia Quarterly Review* 33 (Fall, 1957): 481–96.

Martin, Edwin T. "Thomas Jefferson's Interest in Science and the Useful Arts," *The Emory University Quarterly* 2 (June, 1946): 65–73.

Montgomery, H. C. "Thomas Jefferson as a Philologist," *American Journal of Philology* 65 (October, 1944): 367–71.

Padover, Saul K. "World of the Founding Fathers," *Social Research* 25 (Summer, 1958): 191–214.

Palmer, R. R. "Dubious Democrat: Thomas Jefferson in Bourbon France," *Political Science Quarterly* 72 (Summer, 1957): 388–404.

Peterson, Merrill D. "Henry Adams on Jefferson as President," *Virginia Quarterly Review* 39 (Spring, 1963): 187–201.

Savelle, Max. "Nationalism and Other Loyalties in the American Revolution," *American Historical Review* 67 (July, 1962): 901–23.

Schlesinger, Arthur, Jr. "The Humanist Looks at Empirical Social Research," *American Sociological Review* 27 (December, 1962): 768–71.

Sorokin, Pitirim A. "Sociology of Yesterday, Today and Tomorrow," *American Sociological Review* 30 (December, 1965): 833–43.

Stevenson, Adlai E. "Jefferson and Our National Leadership," *Virginia Quarterly Review* 36 (Summer, 1960) : 337–49.
"Thomas Jefferson." *Encyclopaedia Britannica.* 14th ed. 986–92.
Williams, William Appleton, "The Frontier Thesis and American Foreign Policy," *Pacific Historical Review* 24 (1955) : 379–95.

Index